To Celia

With best wishes + hopes

that you will like the contents!

Cathy Orloff

11/12/2015

The Land Question

Henry George

The Land Question

and related writings

**Viewpoint
and counterviewpoint
on the need
for land reform**

Robert Schalkenbach Foundation

Henry George

The Land Question
  and related writings
  Viewpoint and counterviewpoint
  on the need for land reform

Revised edition

ISBN 978-0-911312-40-9

Library of Congress control number: 2008941365

Cover design by Vajramati
Book design by Lindy Davies

Robert Schalkenbach Foundation
90 John Street, Suite 501
New York NY 10038

Tel: 212-683-6424 Toll-free: 800-269-9555
Fax: 212-683-6454
Email: books@schalkenbach.org
www.schalkenbach.org
www.progressandpoverty.org

FIRST PRINTING, 2009

Contents

Publisher's Preface

by Thomas A. Larkin

IT HAS BEEN SAID that Henry George left a threefold economic legacy: political, intellectual and moral. Nowhere is
this clearer than in this volume which brings together three
famous George works: *The Land Question,* first published
in 1881 under the title *The Irish Land Question; Property in
Land,* a debate between George and the Duke of Argyll
published originally in 1884 in the British periodical *Nineteenth Century;* and *An Open Letter to Pope Leo XIII,* a response to the Pope's 1891 Encyclical *Rerum Novarum* (On
the Condition of Labor).

In *The Land Question* George seized upon the outrage
of the Irish people against absentee landlords as a concrete
example of the misery caused by land abuse to point up
worldwide misappropriation of land. His son has rightly
noted that "in this brief work he gave the first striking evidence of a high order of practical ability, showing that, besides the genius to formulate a philosophy, he had the
wisdom to avail himself of passing events to apply it." While
he urged the Irish to insist upon "The principle that the land
of Ireland belongs of right to the whole people of Ireland,"
and, the principle being accepted, to collect the rent and
"divide it equally, or, what amounts to the same thing, to
apply it to purposes of common benefit," his long-range ob-
jective was to convince the world to recognize his fundamental principle that land belongs to the people — or suffer

a proliferation of the Irish problem in a multitude of places.

Property in Land is a brilliant dispute between two highly intelligent men. The Duke of Argyll, titular chief of the Scottish Campbell Clan whose son was married to a daughter of Queen Victoria, was a philosopher of note. Henry George had read his *The Reign of Law* and in admiration sent him a copy of *Progress and Poverty*. The Duke's courteous acknowledgment left George wholly unprepared for the nobleman's caustic attack on the book, derisively entitled "The Prophet of San Francisco," in the pages of *Nineteenth Century*. George's first reaction was to ignore the attack as more abusive than substantial, but when members of the Scottish Land Restoration League pointed out that the Duke's prominence would insure wide interest in a debate that must of necessity bring George's philosophy and the entire land question before the people, he took up his pen. *Nineteenth Century* published George's reply, "The Reduction to Iniquity," and his delighted followers immediately issued a pamphlet with the Duke's attack and George's answer which they entitled *The Peer and the Prophet*. The pamphlet later appeared in the United States under the title *Property in Land*.

Seven years later Pope Leo XIII's landmark encyclical letter *Rerum Novarum* (On the Condition of Labor) evoked a response of a different order. George and many of his followers thought that the encyclical condemned his teaching, although some of his Catholic friends disagreed, and he decided to reply, not to debate the Pope, but to define his own views. "What I have really aimed at," he informed his son, "is to make a clear, brief explanation of our principles, to show their religious character, and to draw a line between us and the socialists. I have written for such men as Cardinal Manning, General Booth and religious-minded men of all creeds."

The three George works in this volume, then, explore three aspects of his thought. *The Land Question* is a tract on political reform and its implementation, the Argyll debate deals with the intellectual problems of freedom and the dignity of the individual, and the letter to Leo XIII stresses George's concern with religious and moral values.

Taken together, these works reinforce the belief of many of his admirers that the teaching of Henry George is indeed a philosophy of freedom.

THOMAS A. LARKIN wrote this preface for the 1982 edition published by the Robert Schalkenbach Foundation. Larkin was a dedicated student of the Georgist philosophy and a businessman who made a successful career as a Wall Street broker and financial advisor. He served on numerous civic and charitable boards, including that of the Robert Schalkenbach Foundation.

Publisher's Note — 2009

Previous editions of this book included the text of the three collected works by Henry George with their original pagination. This new edition has been reset with continuous pagination and a new index.

Henry George

"The Prophet of San Francisco" shortly after writing *Progress and Poverty* (1879).

The Land Question

What it involves,
and how alone it can be settled

We hold these truths to be self-evident: That all men are created equal; that they are endowed by their Creator with certain unalienable rights; that among these are life, liberty and the pursuit of happiness. That to secure these rights, governments are instituted among men, deriving their just powers from the consent of the governed; that whenever any form of government becomes destructive of these ends, it is the right the people to alter or abolish it. — Declaration of Independence

Preface

This book was first published in the early part of 1881, under the title of *The Irish Land Question*. In order better to indicate the general character of this subject, and to conform to the title under which it had been republished in other countries, the title was subsequently changed to *The Land Question.* — Henry George, 1881

I. Unpalatable Truth

In CHARGING the Dublin jury in the Land League cases, Mr. Justice Fitzgerald told them that the land laws of Ireland were more favorable to the tenant than those of Great Britain, Belgium, or the United States.

As a matter of fact, Justice Fitzgerald is right. For in Ireland certain local customs and the provisions of the Bright Land Act mitigate somewhat the power of the landlord in his dealings with the tenant. In Great Britain, save by custom in a few localities, there are no such mitigations. In Belgium I believe there are none. There are certainly none in the United States.

This fact which Justice Fitzgerald cites will be reechoed by the enemies of the Irish movement. And it is a fact well worth the consideration of its friends. For the Irish movement has passed its first stage, and it is time for a more definite understanding of what is needed and how it is to be got.

It is the fashion of Land League orators and sympathizing newspapers in this country to talk as if the distress and disquiet in Ireland were wholly due to political oppression, and our national House of Representatives recently passed, by unanimous vote, a resolution which censured England for her treatment of Ireland. But, while it is indeed true that Ireland has been deeply wronged and bitterly oppressed by England, it is not true that there is any economic oppression of Ireland by England now. To whatever cause Irish distress may be due, it is certainly not due to the existence of laws which press on industry more heavily in Ireland than in any other part of the United Kingdom.

And, further than this, the Irish land system, which is so much talked of as though it were some peculiarly atrocious system, is essentially the same land system which prevails in all civilized countries, which we of the United States have accepted unquestioningly, and have extended over the whole temperate zone of a new continent — the same system which all over the civilized world men are accustomed to consider natural and just.

Justice Fitzgerald is unquestionably right.

As to England, it is well known that the English landlords exercise freely all the powers complained of in the Irish landlords, without even the slight restrictions imposed in Ireland.

As to Belgium, let me quote the high authority of the distinguished Belgian publicist, M. Emile de Laveleye, of the University of Liége. He says that the Belgian tenant farmers — for tenancy largely prevails even where the land is most minutely divided — are rack-rented with a mercilessness unknown in England or even in Ireland, and are compelled to vote as their landlords dictate!

And as to the United States, let me ask the men who to applauding audiences are nightly comparing the freedom of America with the oppression of Ireland — let me ask the Representatives who voted for the resolution of sympathy with Ireland, this simple question: What would the Irish landlords lose, what would the Irish tenants gain, if, tomorrow, Ireland were made a State in the American Union and American law substituted for English law?

I think it will puzzle them to reply. The truth is that the gain would be to the landlords, the loss to the tenants. The simple truth is, that, under our laws, the Irish landlords could rack-rent, distrain, evict, or absent themselves, as they pleased, and without any restriction from Ulster tenant-right or legal requirement of compensation for improvements. Under our laws they could, just as freely as they can now, impose whatever terms they pleased upon their tenants — whether as to cultivation, as to improvements, as to game, as to marriages, as to voting, or as to anything else. For these powers do not spring from special laws. They are merely incident to the right of property; they result simply from the acknowledgment of the right of the owner of land to do as he pleases with his own — to let it, or not let it. So far as law can give them to him, every American landlord has these powers as fully as any Irish landlord. Cannot the American owner of land make, in letting it, any stipulation he pleases as to how it shall be used, or improved, or cultivated? Can he not reserve any of his own rights upon it, such as the right of entry, or of cutting wood, or shooting game, or catching fish? And, in the absence of special agreement, does not American law give him, what the law of Ireland does not now give him, the ownership at the expiration of the lease of all the improvements made by the tenant?

What single power has the Irish landowner that the American landowner has not as fully? Is not the American landlord just as free as is the Irish landlord to refuse to rent his lands or his houses to any one who does not attend a certain church or vote a certain ticket? Is he not quite as free to do this as he is free to refuse his contributions to all but one particular benevolent society or political committee? Or, if, not liking a certain newspaper, he chooses to give notice to quit to any tenant whom he finds taking that newspaper, what law can be invoked to prevent him? There is none. The property is his, and he can let it, or not let it, as he wills. And, having this power to let or not let, he has power to demand any terms he pleases.

That Ireland is a conquered country; that centuries ago her soil was taken from its native possessors and parceled out among aliens, and that it has been confiscated again and again, has nothing to do with the real question of to-day — no more to do with it than have the confiscations of Marius and Sylla. England, too, is a conquered country; her soil has been confiscated again and again; and, spite of all talk about Saxon and Celt, it is not probable that, after the admixture of generations, the division of landholder and non-landholder any more coincides with distinction of race in the one country than in the other. That Irish land titles rest on force and fraud is true; but so do land titles in every country — even to a large extent in our own peacefully settled country. Even in our most recently settled States, how much land is there to which title has been got by fraud and perjury and bribery — by the arts of the lobbyist or the cunning tricks of hired lawyers, by double-barreled shotguns and repeating rifles!

The truth is that the Irish land system is simply the general system of modern civilization. In no essential feature does it differ from the system that obtains here — in what we are accustomed to consider the freest country under the sun. Entails and primogeniture and family settlements may be in themselves bad things, and may sometimes interfere with putting the land to its best use, but their effects upon the relations of landlord and tenant are not worth talking about. As for rack-rent, which is simply a rent fixed at short intervals by competition, that is in the United States even a more common way of letting land than in Ireland. In our cities the majority of our people live in houses rented from month to month or year to year for the highest price the landlord thinks he can get. The usual term, in the newer States, at least, for the letting of agricultural land is from season to season. And that the rent of land in the United States comes, on the whole, more closely to the standard of rack, or full competition rent, there can be, I think, little doubt. That the land of Ireland is, as the apologists for land-lordism say, largely under-rented (that is, not rented for the

full amount the landlord might get with free competition)
is probably true. Miss C. G. O'Brien, in a recent article in
the *Nineteenth Century,* states that the tenant-farmers generally get for such patches as they sub-let to their laborers twice
the rent they pay the landlords. And we hear incidentally
of many "good landlords," i.e., landlords not in the habit
of pushing their tenants for as much as they might get by
rigorously demanding all that any one would give.

These things, as well as the peculiar bitterness of complaints against middlemen and the speculators who have purchased encumbered estates and manage them solely with a
view to profit, go to show the truth of the statement that the
land of Ireland has been, by its present owners, largely under-
let, when considered from what we would deem a business
point of view. And this is but what might be expected. Human nature is about the same the world over, and the Irish
landlords as a class are no better nor worse than would be
other men under like conditions. An aristocracy such as that
of Ireland has its virtues as well as its vices, and is influenced
by sentiments which do not enter into mere business transactions — sentiments which must often modify and soften
the calculations of cold self-interest. But with us the letting
of land is as much a business matter as the buying or selling
of wheat or of stocks. An American would not think he was
showing his goodness by renting his land for low rates, any
more than he would think he was showing his goodness by
selling wheat for less than the market price, or stocks for less
than the quotations. So in those districts of France and Belgium where the land is most subdivided, the peasant proprietors, says M. de Laveleye, boast to one another of the high
rents they get, just as they boast of the high prices they get for
pigs or for poultry.

The best measure of rent is, of course, its proportion
to the produce. The only estimate of Irish rent as a proportion of which I know is that of Buckle, who puts it at

one-fourth of the produce. In this country I am inclined to think one-fourth would generally be considered a moderate rent. Even in California there is considerable land rented for one-third the crop, and some that rents for one-half the crop; while, according to a writer in the *Atlantic Monthly*, the common rent in that great wheatgrowing section of the New Northwest now being opened up is one-half the crop!

It does not seem to me that Justice Fitzgerald's statement can be disputed, though of course its developments are not yet as strikingly bad, for this is yet a new country, and tenants are comparatively few, and land comparatively easy to get. The American land system is really worse for the tenant than the Irish system. For with us there is neither sentiment nor custom to check the force of competition or mitigate the natural desire of the landlord to get all he can.

Nor is there anything in our system to prevent or check absenteeism, so much complained of in regard to Ireland. Before the modern era, which has so facilitated travel and communication, and made the great cities so attractive to those having money to spend, the prevalence of Irish absenteeism may have been due to special causes, but in the present day there is certainly nothing peculiar in it. Most of the large English and Scotch landholders are absentees for the greater part of the year, and many of them live permanently or for long intervals upon the Continent. So are our large American landowners generally absentees. In New York, in San Francisco, in Washington, Boston, Chicago, and St. Louis, live men who own large tracts of land which they seldom or never see. A resident of Rochester is said to own no less than four hundred farms in different States, one of which (I believe in Kentucky) comprises thirty-five thousand acres. Under the plantation system of farming and that of stock-raising on a grand scale, which are developing so rapidly in our new States, very much of the profits go to professional men and capitalists who live in distant cities. Corporations whose stock is held in the East or in Europe own much greater bodies of land, at much greater distances, than do the London corporations possessing landed estates in Ireland. To say nothing of the great land-grant railroad companies, the Standard Oil Company probably owns more acres of Western land than all the London companies put together own of Irish land. And, although landlordism in its grosser forms is only beginning in the United States, there is probably no American, wherever he may live, who cannot in his immediate vicinity see some instance of absentee landlordism. The tendency to concentration born of the new era ushered in by the application of steam shows itself in this way as in many others. To those who can live where they please, the great cities are becoming more and more attractive.

And it is further to be remarked that too much stress is laid upon absenteeism, and that it might be prevented without much of the evil often attributed to it being cured. That is to say, that to his tenantry and neighborhood the owner of land in Galway or Kilkenny would be as much an absentee if he lived in Dublin as if he lived in London, and that, if Irish landlords were compelled to live in Ireland, all that the Irish people would gain would be, metaphorically speaking, the crumbs that fell from the landlords' tables. For if the butter and eggs, the pigs and the poultry, of the Irish peasant must be taken from him and exported to pay for his landlord's wine and cigars, what difference does it make to him where the wine is drunk or the cigars are smoked?

II. Distress and Famine

BUT IT WILL BE ASKED: If the land system which prevails in Ireland is essentially the same as that which prevails elsewhere, how is it that it does not produce the same results elsewhere?

I answer that it does everywhere produce the same kind of results. As there is nothing essentially peculiar in the Irish land system, so is there nothing essentially peculiar in Irish distress. Between the distress in Ireland and the distress in other countries there may be differences in degree and differences in manifestation; but that is all.

The truth is, that as there is nothing peculiar in the Irish land system, so is there nothing peculiar in the distress which that land system causes. We hear a great deal of Irish emigration, of the millions of sons and daughters of Erin who have been compelled to leave their native soil. But have not the Scottish Highlands been all but depopulated? Do not the English emigrate in the same way, and for the same reasons? Do not the Germans and Italians and Scandinavians also emigrate? Is there not a constant emigration from the Eastern States of the Union to the Western — an emigration impelled by the same motives as that which sets across the Atlantic? Nor am I sure that this is not in some respects a more demoralizing emigration than the Irish, for I do not think there is any such monstrous disproportion of the sexes in Ireland as in Massachusetts. If French and Belgian peasants do not emigrate as do the Irish, is it not simply because they do not have such "long families"?

There has recently been deep and widespread distress in Ireland, and but for the contributions of charity many would have perished for want of food. But, to say nothing of such countries as India, China, Persia, and Syria, is it not true that within the last few years there have been similar spasms of distress in the most highly civilized countries — not merely in Russia and in Poland, but in Germany and England? Yes, even in the United States.

Have there not been, are there not constantly occurring, in all these countries, times when the poorest classes are reduced to the direst straits, and large numbers are saved from starvation only by charity?

When there is famine among savages it is because food enough is not to be had. But this was not the case in Ireland. In any part of Ireland, during the height of what was called the famine, there was food enough for whoever had means to pay for it. The trouble was not in the scarcity of food. There was, as a matter of fact, no real scarcity of food, and the proof of it is that food did not command scarcity prices. During all the so-called famine, food was constantly exported from Ireland to England, which would not have been the case had there been true famine in one country any more than in the other. During all the so-called famine a practically unlimited supply of American meat and grain could have been poured into Ireland, through the existing mechanism of exchange, so quickly that the relief would have been felt instantaneously. Our sending of supplies in a national warship was a piece of vulgar ostentation, fitly paralleled by their ostentatious distribution in British gunboats under the nominal superintendence of a royal prince. Had we been bent on relief, not display, we might have saved our government the expense of fitting up its antiquated warship, the British gunboats their coal, the Lord Mayor his dinner, and the Royal Prince his valuable time. A cable draft, turned

in Dublin into postal orders, would have afforded the relief, not merely much more easily and cheaply, but in less
time than it took our warship to get ready to receive her
cargo; for the reason that so many of the Irish people were
starving was, not that the food was not to be had, but that
they had not the means to buy it. Had the Irish people
had money or its equivalent, the bad seasons might have
come and gone without stinting anyone of a full meal.
Their effect would merely have been to determine toward
Ireland the flow of more abundant harvests.

I wish clearly to bring to view this point. The Irish famine was not a true famine arising from scarcity of food. It
was what an English writer styled the Indian famine — a
"financial famine," arising not from scarcity of food but
from the poverty of the people. The effect of the short crops
in producing distress was not so much in raising the price
of food as in cutting off the accustomed incomes of the
people. The masses of the Irish people get so little in ordinary times that they are barely able to live, and when anything occurs to interrupt their accustomed incomes they
have nothing to fall back on.

Yet is this not true of large classes in all countries? And
are not all countries subject to just such famines as this
Irish famine? Good seasons and bad seasons are in the order of nature, just as the day of sunshine and the day of
rain, the summer's warmth and the winter's snow. But agriculture is, on the whole, as certain as any other pursuit, for
even those industries which may be carried on regardless of
weather are subject to alternations as marked as those to
which agriculture is liable. There are good seasons and bad
seasons even in fishing and hunting, while the alternations
are very marked in mining and in manufacturing. In fact,
the more highly differentiated branches of industry which
advancing civilization tends to develop, though less directly
dependent upon rain and sunshine, heat and cold, seem

increasingly subject to alternations more frequent and intense. Though in a country of more diversified industry the failure of a crop or two could not have such widespread effects as in Ireland, yet the countries of more complex industries are liable to a greater variety of disasters. A war on another continent produces famine in Lancashire; Parisian milliners decree a change of fashion, and Coventry operatives are saved from starvation only by public alms; a railroad combination decides to raise the price of coal, and Pennsylvania miners find their earnings diminished by half or totally cut off; a bank breaks in New York, and in all the large American cities soup-houses must be opened!

In this Irish famine which provoked the land agitation, there is nothing that is peculiar. Such famines on a smaller or a larger scale are constantly occurring. Nay, more! the fact is, that famine, just such famine as this Irish famine, constantly exists in the richest and most highly civilized lands. It persists even in "good times" when trade is "booming;" it spreads and rages whenever from any cause industrial depression comes. It is kept under, or at least kept from showing its worst phases, by poor-rates and almshouses, by private benevolence and by vast organized charities, but it still exists, gnawing in secret when it does not openly rage. In the very centers of civilization, where the machinery of production and exchange is at the highest point of efficiency, where bank vaults hold millions, and show-windows flash with more than a prince's ransom, where elevators and warehouses are gorged with grain, and markets are piled with all things succulent and toothsome, where the dinners of Lucullus are eaten every day, and, if it be but cool, the very greyhounds wear dainty blankets — in these centers of wealth and power and refinement, there are always hungry men and women and little children. Never the sun goes down but on human beings prowling like wolves for food, or huddling together like vermin for shelter and warmth.

"Always with You" is the significant heading under which a New York paper, in these most prosperous times, publishes daily the tales of chronic famine; and in the greatest and richest city in the world — in that very London where the plenty of meat in the butchers' shops seemed to some savages the most wondrous of all its wonderful sights — in that very London, the mortuary reports have a standing column for deaths by starvation.

But no more in its chronic than in its spasmodic forms is famine to be measured by the deaths from starvation. Perfect, indeed, in all its parts must be the human machine if it can run till the last bit of available tissue be drawn on to feed its fires. It is under the guise of disease to which physicians can give less shocking names, that famine — especially the chronic famine of civilization — kills. And the statistics of mortality, especially of infant mortality, show that in the richest communities famine is constantly at its work. Insufficient nourishment, inadequate warmth and clothing, and unwholesome surroundings, constantly, in the very centers of plenty, swell the death rates. What is this but famine — just such famine as the Irish famine? It is not that the needed things are really scarce; but that those whose need is direst have not the means to get them, and, when not relieved by charity, want kills them in its various ways. When, in the hot midsummer, little children die like flies in the New York tenement wards, what is that but famine? And those barges crowded with such children that a noble and tender charity sends down New York Harbor to catch the fresh salt breath of the Atlantic — are they not fighting famine as truly as were our food-laden warship and the Royal Prince's gunboats? Alas! to find famine one has not to cross the sea.

There was bitter satire in the cartoon that one of our illustrated papers published when subscriptions to the Irish famine fund were being made — a cartoon that represented

James Gordon Bennett sailing away for Ireland in a boat loaded down with provisions, while a sad-eyed, hungry-looking, tattered group gazed wistfully on them from the pier. The bite and the bitterness of it, the humiliating sting and satire of it, were in its truth.

This is "the home of freedom," and "the asylum of the oppressed;" our population is yet sparse, our public domain yet wide; we are the greatest of food producers, yet even here there are beggars, tramps, paupers, men torn by anxiety for the support of their families, women who know not which way to turn, little children growing up in such poverty and squalor that only a miracle can keep them pure. "Always with you," even here. What is the week or the day of the week that our papers do not tell of man or woman who, to escape the tortures of want, has stepped out of life unbidden? What is this but famine?

III. A Universal Question

LET ME BE UNDERSTOOD. I am not endeavoring to excuse or belittle Irish distress. I am merely pointing out that distress of the same kind exists elsewhere This is a fact I want to make clear, for it has hitherto, in most of the discussions of the Irish Land Question, been ignored. And without an appreciation of this fact the real nature of the Irish Land Question is not understood, nor the real importance of the agitation seen.

What I contend for is this: That it is a mistake to consider the Irish Land Question as a mere local question, arising out of conditions peculiar to Ireland, and which can be settled by remedies that can have but local application. On the contrary, I contend that what has been brought into prominence by Irish distress, and forced into discussion by Irish agitation, is something infinitely more important than any mere local question could be; it is nothing less than that question of transcendent importance which is everywhere beginning to agitate, and, if not settled, must soon convulse the civilized world — the question whether, their political equality conceded (for, where this has not already been, it soon will be), the masses of mankind are to remain mere hewers of wood and drawers of water for the benefit of a fortunate few? Whether, having escaped from feudalism, modern society is to pass into an industrial organization more grinding and oppressive, more heartless and hopeless, than feudalism? Whether, amid the abundance their labor creates, the producers of wealth are to be content in good times with the barest of livings and in bad times to suffer and to starve? What is involved in this Irish Land Question is not a mere local matter between Irish landlords and Irish tenants, but the great social problem of modern civilization. What is arraigned in the arraignment of the claims of Irish landlords is nothing less than the widespread institution of private property in land. In the assertion of the natural rights of the Irish people is the assertion of the natural rights that, by virtue of his existence, pertain every-where to man.

It is probable that the Irish agitators did not at first perceive the real bearing and importance of the question they took in hand. But they — the more intelligent and ear-nest of them, at least — must now begin to realize it.* Yet, save, perhaps, on the part of the ultra-Tories, who would resist any concession as the opening of a door that cannot again be shut, there is on all sides a disposition to ignore the real nature of the question, and to treat it as springing from conditions peculiar to Ireland. On the one hand, there is a large class in England and elsewhere, who, while willing to concede or even actually desire that something should be done for Ireland, fear any extension of the agitation into a questioning of the rights of landowners elsewhere. And, on the other hand, the Irish leaders seem anxious to con-fine attention in the same way, evidently fearing that, should the question assume a broader aspect, strong forces now with them might fall away and, perhaps to a large extent, become directly and strongly antagonistic.

But it is not possible so to confine the discussion; no more possible than it was possible to confine to France the

---

* The *Irish World*, which, though published in New York, has ex-erted a large influence upon the agitation on both sides of the At-lantic, does realize, and has from the first frankly declared, that the fight must be against landlordism in toto and everywhere.

questions involved in the French Revolution; no more possible than it was possible to keep the discussion which arose over slavery in the Territories confined to the subject of slavery in the Territories. And it is best that the truth be fully stated and clearly recognized. He who sees the truth, let him proclaim it, without asking who is for it or who is against it. This is not radicalism in the bad sense which so many attach to the word. This is conservatism in the true sense.

What gives to the Irish Land Question its supreme significance is that it brings into attention and discussion — nay, that it forces into attention and discussion, not a mere Irish question, but a question of worldwide importance.

What has brought the land question to the front in Ireland, what permits the relation between land and labor to be seen there with such distinctness — to be seen even by those who cannot in other places perceive them — is certain special conditions. Ireland is a country of dense population, so that competition for the use of land is so sharp and high as to produce marked effects upon the distribution of wealth. It is mainly an agricultural country, so that production is concerned directly and unmistakably with the soil. Its industrial organization is largely that simple one in which an employing capitalist does not stand between laborer and landowner, so that the connection between rent and wages is not obscured. Ireland, moreover, was never conquered by the Romans, nor, until comparatively recently, by any people who had felt in their legal system the effect of Roman domination. It is the European country in which primitive ideas as to land tenures have longest held their sway, and the circumstances of its conquest, its cruel misgovernment, and the differences of race and religion between the masses of the people and those among whom the land was parceled, have tended to preserve old traditions and to direct the strength of Irish feeling and the fervor of Irish imagination against a system which forces the descendant of the ancient possessors of the soil to pay tribute for it to the representative of a hated stranger. It is for these reasons that the connection between Irish distress and Irish landlordism is so easily seen and readily realized.

But does not the same relation exist between English pauperism and English landlordism — between American tramps and the American land system? Essentially the same land system as that of Ireland exists elsewhere, and, wherever it exists, distress of essentially the same kind is to be seen. And elsewhere, just as certainly as in Ireland, is the connection between the two that of cause and effect.

When the agent of the Irish landlord takes from the Irish cottier for rent his pigs, his poultry, or his potatoes, or the money that he gains by the sale of these things, it is clear enough that this rent comes from the earnings of labor, and diminishes what the laborer gets. But is not this in reality just as clear when a dozen middlemen stand between laborer and landlord? Is it not just as clear when, instead of being paid monthly or quarterly or yearly, rent is paid in a lumped sum called purchase money? Whence come the incomes which the owners of land in mining districts, in manufacturing districts, or in commercial districts, receive for the use of their land? Manifestly, they must come from the earnings of labor — there is no other source from which they can come. From what are the revenues of Trinity Church corporation drawn, if not from the earnings of labor? What is the source of the income of the Astors, if it is not the labor of laboring men, women, and children? When a man makes a fortune by the rise of real estate, as in New York and elsewhere many men have done within the past few months, what does it mean? It means that he may have fine clothes, costly food, a grand house luxuriously furnished, etc. Now, these things are not the spontaneous fruits of the soil; neither do they fall from heaven, nor are they cast up by the sea. They are products of labor — can be produced only by labor. And hence, if men who do no labor get them, it must necessarily be at the expense of those who do labor.

It may seem as if I were needlessly dwelling upon a truth apparent by mere statement. Yet, simple as this truth is, it is persistently ignored. This is the reason that the true relation, and true importance of the question which has come to the front in Ireland are so little realized.

To give an illustration: In his article in the *North American Review* last year, Mr. Parnell speaks as though the building up of manufactures in Ireland would lessen the competition for land. What justification for such a view is there either in theory or in fact? Can manufacturing be carried on without land any more than agriculture can be carried on without land? Is not competition for land measured by price, and, if Ireland were a manufacturing country, would not the value of her land be greater than now? Had English clamor for "protection to home industry" not been suffered to secure the strangling of Irish industries in their infancy, Ireland might now be more of a manufacturing country with larger population and a greater aggregate production of wealth. But the tribute which the landowners could have taken would likewise have been greater. Put a Glasgow, a Manchester, or a London in one of the Irish agricultural counties, and, where the landlords now take pounds in rent, they would be enabled to demand hundreds and thousands of pounds. And it would necessarily come from the same source — the ultimate source of all incomes — the earnings of labor. That so large a proportion of the laboring-class would not have to compete with each other for agricultural land is true. But they would have to do what is precisely the same thing. They would have to compete with each other for employment — for the opportunity to make a living. And there is no reason to think that this competition would be less intense than now. On the contrary, in the manufacturing districts of England and Scotland, just as in the agricultural districts of Ireland, the competition for the privilege of earning a living forces wages to such a minimum as, even in good times, will give only a living.

What is the difference? The Irish peasant cultivator hires his little farm from a landlord, and pays rent directly. The English agricultural laborer hires himself to an employing farmer who hires the land, and who out of the produce pays to the one his wages and to the other his rent. In both cases competition forces the laborer down to a bare living as a net return for his work, and only stops at that point because, when men do not get enough to live on, they die and cease to compete. And, in the same way, competition forces the employing farmer to give up to the landlord all that he has left after paying wages, save the ordinary returns of capital — for the profits of the English farmer do not, on the average, I understand, exceed five or six per cent. And in other businesses, such as manufacturing, competition in the same way forces down wages to the minimum of a bare living, while rent goes up and up. Thus is it clear that no change in methods or improvements in the processes of industry lessens the landlord's power of claiming the lion's share.

I am utterly unable to see in what essential thing the condition of the Irish peasant would be a whit improved were Ireland as rich as England, and her industries as diversified. For the Irish peasant is not to be compared with the English tenant farmer, who is really a capitalist, but with the English agricultural laborer and the lowest class of factory operatives. Surely their condition is not so much better than that of the Irish peasant as to make a difference worth talking about. On the contrary, miserable as is the condition of the Irish peasantry, sickening as are the stories of their suffering, I am inclined to think that for the worst instances of human degradation one must go to the reports that describe the condition of the laboring poor of England, rather than to the literature of Irish misery. For there are three things for which, in spite of their poverty and wretchedness and occasional famine, the very poorest of Irish peasants are by all accounts remarkable — the physical vigor of their men, the purity of their women, and the strength of the family affections. This, to put it mildly, cannot be said of large classes of the laboring populations of England and Scotland. In those rich manufacturing districts are classes stunted and deteriorated physically by want and unwholesome employments; classes in which the idea of female virtue is all but lost, and the family affections all but trodden out.

But it is needless to compare sufferings and measure miseries. I merely wish to correct that impression which leads so many people to talk and write as though rent and land tenures related solely to agriculture and to agricultural communities. Nothing could be more erroneous. Land is necessary to all production, no matter what be its kind or form; land is the standing-place, the workshop, the storehouse of labor; it is to the human being the only means by which he can obtain access to the material universe or utilize its powers. Without land man cannot exist. To whom the ownership of land is given, to him is given the virtual ownership of the men who must live upon it. When this necessity is absolute, then does he necessarily become their absolute master. And just as this point is neared — that is to say, just as competition increases the demand for land — just in that degree does the power of taking a larger and larger share of the earnings of labor increase. It is this power that gives land its value; this is the power that enables the owner of valuable land to reap where he has not sown — to appropriate to himself wealth which he has had no share in producing. Rent is always the devourer of wages. The owner of city land takes, in the rents he receives for his land, the earnings of labor just as clearly as does the owner of farming land. And whether he be working in a garret ten stories above the street, or in a mining drift thousands of feet below the earth's surface, it is the competition for the use of land that ultimately determines what proportion of the produce of his labor the laborer will get for himself. This is the reason why modern progress does not tend to extirpate poverty; this is the reason why, with all the inventions and improvements and economies which so enormously increase productive power, wages everywhere tend to the minimum of a bare living. The cause that in Ireland produces poverty and distress — the ownership by some of the people of the land on which and from which the whole people must live — everywhere else produces the same results. It is this that produces the hideous squalor of London and Glasgow slums; it is this that makes want jostle luxury in the streets of rich New York, that forces little children to monotonous and stunting toil in Massachusetts mills, and that fills the highways of our newest States with tramps.

IV. Proposed Remedies

THE FACTS we have been considering give to the Irish agitation a significance and dignity that no effort for the redress of merely local grievances, no struggle for mere national independence could have. As the cause which produces Irish distress exists everywhere throughout modern civilization, and everywhere produces the same results, the question as to what measures will fully meet the case of Ireland has for us not merely a speculative and sentimental interest, but a direct and personal interest. For a year and more the English journals and magazines have been teeming with articles on the Irish Land Question; but, among all the remedies proposed, even by men whose reputation is that of clear thinkers and advanced Liberals, I have seen nothing which shows any adequate grasp of the subject. And this is true also of the measures proposed by the agitators, so far as they have proposed any. They are illogical and insufficient to the last degree. They neither disclose any clear principle nor do they aim at any result worth the struggle. From the most timid to the most radical, these schemes are restricted to one or more of the following propositions:

1. To abolish entails and primogenitures and other legal difficulties in the way of sales.
2. To legalize and extend tenant-right.
3. To establish tribunals of arbitrament which shall decide upon appeal the rent to be paid.
4. To have the State buy out the landlords and sell again on time to the tenants.

The first of these propositions is good in itself. To make the transfer of land easy would be to remove obstacles which prevent its passing into the hands of those who would make the most out of it. But, so far as this will have any effect at all, it will not be toward giving the Irish tenants more merciful landlords; nor yet will it be to the diffusion of landed property. Those who think so shut their eyes to the fact that the tendency of the time is to concentration.

As for the propositions which look in various forms to the establishment of tenant-right, it is to be observed that, in so far as they go beyond giving the tenant surety for his improvements, they merely carve out of the estate of the landlord an estate for the tenant. Even if the proposal to empower the courts, in cases of dispute, to decide what is a fair rent were to amount to anything (and the Land Leaguers say it would not), the fixing of a lower rent as the share of the landlord would merely enable the tenant to charge a higher price to his successor. Whatever might thus be done for present agricultural tenants would be of no use to future tenants, and nothing whatever would be done for the masses of the people. In fact, that the effect would be to increase rent in the aggregate there can be no doubt. Whatever modification might be made in the landlord's demands, the sum which the outgoing tenant would ask would be very certain to be all he could possibly get, so that rent in the aggregate, instead of being diminished, would be screwed up to the full competition or rack-rent standard.

What seem to be considered the most radical propositions yet made are those for the creation of a "peasant proprietary" — the State to buy out the landlords and resell to the tenants, for annual payments extending over a term of years, and covering principal and interest. Waiving all practical difficulties, and they are very great, what could thus be accomplished? Nothing real and permanent. For not merely is this, too, but a partial measure, which could not improve

the condition of the masses of the people or help those
most needing help, but no sooner were the lands thus divided than a process of concentration would infallibly set
in which would be all the more rapid from the fact that the
new landholders would be heavily mortgaged. The tendency
to concentration which has so steadily operated in Great
Britain, and is so plainly showing itself in our new States,
must operate in Ireland, and would immediately begin to
weld together again the little patches of the newly created
peasant proprietors. The tendency of the time is against
peasant proprietorships; it is in everything to concentration, not to separation. The tendency which has wiped out
the small landowners, the boasted yeomanry, of England —
which in our new States is uniting the quarter-sections of
preemption and homestead settlers into great farms of thousands of acres — is already too strong to be resisted, and is
constantly becoming stronger and more penetrating. For it
springs from the inventions and improvements and economies which are transforming modern industry — the same
influences which are concentrating population in large cities, business into the hands of great houses, and for the
blacksmith making his own nails or the weaver working his
own loom substitute the factory of the great corporation.

That a great deal that the English advocates of peasant
proprietorship have to say about the results of their favorite
system in continental Europe is not borne out by the facts,
any one who chooses to look over the testimony may see.
But it is useless to discuss that. Peasant proprietorship in
continental Europe is a survival. It exists only among populations which have not felt fully the breath of the new era.
It continues to exist only by virtue of conditions which do
not obtain in Ireland. The Irish peasant is not the French
or Belgian peasant. He is in the habit of having very "long
families;" they very short ones. He has become familiar with
the idea of emigrating; they have not. He can hardly be

expected to have acquired those habits of close economy and careful forethought for which they are so remarkable; and there are various agencies, among which are to be counted the national schools and the reaction from America, that have roused in him aspirations and ambitions which would prevent him from continuing to water his little patch with his sweat, as do the French and Belgian peasant proprietors, when he could sell it for enough to emigrate. Peasant proprietorship, like that of France and Belgium, might possibly have been instituted in Ireland some time ago, before the railroad and the telegraph and the national schools and the establishment of the steam bridge across the Atlantic. But to do it now to any extent, and with any permanency, seems to me about as practicable as to go back to hand-loom weaving in Manchester. Much more in accordance with modern tendencies is the notice I have recently seen of the formation of a company to buy up land in Southern Ireland, and cultivate it on a large scale; for to production on a large scale modern processes more and more strongly tend. It is not merely the steam plow and harvesting machinery that make the cultivation of the large field more profitable than that of the small one; it is the railroad, the telegraph, the manifold inventions of all sorts. Even butter and cheese are now made and chickens hatched and fattened in factories.

But the fatal defect of all these schemes as remedial measures is that they do not go to the cause of the disease. What they propose to do, they propose to do for merely one class of the Irish people — the agricultural tenants. Now, the agricultural tenants are not so large nor so poor a class (among them are in fact many large capitalist farmers of the English type) as the agricultural laborers, while besides these there are the laborers of other kinds — the artisans, operatives, and poorer classes of the cities. What extension of tenant-right or conversion of tenant farmers into partial or absolute proprietors is to benefit them? Even if the number of owners of Irish soil could thus be increased, the soil of Ireland would still be in the hands of a class, though of a somewhat larger class. And the spring of Irish misery would be untouched. Those who had merely their labor would be as badly off as now, if not in some respects worse off. Rent would soon devour wages, and the injustice involved in the present system would be intrenched by the increase in the number who seemingly profit by it.

It is that peasant proprietors would strengthen the existing system that makes schemes for creating them so popular among certain sections of the propertied classes of Great Britain. This is the ground on which these schemes are largely urged. These small landowners are desired that they may be used as a buffer and bulwark against any questioning of the claims of the larger owners. They would be put forward to resist the shock of "agrarianism," just as the women are put forward in resistance to the process-servers. "What! do you propose to rob these poor peasants of their little homesteads?" would be the answer to any one who proposed to attack the system under which the larger landholders draw millions annually from the produce of labor.

And here is the danger in the adoption of measures not based upon correct principles. They fail not only to do any real and permanent good, but they make proper measures more difficult. Even if a majority of the people of Ireland were made the owners of the soil, the injustice to the minority would be as great as now, and wages would still tend to the minimum, which in good times means a bare living, and in bad times means starvation. Even were it possible to cut up the soil of Ireland into those little patches into which the soil of France and Belgium is cut in the districts where the *morcellement* prevails, this would not be the attainment of a just and healthy social state; it would make the attainment of a just and healthy social state much more difficult.

V. Whose Land Is It?

WHAT, THEN, is the true solution of the Irish problem? The answer is as important to other countries as to Ireland, for the Irish problem is but a local phase of the great problem which is everywhere pressing upon the civilized world.

With the leaders of the Irish movement, the question is, of course, not merely what ought to be done, but what can be done. But, to a clear understanding of the whole subject, the question of principle must necessarily precede that of method. We must decide where we want to go before we can decide what is the best road to take.

The first question that naturally arises is that of right. Among whatever kind of people such a matter as this is discussed, the question of right is sure to be raised. This, to me, seems a very significant thing; for I believe it to spring from nothing less than a universal perception of the human mind — a perception often dim and vague, yet still a universal perception, that justice is the supreme law of the universe, so that, as a short road to what is best, we instinctively ask, "What is right?"

Now, what are the rights of this case? To whom rightfully does the soil of Ireland belong? Who are justly entitled to its use and to all the benefits that flow from its use? Let us settle this question clearly and decisively, before we attempt anything else.

Let me go to the heart of this question by asking another question: Has or has not the child born in Ireland a right to live? There can be but one answer, for no one would contend that it was right to drown Irish babies, or that any human law could make it right. Well, then, if every human being born in Ireland has a right to live in Ireland, these rights must be equal. If each one has a right to live, then no one can have any better right to live than any other one. There can be no dispute about this. No one will contend that it would be any less a crime to drown a baby of an Irish peasant woman than it would be to drown the baby of the proudest duchess, or that a law commanding the one would be any more justifiable than a law commanding the other.

Since, then, all the Irish people have the same equal right to life, it follows that they must all have the same equal right to the land of Ireland. If they are all in Ireland by the same equal permission of Nature, so that no one of them can justly set up a superior claim to life than any other one of them; so that all the rest of them could not justly say to any one of them, "You have not the same right to live as we have; therefore we will pitch you out of Ireland into the sea!" then they must all have the same equal rights to the elements which Nature has provided for the sustaining of life — to air, to water, and to land. For to deny the equal right to the elements necessary to the maintaining of life is to deny the equal right to life. Any law that said, "Certain babies have no right to the soil of Ireland; therefore they shall be thrown off the soil of Ireland;" would be precisely equivalent to a law that said, "Certain babies have no right to live; therefore they shall be thrown into the sea." And as no law or custom or agreement can justify the denial of the equal right to life, so no law or custom or agreement can justify the denial of the equal right to land.

It therefore follows, from the very fact of their existence, that the right of each one of the people of Ireland to an equal share in the land of Ireland is equal and inalienable: that is to say, that the use and benefit of the land of Ireland belong rightfully to the whole people of Ireland, to each one as much as to every other; to no one more than to any other — not to some individuals, to the exclusion of other individuals; not to one class, to the exclusion of other classes; not to landlords, not to tenants, not to cultivators, but to the whole people.

This right is irrefutable and indefeasible. It pertains to and springs from the fact of existence, the right to live. No law, no covenant, no agreement, can bar it. One generation cannot stipulate away the rights of another generation. If the whole people of Ireland were to unite in bargaining away their rights in the land, how could they justly bargain away the right of the child who the next moment is born? No one can bargain away what is not his; no one can stipulate away the rights of another. And if the newborn infant has an equal right to life, then has it an equal right to land. Its warrant, which comes direct from Nature, and which sets aside all human laws or title-deeds, is the fact that it is born.

Here we have a firm, self-apparent principle from which we may safely proceed. The land of Ireland does not belong to one individual more than to another individual; to one class more than to another class; to one generation more than to the generations that come after. It belongs to the whole people who at the time exist upon it.

VI. Landlords' Right Is Labor's Wrong

I DO NOT DWELL upon this principle because it has not yet been asserted. I dwell upon it because, although it has been asserted, no proposal to carry it out has yet been made. The cry has indeed gone up that the land of Ireland belongs to the people of Ireland, but there the recognition of the principle has stopped. To say that the land of Ireland belongs to the people of Ireland, and then merely to ask that rents shall be reduced, or that tenant right be extended, or that the State shall buy the land from one class and sell it to another class, is utterly illogical and absurd.

Either the land of Ireland rightfully belongs to the Irish landlords, or it rightfully belongs to the Irish people; there can be no middle ground. If it rightfully belongs to the landlords, then is the whole agitation wrong, and every scheme for interfering in any way with the landlords is condemned. If the land rightfully belongs to the landlords, then it is nobody else's business what they do with it, or what rent they charge for it, or where or how they spend the money they draw from it, and whoever does not want to live upon it on the landlords' terms is at perfect liberty to starve or emigrate. But if, on the contrary, the land of Ireland rightfully belongs to the Irish people, then the only logical demand is, not that the tenants shall be made joint owners with the landlords, not that it be bought from a smaller class and sold to a larger class, but that it be resumed by the whole people. To propose to pay the landlords for it is to deny the right of the people to it. The real fight for Irish rights must be made outside of Ireland; and, above all things, the Irish agitators ought to take a logical position, based upon a broad, clear principle which can be everywhere understood and appreciated. To ask for tenant-right or peasant proprietorship is not to take such a position; to concede that the landlords ought to be paid is utterly to abandon the principle that the land belongs rightfully to the people.

To admit, as even the most radical of the Irish agitators seem to admit, that the landlords should be paid the value of their lands, is to deny the rights of the people. It is an admission that the agitation is an interference with the just rights of property. It is to ignore the only principle on which the agitation can be justified, and on which it can gather strength for the accomplishment of anything real and permanent. To admit this is to admit that the Irish people have no more right to the soil of Ireland than any outsider. For, any outsider can go to Ireland and buy land, if he will give its market value. To propose to buy out the landlords is to propose to continue the present injustice in another form. They would get in interest on the debt created what they now get in rent. They would still have a lien upon Irish labor.

And why should the landlords be paid? If the land of Ireland belongs of natural right to the Irish people, what valid claim for payment can be set up by the landlords? No one will contend that the land is theirs of natural right, for the day has gone by when men could be told that the Creator of the universe intended his bounty for the exclusive use and benefit of a privileged class of his creatures — that he intended a few to roll in luxury while their fellows toiled and starved for them. The claim of the landlords to the land rests not on natural right, but merely on municipal law — on municipal law which contravenes natural right. And, whenever the sovereign power changes municipal law

so as to conform to natural right, what claim can they assert
to compensation? Some of them bought their lands, it is
true; but they got no better title than the seller had to give.
And what are these titles? Titles based on murder and robbery, on blood and rapine — titles which rest on the most
atrocious and wholesale crimes. Created by force and maintained by force, they have not behind them the first shadow
of right. That Henry II and James I and Cromwell and the
Long Parliament had the power to give and grant Irish lands
is true; but will any one contend they had the right? Will
any one contend that in all the past generations there has
existed on the British Isles or anywhere else any human
being, or any number of human beings, who had the right
to say that in the year 1881 the great mass of Irishmen should
be compelled to pay — in many cases to residents of England, France, or the United States — for the privilege of
living in their native country and making a living from their
native soil? Even if it be said that might makes right; even if
it be contended that in the twelfth, or seventeenth, or eigh-
teenth century lived men who, having the power, had therefore the right, to give away the soil of Ireland, it cannot be
contended that their right went further than their power,
or that their gifts and grants are binding on the men of the
present generation. No one can urge such a preposterous
doctrine. And, if might makes right, then the moment the
people get power to take the land the rights of the present
landholders utterly cease, and any proposal to compensate
them is a proposal to do a fresh wrong.

Should it be urged that, no matter on what they originally rest, the lapse of time has given to the legal owners of
Irish land a title of which they cannot now be justly deprived without compensation, it is sufficient to ask, with
Herbert Spencer, at what rate per annum wrong becomes
right? Even the shallow pretense that the acquiescence of
society can vest in a few the exclusive right to that element

on which and from which Nature has ordained that all must live, cannot be urged in the case of Ireland. For the Irish people have never acquiesced in their spoliation, unless the bound and gagged victim may be said to acquiesce in the robbery and maltreatment which he cannot prevent. Though the memory of their ancient rights in the land of their country may have been utterly stamped out among the people of England, and have been utterly forgotten among their kin on this side of the sea, it has long survived among the Irish. If the Irish people have gone hungry and cold and ignorant, if they have been evicted from lands on which their ancestors had lived from time immemorial, if they have been forced to emigrate or to starve, it has not been for the want of protest. They have protested all they could; they have struggled all they could. It has been but superior force that has stifled their protests and made their struggles vain. In a blind, dumb way, they are protesting now and struggling now, though even if their hands were free they might not at first know how to untie the knots in the cords that bind them. But acquiesce they never have.

Yet, even supposing they had acquiesced, as in their ignorance the working-classes of such countries as England and the United States now acquiesce, in the iniquitous system which makes the common birthright of all the exclusive property of some. What then? Does such acquiescence turn wrong into right? If the sleeping traveler wake to find a robber with his hand in his pocket, is he bound to buy the robber off — bound not merely to let him keep what he has previously taken, but pay him the full value of all he expected the sleep of his victim to permit him to get? If the stockholders of a bank find that for a long term of years their cashier has been appropriating the lion's share of the profits, are they to be told that they cannot discharge him without paying him for what he might have got, had his peculations not been discovered?

VII. The Great-Great Grandson of Captain Kidd

I APOLOGIZE to the Irish landlords and to all other landlords for likening them to thieves and robbers. I trust they will understand that I do not consider them as personally worse than other men, but that I am obliged to use such illustrations because no others will fit the case. I am concerned not with individuals, but with the system. What I want to do is, to point out a distinction that in the plea for the vested rights of landowners is ignored — a distinction which arises from the essential difference between land and things that are the produce of human labor, and which is obscured by our habit of classing them all together as property.

The galleys that carried Cæsar to Britain, the accoutrements of his legionaries, the baggage that they carried, the arms that they bore, the buildings that they erected; the scythed chariots of the ancient Britons, the horses that drew them, their wicker boats and wattled houses — where are they now? But the land for which Roman and Briton fought, there it is still. That British soil is yet as fresh and as new as it was in the days of the Romans. Generation after generation has lived on it since, and generation after generation will live on it yet. Now, here is a very great difference. The right to possess and to pass on the ownership of things that in their nature decay and soon cease to be is a very different thing from the right to possess and to pass on the ownership of that which does not decay, but from which each successive generation must live.

To show how this difference between land and such

other species of property as are properly styled wealth bears upon the argument for the vested rights of landholders, let me illustrate again.

Captain Kidd was a pirate. He made a business of sailing the seas, capturing merchantmen, making their crews walk the plank, and appropriating their cargoes. In this way he accumulated much wealth, which he is thought to have buried. But let us suppose, for the sake of the illustration, that he did not bury his wealth, but left it to his legal heirs, and they to their heirs and so on, until at the present day this wealth or a part of it has come to a great-great-grandson of Captain Kidd. Now, let us suppose that someone — say a great-great-grandson of one of the shipmasters whom Captain Kidd plundered, makes complaint, and says: "This man's great-great-grandfather plundered my great-great-grandfather of certain things or certain sums, which have been transmitted to him, whereas but for this wrongful act they would have been transmitted to me; therefore, I demand that he be made to restore them." What would society answer?

Society, speaking by its proper tribunals, and in accordance with principles recognized among all civilized nations, would say: "We cannot entertain such a demand. It may be true that Mr. Kidd's great-great-grandfather robbed your great-great-grandfather, and that as the result of this wrong he has got things that otherwise might have come to you. But we cannot inquire into occurrences that happened so long ago. Each generation has enough to do to attend to its own affairs. If we go to righting the wrongs and reopening the controversies of our great-great-grandfathers, there will be endless disputes and pretexts for dispute. What you say may be true, but somewhere we must draw the line, and have an end to strife. Though this man's great-great-grandfather may have robbed your great-great-grandfather, he has not robbed you. He came into possession of these things peacefully, and has held them peacefully, and we must take this peaceful possession, when it has been continued for a certain time, as absolute evidence of just title; for, were we not to do that, there would be no end to dispute and no secure possession of anything."

Now, it is this commonsense principle that is expressed in the statute of limitations — in the doctrine of vested rights. This is the reason why it is held — and as to most things held justly — that peaceable possession for a certain time cures all defects of title.

But let us pursue the illustration a little further:

Let us suppose that Captain Kidd, having established a large and profitable piratical business, left it to his son, and he to his son, and so on, until the great-great-grandson, who now pursues it, has come to consider it the most natural thing in the world that his ships should roam the sea, capturing peaceful merchantmen, making their crews walk the plank, and bringing home to him much plunder, whereby he is enabled, though he does no work at all, to live in very great luxury, and look down with contempt upon people who have to work. But at last, let us suppose, the merchants get tired of having their ships sunk and their goods taken, and sailors get tired of trembling for their lives every time a sail lifts above the horizon, and they demand of society that piracy be stopped.

Now, what should society say if Mr. Kidd got indignant, appealed to the doctrine of vested rights, and asserted that society was bound to prevent any interference with the business that he had inherited, and that, if it wanted him to stop, it must buy him out, paying him all that his business was worth — that is to say, at least as much as he could make in twenty years' successful pirating, so that if he stopped pirating he could still continue to live in luxury off of the profits of the merchants and the earnings of the sailors?

What ought society to say to such a claim as this? There

will be but one answer. We will all say that society should
tell Mr. Kidd that his was a business to which the statute of
limitations and the doctrine of vested rights did not apply;
that because his father, and his grandfather, and his great-
and great- great-grandfather pursued the business of capturing ships and making their crews walk the plank, was no
reason why he should be permitted to pursue it. Society, we
will all agree, ought to say he would have to stop piracy and
stop it at once, and that without getting a cent for stopping.

Or supposing it had happened that Mr. Kidd had sold
out his piratical business to Smith, Jones, or Robinson, we
will all agree that society ought to say that their purchase of
the business gave them no greater right than Mr. Kidd had.

We will all agree that that is what society ought to say.
Observe, I do not ask what society would say.

For, ridiculous and preposterous as it may appear, I am
satisfied that, under the circumstances I have supposed,
society would not for a long time say what we have agreed it
ought to say. Not only would all the Kidds loudly claim that
to make them give up their business without full recompense would be a wicked interference with vested rights,
but the justice of this claim would at first be assumed as a
matter of course by all or nearly all the influential classes —
the great lawyers, the able journalists, the writers for the
magazines, the eloquent clergymen, and the principal pro-
fessors in the principal universities. Nay, even the merchants
and sailors, when they first began to complain, would be
so tyrannized and browbeaten by this public opinion that
they would hardly think of more than of buying out the
Kidds, and, wherever here and there any one dared to raise
his voice in favor of stopping piracy at once and without
compensation, he would only do so under penalty of being
stigmatized as a reckless disturber and wicked foe of social
order.

If any one denies this, if any one says mankind are not

such fools, then I appeal to universal history to bear me witness. I appeal to the facts of today.

Show me a wrong, no matter how monstrous, that ever yet, among any people, became ingrafted in the social system, and I will prove to you the truth of what I say.

The majority of men do not think; the majority of men have to expend so much energy in the struggle to make a living that they do not have time to think. The majority of men accept, as a matter of course, whatever is. This is what makes the task of the social reformer so difficult, his path so hard. This is what brings upon those who first raise their voices in behalf of a great truth the sneers of the powerful and the curses of the rabble, ostracism and martyrdom, the robe of derision and the crown of thorns.

Am I not right? Have there not been states of society in which piracy has been considered the most respectable and honorable of pursuits? Did the Roman populace see anything more reprehensible in a gladiatorial show than we do in a horse-race? Does public opinion in Dahomey see anything reprehensible in the custom of sacrificing a thousand or two human beings by way of signalizing grand occasions? Are there not states of society in which, in spite of the natural proportions of the sexes, polygamy is considered a matter of course? Are there not states of society in which it would be considered the most ridiculous thing in the world to say that a man's son was more closely related to him than his nephew? Are there not states of society in which it would be considered disreputable for a man to carry a burden while a woman who could stagger under it was around? — states of society in which the husband who did not occasionally beat his wife would be deemed by both sexes a weak-minded, low-spirited fellow? What would Chinese fashionable society consider more outrageous than to be told that mothers should not be permitted to squeeze their daughters' feet, or Flathead women than being restrained from tying a board on their infants' skulls? How long has it been since the monstrous doctrine of the divine right of kings was taught through all Christendom?

What is the slave trade but piracy of the worst kind? Yet it is not long since the slave-trade was looked upon as a perfectly respectable business, affording as legitimate an opening for the investment of capital and the display of enterprise as any other. The proposition to prohibit it was first looked upon as ridiculous, then as fanatical, then as wicked. It was only slowly and by hard fighting that the truth in regard to it gained ground. Does not our very Constitution bear witness to what I say? Does not the fundamental law of the nation, adopted twelve years after the enunciation of the Declaration of Independence, declare that for twenty years the slave-trade shall not be prohibited nor restricted? Such dominion had the idea of vested interests over the minds of those who had already proclaimed the inalienable right of man to life, liberty, and the pursuit of happiness!

Is it not but yesterday that in the freest and greatest republic on earth, among the people who boast that they lead the very van of civilization, this doctrine of vested rights was deemed a sufficient justification for all the cruel wrongs of human slavery? Is it not but yesterday when whoever dared to say that the rights of property did not justly attach to human beings; when whoever dared to deny that human beings could be rightfully bought and sold like cattle — the husband torn from the wife and the child from the mother; when whoever denied the right of whoever had paid his money for him to work or whip his own nigger was looked upon as a wicked assailant of the rights of property? Is it not but yesterday when in the South whoever whispered such a thought took his life in his hands; when in the North the abolitionist was held by the churches as worse than an infidel, was denounced by the politicians and rotten-egged by the mob? I was born in a Northern State, I have never lived in the South, I am not yet gray; but I well remember, as every American of middle age must remember, how over and over again I have heard all questionings of slavery silenced by the declaration that the negroes were the property of their masters, and that to take away a man's slave without payment was as much a crime as to take away his horse without payment. And whoever does not remember that far back, let him look over American literature previous to the war, and say whether, if the business of piracy had been a flourishing business, it would have lacked defenders? Let him say whether any proposal to stop the business of piracy without compensating the pirates would not have been denounced at first as a proposal to set aside vested rights?

But I am appealing to other states of society and to times that are past merely to get my readers, if I can, out of their accustomed ruts of thought. The proof of what I assert about the Kidds and their business is in the thought and speech of today.

Here is a system which robs the producers of wealth as remorselessly and far more regularly and systematically than the pirate robs the merchantman. Here is a system that steadily condemns thousands to far more lingering and horrible deaths than that of walking the plank — to death of the mind and death of the soul, as well as death of the body. These things are undisputed. No one denies that Irish pauperism and famine are the direct results of this land system, and no one who will examine the subject will deny that the chronic pauperism and chronic famine which everywhere mark our civilization are the results of this system. Yet we are told — nay, it seems to be taken for granted — that this system cannot be abolished without buying off those who profit by it. Was there ever more degrading abasement of the human mind before a fetish? Can we wonder, as we see it, at any perversion of ideas?

Consider: is not the parallel I have drawn a true one? Is it not just as much a perversion of ideas to apply the doctrine of vested rights to property in land, when these are its admitted fruits, as it was to apply it to property in human flesh and blood; as it would be to apply it to the business of piracy? In what does the claim of the Irish landholders differ from that of the hereditary pirate or the man who has bought out a piratical business? "Because I have inherited or purchased the business of robbing merchantmen," says the pirate, "therefore respect for the rights of property must compel you to let me go on robbing ships and making sailors walk the plank until you buy me out." "Because we have inherited or purchased the privilege of appropriating to ourselves the lion's share of the produce of labor," says the landlord, "therefore you must continue to let us do it, even though poor wretches shiver with cold and faint with hunger, even though, in their poverty and misery, they are reduced to wallow with the pigs." What is the difference?

This is the point I want to make clearly and distinctly, for it shows a distinction that in current thought is overlooked. Property in land, like property in slaves, is essentially different from property in things that are the result of labor. Rob a man or a people of money, or goods, or cattle, and the robbery is finished there and then. The lapse of time does not, indeed, change wrong into right, but it obliterates the effects of the deed. That is done; it is over; and, unless it be very soon righted, it glides away into the past, with the men who were parties to it, so swiftly that nothing save omniscience can trace its effects; and in attempting to right it we would be in danger of doing fresh wrong. The past is forever beyond us. We can neither punish nor recompense the dead. But rob a people of the land on which they must live, and the robbery is continuous. It is a fresh robbery of every succeeding generation — a new robbery every year and every day; it is like the robbery which condemns to slavery the children of the slave. To apply to it the statute of limitations, to acknowledge for it the title of prescription, is not to condone the past; it is to legalize robbery in the present, to justify it in the future. The indictment which really lies against the Irish landlords is not that their ancestors, or the ancestors of their grantors, robbed the ancestors of the Irish people. That makes no difference. "Let the dead bury their dead." The indictment that truly lies is that here, now, in the year 1881, they rob the Irish people. And shall we be told that there can be a vested right to continue such robbery?

VIII. The Only Way, The Easy Way

I HAVE DWELT so long upon this question of compensating landowners, not merely because it is of great practical importance, but because its discussion brings clearly into view the principles upon which the land question, in any country, can alone be justly and finally settled. In the light of these principles we see that landowners have no rightful claim either to the land or to compensation for its resumption by the people, and, further than that, we see that no such rightful claim can ever be created. It would be wrong to pay the present landowners for "their" land at the expense of the people; it would likewise be wrong to sell it again to smaller holders. It would be wrong to abolish the payment of rent, and to give the land to its present cultivators. In the very nature of things, land cannot rightfully be made individual property. This principle is absolute. The title of a peasant proprietor deserves no more respect than the title of a great territorial noble. No sovereign political power, no compact or agreement, even though consented to by the whole population of the globe, can give to an individual a valid title to the exclusive ownership of a square inch of soil. The earth is an entailed estate — entailed upon all the generations of the children of men, by a deed written in the constitution of Nature, a deed that no human proceedings can bar, and no prescription determine. Each succeeding generation has but a tenancy for life. Admitting that any set of men may barter away their own natural rights (and this logically involves an admission of the right of suicide), they can no more barter away the rights of their successors than they can barter away the rights of the inhabitants of other worlds.

What should be aimed at in the settlement of the Irish Land Question is thus very clear. The "three F's" are, what they have already been called, three frauds; and the proposition to create peasant proprietorship is no better. It will not do merely to carve out of the estates of the landlords minor estates for the tenants; it will not do merely to substitute a larger for a smaller class of proprietors; it will not do to confine the settlement to agricultural land, leaving to its present possessors the land of the towns and villages. None of these lame and impotent conclusions will satisfy the demands of justice or cure the bitter evils now so apparent. The only true and just solution of the problem, the only end worth aiming at, is to make all the land the common property of all the people.

This principle conceded, the question of method arises. How shall this be done? Nothing is easier. It is merely necessary to divert the rent which now flows into the pockets of the landlords into the common treasury of the whole people. It is not possible so to divide up the land of Ireland as to give each family, still less each individual, an equal share. And, even if that were possible, it would not be possible to maintain equality, for old people are constantly dying and new people constantly being born, while the relative value of land is constantly changing. But it is possible to divide the rent equally, or, what amounts to the same thing, to apply it to purposes of common benefit. This is the way, and this is the only way, in which absolute justice can be done. This is the way, and this is the only way, in which the equal right of every man, woman, and child can be acknowledged and secured. As Herbert Spencer says of it:

> Such a doctrine is consistent with the highest state of civilization; may be carried out without involving a community of

goods, and need cause no very serious revolution in existing arrangements. The change required would simply be a change of landlords. Separate ownership would merge into the joint-stock ownership of the public. Instead of being in the possession of individuals, the country would be held by the great corporate body – society. Instead of leasing his acres from an isolated proprietor, the farmer would lease them from the nation. Instead of paying his rent to the agent of Sir John or his Grace, he would pay it to an agent or deputy agent of the community. Stewards would be public officials instead of private ones, and tenancy the only land tenure. A state of things so ordered would be in perfect harmony with the moral law. Under it, all men would be equally landlords; all men would be alike free to become tenants. . . . Clearly, therefore, on such a system, the earth might be inclosed, occupied, and cultivated, in entire subordination to the law of equal freedom. *

Now, it is a very easy thing thus to sweep away all private ownership of land, and convert all occupiers into tenants of the State, by appropriating rent. No complicated laws or cumbersome machinery is necessary. It is necessary only to tax land up to its full value. Do that, and without any talk about dispossessing landlords, without any use of the ugly word "confiscation," without any infringement of the just rights of property, the land would become virtually the people's, while the landlords would be left the absolute and unqualified possessors of — their deeds of title and conveyance! They could continue to call themselves landlords, if they wished to, just as that poor old Bourbon, the *Comte de Chambord,* continues to call himself King of France; but, as what, under this system, was paid by the tenant would be taken by the State, it is pretty clear that middlemen would not long survive, and that very soon the occupiers of land would come to be nominally the owners, though, in reality, they would be the tenants of the whole people.

---

* *Social Statics,* Chapter IX., sec. 8.

How beautifully this simple method would satisfy every economic requirement; how, freeing labor and capital from the fetters that now oppress them (for all other taxes could be easily remitted), it would enormously increase the production of wealth; how it would make distribution conform to the law of justice, dry up the springs of want and misery, elevate society from its lowest stratum, and give all their fair share in the blessings of advancing civilization, can perhaps be fully shown only by such a detailed examination of the whole social problem as I have made in a book* which I hope will be read by all the readers of this, since in it I go over much ground and treat many subjects which cannot be even touched upon here. Nevertheless, any one can see that to tax land up to its full rental value would amount to precisely the same thing as formally to take possession of it, and then let it out to the highest bidders.

---

* *Progress and Poverty.*

IX. Principle the Best Policy

WE HAVE NOW SEEN the point that should be aimed at, and the method by which it is to be reached. There is another branch of the subject which practical men must consider: the political forces that may be marshaled; the political resistance that must be overcome. It is one thing to work out such a problem in the closet to demonstrate its proper solution to the satisfaction of a few intelligent readers. It is another thing to solve it in the field of action, where ignorance, prejudice, and powerful interests must be met.

It cannot be that the really earnest men in the Irish movement are satisfied with any program yet put forth. But they are doubtless influenced by the fear that the avowal of radical views and aims would not merely intensify present opposition, but frighten away from their cause large numbers and important influences now with it. To say nothing of English conservatism, there is in Ireland a large class now supporting the movement who are morbidly afraid of anything which savors of "communism" or "socialism," while in the United States, whence much moral support and pecuniary aid have been derived, it is certain that many of those who are now loudest in their expressions of sympathy would slink away from a movement which avowed the intention of abolishing private property in land. A resolution expressive of sympathy with the Irish people in their "struggle for the repeal of oppressive land laws" was, by a unanimous vote of the National House of Representatives, flung full in the face of the British lion. How many votes would that resolution have got had it involved a declaration of hostility to the institution of individual property in land?

I understand all this. Nevertheless, I am convinced that the Irish land movement would gain, not lose, were its earnest leaders, disdaining timid counsels, boldly to avow the principle that the land of Ireland belongs of right to the whole people of Ireland, and, without bothering about compensation to the landholders, to propose its resumption by the people in the simple way I have suggested. That, in doing this, they would lose strength and increase antagonism in some directions is true, but they would in other directions gain strength and allay antagonisms. And, while the loss would constantly tend to diminish, the gain would constantly tend to increase. They would, to use the phrase of Emerson, have hitched their wagon to a star."

I admit, as will be urged by those who would hold back from such an avowal as I propose, that political progress must be by short steps rather than by great leaps; that those who would have the people follow them readily, and especially those who would enjoy a present popularity and preferment, must not go too far in advance; and that to demand a little at first is often the surest way to obtain much at last.

So far as personal consideration is concerned, it is only to earnest men capable of feeling the inspiration of a great principle that I care to talk, or that I can hope to convince. To them I wish to point out that caution is not wisdom when it involves the ignoring of a great principle; that it is not every step that involves progression, but only such steps as are in the right line and make easier the next; that there are strong forces that wait but the raising of the true standard to rally on its side.

Let the time-servers, the demagogues, the compromisers, to whom nothing is right and nothing is wrong, but who are always seeking to find some halfway house between right and wrong — let them all go their ways. Any cause which can lay hold of a great truth is the stronger without them. If the earnest men among the Irish leaders abandon their present half-hearted, illogical position, and take their stand frankly and firmly upon the principle that the youngest child of the poorest peasant has as good a right to tread the soil and breathe the air of Ireland as the eldest son of the proudest duke, they will have put their fight on the right line. Present defeat will but pave the way for future victory, and each step won makes easier the next. Their position will be not only logically defensible, but will prove the stronger the more it is discussed; for private property in land — which never arises from the natural perceptions of men, but springs historically from usurpation and robbery — is something so utterly absurd, so outrageously unjust, so clearly a waste of productive forces and a barrier to the most profitable use of natural opportunities, so thoroughly opposed to all sound maxims of public policy, so glaringly in the way of further progress, that it is only tolerated because the majority of men never think about it or hear it questioned. Once fairly arraign it, and it must be condemned; once call upon its advocates to exhibit its claims, and their cause is lost in advance. There is today no political economist of standing who dare hazard his reputation by defending it on economic grounds; there is today no thinker of eminence who either does not, like Herbert Spencer, openly declare the injustice of private property in land, or tacitly make the same admission.

Once force the discussion on this line, and the Irish reformers will compel to their side the most active and powerful of the men who mold thought.

And they will not merely close up their own ranks, now in danger of being broken; they will "carry the war into Africa," and make possible the most powerful of political combinations.

It is already beginning to be perceived that the Irish

movement, so far as it has yet gone, is merely in the interest of a class; that, so far as it has yet voiced any demand, it promises nothing to the laboring and artisan classes. Its opponents already see this opportunity for division, which, even without their efforts, must soon show itself, and which, now that the first impulse of the movement is over, will the more readily develop. To close up its ranks, and hold them firm, so that, even though they be forced to bend, they will not break and scatter, it must cease to be a movement looking merely to the benefit of the tenant-farmer, and become a movement for the benefit of the whole laboring class.

And the moment this is done the Irish land agitation assumes a new and a grander phase. It ceases to be an Irish movement; it becomes but the van of a worldwide struggle. Count the loss and the gain.

X. Appeals to Animosity

THE LAND LEAGUE movement, as an Irish movement, has in its favor the strength of Irish national feeling. In assuming the radical ground I urge, it would lose some of this; for there are doubtless a considerable number of Irishmen on both sides of the Atlantic who would shrink at first from the proposal to abolish private property in land. But all that is worth having would soon come back to it. And its strength would be more compact and intense — animated by a more definite purpose and a more profound conviction.

But in ceasing to be a movement having relation simply to Ireland — in proclaiming a truth and proposing a remedy which apply as well to every other country — it would allay opposition, which, as a mere local movement, it arouses, and bring to its support powerful forces.

The powerful landed interest of England is against the movement anyhow. The natural allies of the Irish agitators are the English working classes — not merely the Irishmen and sons of Irishmen who, in the larger English cities, are numerous enough to make some show and exert some voting power, without being numerous enough to effect any important result — but the great laboring masses of Great Britain. So long as merely Irish measures are proposed, they cannot gain the hearty support even of the English radicals; so long as race prejudices and hatreds are appealed to, counter-prejudices and hatreds must be aroused.

It is the very madness of folly, it is one of those political blunders worse than crimes, to permit in this land agitation

that indiscriminating denunciation of England and everything English which is so common at Land League meetings
and in the newspapers which voice Irish sentiment. The men
who do this may be giving way to a natural sentiment; but
they are most effectually doing the work of the real oppressors of Ireland. Were they secret emissaries of the London
police, were they bribed with the gold which the British oli-
garchy grinds out of the toil of its white slaves in mill and
mine and field, they could not better be doing its work. "Divide and conquer" is the golden maxim of the oppressors of
mankind. It is by arousing race antipathies and exciting national animosities, by appealing to local prejudices and setting people against people, that aristocracies and despotisms
have been founded and maintained. They who would free
men must rise above such feelings if they would be successful. The greatest enemy of the people's cause is he who appeals to national passion and excites old hatreds. He is its
best friend who does his utmost to bury them out of sight.
For that action and reaction are equal and uniform is the law
of the moral as of the physical world. Herein lies the far-
reaching sweep of those sublime teachings that, after centuries of nominal acceptance, the so-called Christian world yet
ignores, and which call on us to answer not revilings with
revilings, but to meet hatred with love. "For," as say the Scriptures of the Buddhists, "hatred never ceases by hatred at any
time; hatred ceases by love; that is an old rule." To
undiscriminately denounce Englishmen is simply to arouse
prejudices and excite animosities — to separate forces that
sought to be united. To make this the fight of the Irish people
against the English people is to doom it to failure. To make it
the common cause of the people everywhere against a system
which everywhere oppresses and robs them is to make its
success assured. Had this been made to appear, the Irish
members would not have stood alone when it came to the
final resistance to coercion. Had this been made to appear,

Great Britain would be in a ferment at the proposal to give the government despotic powers. If the Irish leaders are wise, they may yet avail themselves of the rising tide of British democracy. Let the Land Leaguers adopt the noble maxim of the German Social Democrats. Let them be Land Leaguers first, and Irishmen afterward. Let them account him an enemy of their cause who seeks to pander to prejudice and arouse hate. Let them arouse to a higher love than the mere love of country; to a wider patriotism than that which exhausts itself on one little sub-division of the human race, one little spot on the great earth's surface; and in this name, and by this sign, call upon their brothers, not so much to aid them, as to strike for themselves.

The Irish people have the same inalienable right to govern themselves as have every other people; but the full recognition of this right need not necessarily involve separation, and to talk of separation first is to arouse passions that will be utilized by the worst enemies of Ireland. The demand for the full political rights of the Irish people will be the stronger if it be made to line with and include the demand for the full political rights of the unenfranchised British people. And it must be remembered that all the tendencies of the time are not to separation, but to integration; not to independence, but to interdependence. This is observable wherever modern influences reach, and in all things. To attempt to resist it is to attempt to turn back the tide of progress.

It is not with the English people that the Irish people have cause of quarrel. It is with the system that oppresses both. That is the thing to denounce; that is the thing to fight. And it is to be fought most effectually by uniting the masses against it. Monarchy, aristocracy, landlordism, would get but a new lease of life by the arousing of sectional passions. The greatest blow that could be struck against them would be, scrupulously avoiding everything that could excite antagonistic popular feeling, to carry this land agitation into Great Britain, not as a mere Irish question, but as a home question as well. To proclaim the universal truth that land is of natural right common property; to abandon all timid and half-way schemes which attempt to compromise between justice and injustice, and to demand nothing more nor less than a full recognition of this natural right would be to do this. It would inevitably be to put the British masses upon inquiry; to put British landholders upon the defensive, and give them more than enough to do at home. Both England and Scotland are ripe for such an agitation, and, once fairly begun, it can have but one result — the victory of the popular cause.

XI. How to Win

NOR IS IT merely the laboring classes of Great Britain who may thus be brought into the fight, if the true standard be raised. To demand the nationalization of land by the simple means I have proposed makes possible — nay, as the discussion goes on, makes inevitable — an irresistible combination, the combination of labor and capital against landlordism. This combination proved its power by winning the battle of free trade in 1846 against the most determined resistance of the landed interest. It would be much more powerful now, and, if it can again be made on the land question, it can again force the intrenchments of the landed aristocracy.

This combination cannot be made on any of the timid, illogical schemes as yet proposed; but it can be made on the broad principle that land is rightfully common property. Paradoxical as it may seem, it is yet true that, while the present position of the Irish agitators does involve a menace to capital, the absolute denial of the right of private property in land would not.

In admitting that the landlords ought to get any rent at all, in admitting that, if the land is taken from them, they must be paid for it, the Irish agitators give away their whole case. For in this they admit that the land really belongs to the landlords, and put property in land in the same category with other property. Thus they place themselves in an indefensible position; thus they give to the agitation a "communistic"* character, and excite against it that natural and proper feeling which strongly resents any attack upon the rights of property as an attack upon the very foundations of society. It was doubtless this mistake of the agitators in admitting the right of private property in land to which Archbishop McCabe recently alluded in saying that some of the utterances of the agitators excited the solicitude of the Holy See. For this mistake gives to the agitation the character of an attack upon the rights of property. If the land is really the property of the landlords (and this is admitted when it is admitted that they are entitled to any rent or to any compensation), then to limit the rent which they shall get, or to interfere with their freedom to make what terms they please with tenants, is an attack upon property rights. If the land is rightfully the landlords', then is any compulsion as to how they shall let it, or on what terms they shall part with it, a bad and dangerous precedent, which naturally alarms capital and excites the solicitude of those who are concerned for good morals and social order. For, if a man may be made to part with one species of property by boycotting or agitation, why not with another! If a man's title to land is as rightful as his title to his watch, what is the difference between agitation by Land League meetings and Parliamentary filibustering to make him give up the one and agitation with a cocked pistol to make him give up the other?

But, if it be denied that land justly is, or can be, private property, if the equal rights of the whole people to the use of the elements gratuitously furnished by Nature be asserted without drawback or compromise, then the essential difference between property in land and property in things of

---

* I use the word in the usual sense in which it is used by the vulgar, and in which a communist is understood as one who wants to divide up other people's property.

human production is at once brought out. Then will it clearly appear not only that the denial of the right of individual property in land does not involve any menace to legitimate property rights, but that the maintenance of private property in land necessarily involves a denial of the right to all other property, and that the recognition of the claims of the landlords means a continuous robbery of capital as well as of labor.

All this will appear more and more clearly as the practical measures necessary to make land common property are proposed and discussed. These simple measures involve no harsh proceedings, no forcible dispossession, no shock to public confidence, no retrogression to a lower industrial organization, no loaning of public money, or establishment of cumbrous commissions. Instead of doing violence to the rightful sense of property, they assert and vindicate it. The way to make land common property is simply to take rent for the common benefit. And to do this, the easy way is to abolish one tax after another, until the whole weight of taxation falls upon the value of land. When that point is reached, the battle is won. The hare is caught, killed, and skinned, and to cook him will be a very easy matter. The real fight will come on the proposition to consolidate existing taxation upon land values. When that is once won, the landholders will not merely have been decisively defeated, they will have been routed; and the nature of land values will be so generally understood that to raise taxation so as to take the whole rent for common purposes will be a mere matter of course.

The political art is like the military art. It consists in combining the greatest strength against the point of least resistance. I have pointed out the way in which, in the case we are considering, this can be done. And, the more the matter is considered, the clearer and clearer will it appear that there is every practical reason, as there is every theoretical reason,

why the Irish reformers should take this vantage-ground of
principle. To propose to put the public burdens upon the
landholders is not a novel and unheard-of thing against which
English prejudice would run as something "newfangled,"
some new invention of modern socialism. On the contrary,
it is the ancient English practice. It would be but a return, in
a form adapted to modern times, to the system under which
English land was originally parceled out to the predecessors
of the present holders — the just system, recognized for centuries, that those who enjoy the common property should
bear the common burdens. The putting of property in land
in the same category as property in things produced by labor
is comparatively modern. In England, as in Ireland and Scotland, as in fact among every people of whom we know anything, the land was originally treated as common property,
and this recognition ran all through the feudal system. The
essence of the feudal system was in treating the landholder
not as an owner, but as a lessee. William the Conqueror did
not give away the land of England as the Church lands were
given away by Henry VIII, when he divided among his sycophants the property of the people, which, after the manner
of the times, had been set apart for the support of religious,
educational, and charitable institutions. To every grant of
land made by the Conqueror was annexed a condition which
amounted to a heavy perpetual tax or rent. One of his first
acts was to divide the soil of England into sixty thousand
knights' fees; and thus, besides many other dues and obligations, was thrown upon the landholders the cost of providing and maintaining the army. All the long, costly wars that
England fought during feudal times involved no public debt.
Public debt, pauperism, and the grinding poverty of the poorer
classes came in as the landholders gradually shook off the
obligations on which they had received their land, an operation culminating in the abolition after the Restoration of the
feudal tenures, for which were substituted indirect taxes that

still weigh upon the whole people. To now reverse this process, to abolish the taxes which are borne by labor and capital, and to substitute for them a tax on rent, would be not the adoption of anything new, but a simple going back to the old plan. In England, as in Ireland, the movement would appeal to the popular imagination as a demand for the reassertion of ancient rights.

There are other most important respects in which this measure will commend itself to the English mind. The tax upon land values or rent is in all economic respects the most perfect of taxes. No political economist will deny that it combines the maximum of certainty with the minimum of loss and cost; that, unlike taxes upon capital or exchange or improvement, it does not check production or enhance prices or fall ultimately upon the consumer. And, in proposing to abolish all other taxes in favor of this theoretically perfect tax, the Land Reformers will have on their side the advantage of ideas already current, while they can bring the *argumentum ad hominem* to bear on those who might never comprehend an abstract principle. Englishmen of all classes have happily been educated up to a belief in free trade, though a very large amount of revenue is still collected from customs. Let the Land Reformers take advantage of this by proposing to carry out the doctrine of free trade to its fullest extent. If a revenue tariff is better than a protective tariff, then no tariff at all is better than a revenue tariff. Let them propose to abolish the customs duties entirely, and to abolish as well harbor dues and lighthouse dues and dock charges, and in their place to add to the tax on rent, or the value of land exclusive of improvements. Let them in the same way propose to get rid of the excise, the various license taxes, the tax upon buildings, the onerous and unpopular income tax, etc., and to saddle all public expenses on the landlords.

This would bring home the land question to thousands

and thousands who have never thought of it before; to thousands and thousands who have heretofore looked upon the land question as something peculiarly Irish, or something that related exclusively to agriculture and to farmers, and have never seen how, in various direct and indirect ways, they have to contribute to the immense sums received by the landlords as rent. It would be putting the argument in a shape in which even the most stupid could understand it. It would be directing the appeal to a spot where even the unimaginative are sensitive — the pocket. How long would a merchant or banker or manufacturer or annuitant regard as dangerous and wicked an agitation which proposed to take taxation off of him? Even the most prejudiced can be relied on to listen with patience to an argument in favor of making some one else pay what they now are paying.

Let me illustrate by a little story what I feel confident would be the effect of the policy I propose:

Once upon a time I was the Pacific coast agent of an Eastern news association, which took advantage of an opposition telegraph company to run against the Associated Press monopoly. The association in California consisted of one strong San Francisco paper, to which telegraphic news was of much importance, and a number of interior papers, to which it was of minor importance, if of any importance at all. It became necessary to raise more money for the expenses of collecting and transmitting these dispatches, and, thinking it only fair, I assessed the increased cost to the strong metropolitan paper. The proprietor of this paper was very indignant. He appealed to the proprietors of all the other papers, and they all joined in his protest. I replied by calling a meeting. At this meeting the proprietor of the San Francisco paper led off with an indignant speech. He was seconded by several others, and evidently had the sympathy of the whole crowd. Then came my turn. I said, in effect: "Gentlemen, you can do what you please about this matter.

Whatever satisfies you satisfies me. The only thing fixed is, that more money has to be raised. As this San Francisco paper pays now a much lower relative rate than you do, I thought it only fair that it should pay the increased cost. But, if you think otherwise, there is no reason in the world why you should not pay it yourselves." The debate immediately took another turn, and in a few minutes my action was indorsed by a unanimous vote, for the San Francisco man was so disgusted by the way his supporters left him that he would not vote at all.

Now, that is just about what will happen to the British landlords if the question be put in the way I propose. The British landowners are in numbers but an insignificant minority. And, the more they protested against the injustice of having to pay all the taxes, the quicker would the public mind realize the essential injustice of private property in land, the quicker would the majority of the people come to see that the landowners ought not only to pay all the taxes, but a good deal more besides. Once put the question in such a way that the British workingman will realize that he pays two prices for his ale and half a dozen prices for his tobacco, because a landowners' Parliament in the time of Charles II shook off their ancient dues to the State, and imposed them in indirect taxation on him; once bring to the attention of the well-to-do Englishman, who grunts as he pays his income tax, the question as to whether the landowner, who draws his income from property that of natural right belongs to the whole people, ought not to pay it instead of him, and it will not be long before the absurd injustice of allowing rent to be appropriated by individuals will be thoroughly understood. This is a very different thing from asking the British taxpayer to buy out the Irish landlord for the sake of the Irish peasant.

I have been speaking as though all landholders would resist the change which would sacrifice their special interests to the larger interests of society. But I am satisfied that to think this is to do landholders a great injustice. For landholders as a class are not more stupid nor more selfish than any other class. And as they saw, as they must see, as the discussion progresses, that they also would be the gainers in the great social change which would abolish poverty and elevate the very lowest classes — the "mudsills" of society, as a Southern Senator expressively called them during the Slavery discussion — above the want, the misery, the vice, and degradation in which they are now plunged, there are many landowners who would join heartily and unreservedly in the effort to bring this change about. This I believe, not merely because my reading and observation both teach me that low, narrow views of self-interest are not the strongest of human motives, but because I know that today among those who see the truth I have here tried to set forth, and who would carry out the reform I have proposed, are many landholders.* And, if they be earnest men, I appeal to landholders as confidently as to any other class. There is that in a great truth that can raise a human soul above the mists of selfishness.

The course which I suggest is the only course which can be logically based on principle. It has everything to commend it. It will concentrate the greatest strength against the least resistance. And it will be on the right line. Every step gained will be an advance toward the ultimate goal; every step gained will make easier the next.

---

* Among the warm friends my book *Progress and Poverty* has found are many landholders — some of them large landholders. As types I may mention the names of D. A. Learnard, of San Joaquin, a considerable farmer, who had no sooner read it than he sent for a dozen copies to circulate among his neighbors; Hiram Tubbs, of San Francisco, the owner of much valuable real estate in and near that city; and Sir George Grey, of New Zealand, the owner of a good deal of land in that colony, of which he was formerly governor, as well as, I understand, of valuable estates in England.

XII. In the United States

IN SPEAKING with special reference to the case of Ireland, I have, so far as general principles are concerned, been using it as a stalking-horse. In discussing the Irish Land Question, we really discuss the most vital of American questions. And if we of the United States cannot see the beam in our own eye, save by looking at the mote in our brother's, then let us look at the mote; and let us take counsel together how he may get it out. For, at least, we shall in this way learn how we may deal with our own case when we wake up to the consciousness of it.

And never had the parable of the mote and the beam a better illustration than in the attitude of so many Americans toward this Irish Land Question. We denounce the Irish land system! We express our sympathy with Ireland! We tender our advice by Congressional and legislative resolution to our British brethren across the sea! Truly our indignation is cheap and our sympathy is cheap, and our advice is very, very cheap! For what are we doing? Extending over new soil the very institution that to them descended from a ruder and a darker time. With what conscience can we lecture them? With all power in the hands of the people, with institutions yet plastic, with millions of virgin acres yet to settle, it should be ours to do more than vent denunciation, and express sympathy, and give advice. It should be ours to show the way. This we have not done; this we do not do. Out in our new States may be seen the growth of a system of cultivation worse in its social effects than that

which prevails in Ireland. In Ireland the laborer has some
sort of a home, and enjoys some of the family affections. In
these great "wheat-manufacturing" districts the laborer is a
nomad, his home is in his blankets, which he carries around
with him. The soil bears wheat, crop after crop, till its fertility is gone. It does not bear children. These machine-worked
"grain factories" of the great Republic of the New World
are doing just what was done by the slave-worked latifundia
of the Roman world. Here they prevent, where there they
destroyed, "the crop of men." And in our large cities may
we not see misery of the same kind as exists in Ireland? If it
is less in amount, is it not merely because our country is yet
newer; because we have yet a wide territory and a sparse
population — conditions past which our progress is rapidly
carrying us? As for evictions, is it an unheard-of thing, even
in New York, for families to be turned out of their homes
because they cannot pay the rent? Are there not many acres
in this country from which those who made homes have
been driven by sheriffs' posses, and even by troops? Do not
a number of the Mussell Slough settlers lie in Santa Clara
jail today because a great railroad corporation set its envious eyes on soil which they had turned from desert into
garden, and they in their madness tried to resist ejectment?

And the men on the other side of the Atlantic who
vainly imagine that they may settle the great question now
pressing upon them by free trade in land, or tenant right,
or some mild device for establishing a peasant proprietary
— they may learn something about their own case if they
will turn their eyes to us.

We have had free trade in land; we have had in our
American farmer, owning his own acres, using his own capital, and working with his own hands, something far better
than peasant proprietorship. We have had, what no legislation can give the people of Great Britain, vast areas of virgin soil. We have had all of these under democratic

institutions. Yet we have here social disease of precisely the same kind as that which exists in Ireland and England. And the reason is that we have had here precisely the same cause — that we have made land private property. So long as this exists, our democratic institutions are vain, our pretense of equality but cruel irony, our public schools can but sow the seeds of discontent. So long as this exists, material progress can but force the masses of our people into a harder and more hopeless slavery. Until we in some way make the land what Nature intended it to be, common property; until we in some way secure to every child born among us his natural birthright; we have not established the Republic in any sense worthy of the name, and we cannot establish the Republic. Its foundations are quicksand.

XIII. A Little Island or a Little World

IMAGINE AN ISLAND girt with ocean; imagine a little world swimming in space. Put on it, in imagination, human beings. Let them divide the land, share and share alike, as individual property. At first, while population is sparse and industrial processes rude and primitive, this will work well enough.

Turn away the eyes of the mind for a moment, let time pass, and look again. Some families will have died out, some have greatly multiplied; on the whole, population will have largely increased, and even supposing there have been no important inventions or improvements in the productive arts, the increase in population, by causing the division of labor, will have made industry more complex. During this time some of these people will have been careless, generous, improvident; some will have been thrifty and grasping. Some of them will have devoted much of their powers to thinking of how they themselves and the things they see around them came to be, to inquiries and speculations as to what there is in the universe beyond their little island or their little world, to making poems, painting pictures, or writing books; to noting the differences in rocks and trees and shrubs and grasses; to classifying beasts and birds and fishes and insects — to the doing, in short, of all the many things which add so largely to the sum of human knowledge and human happiness, without much or any gain of wealth to the doer. Others again will have devoted all their energies to the extending of their possessions. What, then, shall we see, land having been all this time treated as private property? Clearly, we shall see that the primitive equality has given way to inequality. Some will have very much more than one of the original shares into which the land was divided; very many will have no land at all. Suppose that, in all things save this, our little island or our little world is Utopia — that there are no wars or robberies; that the government is absolutely pure and taxes nominal; suppose, if you want to, any sort of a currency; imagine, if you can imagine such a world or island, that interest is utterly abolished; yet inequality in the ownership of land will have produced poverty and virtual slavery.

For the people we have supposed are human beings — that is to say, in their physical natures at least, they are animals who can live only on land and by the aid of the products of land. They may make machines which will enable them to float on the sea, or perhaps to fly in the air, but to build and equip these machines they must have land and the products of land, and must constantly come back to land. Therefore those who own the land must be the masters of the rest. Thus, if one man has come to own all the land, he is their absolute master even to life or death. If they can live on the land only on his terms, then they can live only on his terms, for without land they cannot live. They are his absolute slaves, and so long as his ownership is acknowledged, if they want to live, they must do in everything as he wills.

If, however, the concentration of landownership has not gone so far as to make one or a very few men the owners of all the land — if there are still so many landowners that there is competition between them as well as between those who have only their labor — then the terms on which these non-landholders can live will seem more like free contract. But it will not be free contract. Land can yield no wealth without the application of labor; labor can produce no wealth without land. These are the two equally necessary factors of production. Yet, to say that they are equally necessary factors of production is not to say that, in the making of contracts as to how the results of production are divided, the possessors of these two meet on equal terms. For the nature of these two factors is very different. Land is a natural element; the human being must have his stomach filled every few hours. Land can exist without labor, but labor cannot exist without land. If I own a piece of land, I can let it lie idle for a year or for years, and it will eat nothing. But the laborer must eat every day, and his family must eat. And so, in the making of terms between them, the landowner has an immense advantage over the laborer. It is on the side of the laborer that the intense pressure of competition comes, for in his case it is competition urged by hunger. And, further than this: As population increases, as the competition for the use of land becomes more and more intense, so are the owners of land enabled to get for the use of their land a larger and larger part of the wealth which labor exerted upon it produces. That is to say, the value of land steadily rises. Now, this steady rise in the value of land brings about a confident expectation of future increase of value, which produces among landowners all the effects of a combination to hold for higher prices. Thus there is a constant tendency to force mere laborers to take less and less or to give more and more (put it which way you please, it amounts to the same thing) of the products of their work for the opportunity to work. And thus, in the very nature of things, we should see on our little island or our little world that, after a time had passed, some of the people would be able to take and enjoy a superabundance of all the fruits of labor without doing any labor at all, while others would be forced to work the livelong day for a pitiful living.

But let us introduce another element into the supposition. Let us suppose great discoveries and inventions — such as the steam engine, the power loom, the Bessemer process, the reaping machine, and the thousand and one labor-saving devices that are such a marked feature of our era. What would be the result?

Manifestly, the effect of all such discoveries and inventions is to increase the power of labor in producing wealth — to enable the same amount of wealth to be produced by less labor, or a greater amount with the same labor. But none of them lessen, or can lessen, the necessity for land. Until we can discover some way of making something out of nothing — and that is so far beyond our powers as to be absolutely unthinkable — there is no possible discovery or invention which can lessen the dependence of labor upon land. And, this being the case, the effect of these labor-saving devices, land being the private property of some, would simply be to increase the proportion of the wealth produced that landowners could demand for the use of their land. The ultimate effect of these discoveries and inventions would be not to benefit the laborer, but to make him more dependent.

And, since we are imagining conditions, imagine labor-saving inventions to go to the farthest imaginable point, that is to say, to perfection. What then? Why then, the necessity for labor being done away with, all the wealth that the land could produce would go entire to the landowners. None of it whatever could be claimed by anyone else. For the laborers there would be no use at all. If they continued to exist, it would be merely as paupers on the bounty of the landowners!

XIV. The Civilization that is Possible

IN THE EFFECTS upon the distribution of wealth, of making land private property, we may thus see an explanation of that paradox presented by modern progress. The perplexing phenomena of deepening want with increasing wealth, of labor rendered more dependent and helpless by the very introduction of labor-saving machinery, are the inevitable result of natural laws as fixed and certain as the law of gravitation. Private property in land is the primary cause of the monstrous inequalities which are developing in modern society. It is this, and not any miscalculation of Nature in bringing into the world more mouths than she can feed, that gives rise to that tendency of wages to a minimum — that "iron law of wages," as the Germans call it — that, in spite of all advances in productive power, compels the laboring-classes to the least return on which they will consent to live. It is this that produces all those phenomena that are so often attributed to the conflict of labor and capital. It is this that condemns Irish peasants to rags and hunger, that produces the pauperism of England and the tramps of America. It is this that makes the almshouse and the penitentiary the marks of what we call high civilization; that in the midst of schools and churches degrades and brutalizes men, crushes the sweetness out of womanhood and the joy out of childhood. It is this that makes lives that might be a blessing a pain and a curse, and every year drives more and more to seek unbidden refuge in the gates of death. For, a permanent tendency to inequality once set up, all the forces of progress tend to greater and greater inequality.

All this is contrary to Nature. The poverty and misery, the vice and degradation, that spring from the unequal distribution of wealth, are not the results of natural law; they spring from our defiance of natural law. They are the fruits of our refusal to obey the supreme law of justice. It is because we rob the child of his birthright; because we make the bounty which the Creator intended for all the exclusive property of some, that these things come upon us, and, though advancing and advancing, we chase but the mirage.

When, lit by lightning-flash or friction amid dry grasses, the consuming flames of fire first flung their lurid glow into the face of man, how must he have started back in affright! When he first stood by the shores of the sea, how must its waves have said to him, "Thus far shalt thou go, but no farther"! Yet, as he learned to use them, fire became his most useful servant, the sea his easiest highway. The most destructive element of which we know — that which for ages and ages seemed the very thunderbolt of the angry gods — is, as we are now beginning to learn, fraught for us with untold powers of usefulness. Already it enables us to annihilate space in our messages, to illuminate the night with new suns; and its uses are only beginning. And throughout all Nature, as far as we can see, whatever is potent for evil is potent for good. "Dirt," said Lord Brougham, "is matter in the wrong place." And so the squalor and vice and misery that abound in the very heart of our civilization are but results of the misapplication of forces in their nature most elevating.

I doubt not that whichever way a man may turn to inquire of Nature, he will come upon adjustments which will arouse not merely his wonder, but his gratitude. Yet what has most impressed me with the feeling that the laws of Nature are the laws of beneficent intelligence is what I see of the social possibilities involved in the law of rent.

Rent* springs from natural causes. It arises, as society develops, from the differences in natural opportunities and
the differences in the distribution of population. It increases with the division of labor, with the advance of the
arts, with the progress of invention. And thus, by virtue of
a law impressed upon the very nature of things, has the
Creator provided that the natural advance of mankind
shall be an advance toward equality, an advance toward
cooperation, an advance toward a social state in which
not even the weakest need be crowded to the wall, in which
even for the unfortunate and the cripple there may be
ample provision. For this revenue, which arises from the
common property, which represents not the creation of
value by the individual, but the creation by the community as a whole, which increases just as society develops,
affords a common fund, which, properly used, tends constantly to equalize conditions, to open the largest opportunities for all, and utterly to banish want or the fear of
want.

The squalid poverty that festers in the heart of our civilization, the vice and crime and degradation and ravening
greed that flow from it, are the results of a treatment of
land that ignores the simple law of justice, a law so clear
and plain that it is universally recognized by the veriest savages. What is by nature the common birthright of all, we
have made the exclusive property of individuals; what is by
natural law the common fund, from which common wants
should be met, we give to a few that they may lord it over
their fellows. And so some are gorged while some go hungry, and more is wasted than would suffice to keep all in
luxury.

In this nineteenth century, among any people who have

---

* I, of course, use the word "rent" in its economic, not in its common sense, meaning by it what is commonly called ground-rent.

begun to utilize the forces and methods of modern production, there is no necessity for want. There is no good reason why even the poorest should not have all the comforts, all the luxuries, all the opportunities for culture, all the gratifications of refined taste that only the richest now enjoy. There is no reason why any one should be compelled to long and monotonous labor. Did invention and discovery stop today, the forces of production are ample for this. What hampers production is the unnatural inequality in distribution. And, with just distribution, invention and discovery would only have begun.

Appropriate rent in the way I propose, and speculative rent would be at once destroyed. The dogs in the manger who are now holding so much land they have no use for, in order to extract a high price from those who do want to use it, would be at once choked off, and land from which labor and capital are now debarred under penalty of a heavy fine would be thrown open to improvement and use. The incentive to land monopoly would be gone. Population would spread where it is now too dense, and become denser where it is now too sparse.

Appropriate rent in this way, and not only would natural opportunities be thus opened to labor and capital, but all the taxes which now weigh upon production and rest upon the consumer could be abolished. The demand for labor would increase, wages would rise, every wheel of production would be set in motion.

Appropriate rent in this way, and the present expenses of government would be at once very much reduced — reduced directly by the saving in the present cumbrous and expensive schemes of taxation, reduced indirectly by the diminution in pauperism and in crime. This simplification in governmental machinery, this elevation of moral tone which would result, would make it possible for government to assume the running of railroads, telegraphs, and other businesses which, being in their nature monopolies, cannot, as experience is showing, be safely left in the hands of private individuals and corporations. In short, losing its character as a repressive agency, government could thus gradually pass into an administrative agency of the great cooperative association — society.

For, appropriate rent in this way, and there would be at once a large surplus over and above what are now considered the legitimate expenses of government. We could divide this, if we wanted to, among the whole community, share and share alike. Or we could give every boy a small capital for a start when he came of age, every girl a dower, every widow an annuity, every aged person a pension, out of this common estate. Or we could do with our great common fund many, many things that would be for the common benefit, many, many things that would give to the poorest what even the richest cannot now enjoy. We could establish free libraries, lectures, museums, art galleries, observatories, gymnasiums, baths, parks, theaters; we could line our roads with fruit trees, and make our cities clean and wholesome and beautiful; we could conduct experiments, and offer rewards for inventions, and throw them open to public use.*

Think of the enormous wastes that now go on: The waste of false revenue systems, which hamper production and bar exchange, which fine a man for erecting a building where none stood before, or for making two blades of grass grow where there was but one. The waste of unemployed labor, of idle machinery, of those periodical depressions of industry almost as destructive as war. The waste entailed by poverty, and the vice and crime and thriftlessness and drunkenness that spring from it; the waste entailed by that greed

_____

* A million dollars spent in premiums and experiments would, in all probability, make aerial navigation an accomplished fact.

of gain that is its shadow, and which makes business in large part but a masked war. The waste entailed by the fret and worry about the mere physical necessities of existence, to which so many of us are condemned; the waste entailed by ignorance, by cramped and undeveloped faculties, by the turning of human beings into mere machines!

Think of these enormous wastes, and of the others which, like these, are due to the fundamental wrong which produces an unjust distribution of wealth and distorts the natural development of society, and you will begin to see what a higher, purer, richer civilization would be made possible by the simple measure that will assert natural rights. You will begin to see how, even if no one but the present landholders were to be considered, this would be the greatest boon that could be vouchsafed them by society, and that, for them to fight it, would be as if the dog with a tin kettle tied to his tail should snap at the hand that offered to free him. Even the greatest landholder! As for such landholders as our working farmers and homestead-owners, the slightest discussion would show them that they had everything to gain by the change. But even such landholders as the Duke of Westminster and the Astors would be gainers.

For it is of the very nature of injustice that it really profits no one. When and where was slavery good for slaveholders? Did her cruelties in America, her expulsions of Moors and Jews, her burnings of heretics, profit Spain? Has England gained by her injustice toward Ireland? Did not the curse of an unjust social system rest on Louis XIV and Louis XV as well as on the poorest peasant whom it condemned to rags and starvation — as well as on that Louis whom it sent to the block? Is the Czar of Russia to be envied?

This we may know certainly, this we may hold to confidently: that which is unjust can really profit no one; that which is just can really harm no one. Though all other lights move and circle, this is the pole star by which we may safely steer.

XV. The Civilization That Is

WHEN WE THINK of the civilization that might be, how poor and pitiful, how little better than utter barbarism, seems this civilization of which we boast! Even here, where it has had the freest field and fullest development! Even here!

This is a broad land and a rich land. How wide it is, how rich it is, how the fifty millions of us already here are but beginning to scratch it, a man cannot begin to realize, till he does some thousands of miles of traveling over it. There are a school and a church and a newspaper in every hamlet; we have no privileged orders, no legacies of antiquated institutions, no strong and covertly hostile neighbors, who in fancy or reality oblige us to keep up great standing armies. We have had the experience of all other nations to guide us in selecting what is good and rejecting what is bad. In politics, in religion, in science, in mechanism, everything shows the latest improvements. We think we stand, and in fact we do stand, in the very van of civilization. Food here is cheaper, wages higher, than anywhere else. There is here a higher average of education, of intelligence, of material comfort, and of individual opportunity, than among any other of the great civilized nations. Here modern civilization is at its very best. Yet even here!

Last winter I was in San Francisco. There are in San Francisco citizens who can build themselves houses that cost a million and a half; citizens who can give each of their children two millions of registered United States bonds for a Christmas present; citizens who can send their wives to

Paris to keep house there, or rather to "keep palace" in a style that outdoes the lavishness of Russian grand dukes; citizens whose daughters are golden prizes to the bluest-blooded of English aristocrats; citizens who can buy seats in the United States Senate and leave them empty, just to show their grandeur. There are, also, in San Francisco other citizens. Last winter I could hardly walk a block without meeting a citizen begging for ten cents. And, when a charity fund was raised to give work with pick and shovel to such as would rather work than beg, the applications were so numerous that, to make the charity fund go as far as possible, one set of men was discharged after having been given a few days' work, in order to make room for another set. This and much else of the same sort I saw in San Francisco last winter. Likewise in Sacramento, and in other towns.

Last summer, on the plains, I took from its tired mother, and held in my arms, a little sun-browned baby, the youngest of a family of the sturdy and keen Western New England stock, who alone in their two wagons had traveled nearly three thousand miles looking for some place to locate and finding none, and who were now returning to where the father and his biggest boy could go to work on a railroad, what they had got by the sale of their Nebraska farm all gone. And I walked awhile by the side of long, lank Southwestern men who, after similar fruitless journeys way up into Washington Territory, were going back to the Choctaw Nation.

This winter I have been in New York. New York is the greatest and richest of American cities — the third city of the modern world, and moving steadily toward the first place. This is a time of great prosperity. Never before were so many goods sold, so much business done. Real estate is advancing with big jumps, and within the last few months many fortunes have been made in buying and selling vacant lots. Landlords nearly everywhere are demanding increased rents; asking in some of the business quarters an increase of three hundred per cent. Money is so plenty that government four per cents sell for 114, and a bill is passing Congress for refunding the maturing national debt at three per cent per annum, a rate that a while ago in California was not thought exorbitant per month. All sorts of shares and bonds have been going up and up. You can sell almost anything if you give it a high-sounding corporate name and issue well-printed shares of stock. Seats in the Board of Brokers are worth thirty thousand dollars, and are cheap at that. There are citizens here who rake in millions at a single operation with as much ease as a faro-dealer rakes in a handful of chips.

Nor is this the mere seeming prosperity of feverish speculation. The country is really prosperous. The crops have been enormous, the demand insatiable. We have at last a sound currency; gold has been pouring in. The railroads have been choked with produce, steel rails are being laid faster than ever before; all sorts of factories are running full time or overtime. So prosperous is the country, so good are the times, that, at the Presidential election a few months since, the determining argument was that we could not afford to take the chance of disturbing so much material prosperity by a political change.

Nevertheless, prosperous as are these times, citizens of the United States beg you on the streets for ten cents and five cents, and although you know that there are in this city two hundred charitable societies, although you realize that on general principles to give money in this way is to do evil rather than good, you are afraid to refuse them when you read of men in this great city freezing to death and starving to death. Prosperous as are these times, women are making overalls for sixty cents a dozen, and you can hire citizens for trivial sums to parade up and down the streets all day with advertising placards on their backs. I get on a horse-car and ride with the driver. He is evidently a sober, steady man, as intelligent as a man can be who drives a horse-car all the time he is not asleep or eating his meals. He tells me he has a wife and four children. He gets home (if a couple of rooms can be called a home) at two o'clock in the morning; he has to be back on his car at nine. Sunday he has a couple of hours more, which he has to put in in sleep, else, as he says, he would utterly break down. His children he never sees, save when one of them comes at noon or supper-time to the horse-car route with something for him to eat in a tin pail. He gets for his day's work one dollar and seventy-five cents — a sum that will buy at Delmonico's a beefsteak and cup of coffee. I say to him that it must be pretty hard to pay rent and keep six persons on one dollar and seventy-five cents a day. He says it is; that he has been trying for a month to get enough ahead to buy a new pair of shoes, but he hasn't yet succeeded. I ask why he does not leave such a job. He says, "What can I do? There are a thousand men ready to step into my place!" And so, in this time of prosperity, he is chained to his car. The horses that he drives, they are changed six times during his working-day. They have lots of time to stretch themselves and rest themselves and eat in peace their plentiful meals, for they are worth from one to two hundred dollars each, and it would be a loss to the company for them to fall ill. But this driver, this citizen of the United States, he may fall ill or drop dead, and the company would not lose a cent. As between him and the beasts he drives, I am inclined to think that this most prosperous era is more prosperous for horses than for men.

Our Napoleon of Wall Street, our rising Charlemagne of railroads, who came to this city with nothing but a new kind of mouse trap in a mahogany box, but who now, though yet in the vigor of his prime, counts his wealth by hundreds of millions, if it can be counted at all, is interviewed by a reporter just as he is about to step aboard his palace-car for a grand combination expedition into the Southwest. He

descants upon the services he is rendering in welding into
one big machine a lot of smaller machines, in uniting into
one vast railroad empire the separated railroad kingdoms.
He likewise descants upon the great prosperity of the whole
country. Everybody is prosperous and contented, he says:
there is, of course, a good deal of misery in the big cities,
but, then, there always is!

Yet not alone in the great cities. I ride on the Hudson
River Railroad on a bitter cold day, and from one of the
pretty towns with Dutch names gets in a constable with a
prisoner, whom he is to take to the Albany penitentiary. In
this case justice has been swift enough, for the crime, the
taking of a shovel, has been committed only a few hours
before. Such coat as the man has he keeps buttoned up,
even in the hot car, for, the constable says, he has no under-
clothes at all. He stole the shovel to get to the penitentiary,
where it is warm. The constable says they have lots of such
cases, and that even in these good times these pretty country towns are infested with such tramps. With all our vast
organizing, our developing of productive powers and cheapening of transportation, we are yet creating a class of utter
pariahs. And they are to be found not merely in the great
cities, but wherever the locomotive runs.

Is it real advance in civilization which, on the one hand,
produces these great captains of industry, and, on the other,
these social outcasts?

It is the year of grace 1881, and of the Republic the
105th. The girl who has brought in coal for my fire is twenty
years old. She was born in New York, and can neither read
nor write. To me, when I heard it, this seemed sin and shame,
and I got her a spelling-book. She is trying what she can,
but it is uphill work. She has really no time. Last night when
I came in, at eleven, she was not through scrubbing the
halls. She gets four dollars a month. Her shoes cost two
dollars a pair. She says she can sew; but I guess it is about as

I can. In the natural course of things, this girl will be a mother of citizens of the Republic.

Underneath are girls who can sew; they run sewing machines with their feet all day. I have seen girls in Asia carrying water-jugs on their heads and young women in South America bearing burdens. They were lithe and strong and symmetrical; but to turn a young woman into motive power for a sewing-machine is to weaken and injure her physically. And these girls are to rear, or ought to rear, citizens of the Republic.

But there is worse and worse than this. Go out into the streets at night, and you will find them filled with girls who will never be mothers. To the man who has known the love of mother, of sister, of sweetheart, wife, and daughter, this is the saddest sight of all.

The ladies of the Brooklyn churches — they are getting up petitions for the suppression of Mormon polygamy; they would have it rooted out with pains and penalties, trampled out, if need be, with fire and sword; and their reverend Congressman-elect is going, when he takes his seat, to introduce a most stringent bill to that end; for that a man should have more wives than one is a burning scandal in a Christian country. So it is; but there are also other burning scandals. As for scandals that excite talk, I will spare Brooklyn a comparison with Salt Lake. But as to ordinary things: I have walked through the streets of Salt Lake City, by day and by night, without seeing what in the streets of New York or Brooklyn excites no comment. Polygamy is unnatural and wrong, no doubt of that, for Nature brings into the world something over twenty-two boys for every twenty girls. But is not a state of society unnatural and wrong in which there are thousands and thousands of girls for whom no husband ever offers? Can we brag of a state of society in which one citizen can load his wife with more diamonds than an Indian chief can put beads on his squaw, while many other citizens are afraid to marry lest they cannot support a wife — a state of society in which prostitution flourishes? Polygamy is bad, but is it not better than that? Civilization is advancing day by day; never was such progress as we are making! Yet divorces are increasing and insanity is increasing. What is the goal of a civilization that tends toward free love and the madhouse?

This is a most highly civilized community. There is not a bear nor wolf on Manhattan Island, save in a menagerie. Yet it is easier, where they are worst, to guard against bears and wolves than it is to guard against the human beasts of prey that roam this island. In this highly civilized city every lower window has to be barred, every door locked and bolted; even doormats, not worth twenty-five cents, you will see chained to the steps. Stop for a moment in a crowd and your watch is gone as if by magic; shirt-studs are taken from their owners' bosoms, and earrings cut from ladies' ears. Even a standing army of policemen do not prevent highway robbery; there are populous districts that to walk through after nightfall is a risk, and where you have far more need to go armed and to be wary than in the backwoods. There are dens into which men are lured only to be drugged and robbed, sometimes to be murdered. All the resources of science and inventive genius are exhausted in making burglar-proof strong rooms and safes, yet, as the steel plate becomes thicker and harder, so does the burglar's tool become keener. If the combination lock cannot be picked, it is blown open. If not a crack large enough for the introduction of powder is left, then the air-pump is applied and a vacuum is created. So that those who in the heart of civilization would guard their treasures safely must come back to the most barbarous device, and either themselves, or by proxy, sleeplessly stand guard. What sort of a civilization is this? In what does civilization essentially consist if not in civility — that is to say, in respect for the rights of person and of property?

Yet this is not all, nor the worst. These are but the grosser forms of that spirit that in the midst of our civilization compels every one to stand on guard. What is the maxim of business intercourse among the most highly respectable classes? That if you are swindled it will be your own fault; that you must treat every man you have dealings with as though he but wanted the chance to cheat and rob you. *Caveat emptor.* "Let the buyer beware." If a man steal a few dollars he may stand a chance of going to the penitentiary — I read the other day of a man who was sent to the penitentiary for stealing four cents from a horse-car company. But, if he steal a million by business methods, he is courted and flattered, even though he steal the poor little savings which washerwomen and sewing-girls have brought to him in trust, even though he rob widows and orphans of the security which dead men have struggled and stinted to provide.

This is a most Christian city. There are churches and churches. All sorts of churches, where are preached all sorts of religions, save that which once in Galilee taught the arrant socialistic doctrine that it is easier for a camel to pass through the eye of a needle than for a rich man to enter the kingdom of God; all save that which once in Jerusalem drove the moneychangers from the temple. Churches of brown and gray and yellow stone, lifting toward heaven in such noble symmetry that architecture seems invocation and benison; where, on stained-glass windows, glow angel and apostle, and the entering light is dimmed to a soft glory; where such music throbs and supplicates and bursts in joy as once in St. Sophia ravished the souls of heathen Northmen; churches where richly cushioned pews let for the very highest prices, and the auctioneer determines who shall sit in the foremost seats; churches outside of which on Sunday stand long lines of carriages, on each carriage a coachman. And there are white marble churches, so pure and shapely that the stone seems to have bloomed and flowered — the concrete expression of a grand, sweet thought. Churches restful to the very eye, and into which the weary and heavy-laden can enter and join in the worship of their Creator for no larger an admission fee than it costs on the Bowery to see the bearded lady or the Zulu giant eight feet high. And then there are mission churches, run expressly for poor people, where it does not cost a cent. There is no lack of churches. There are, in fact, more churches than there are people who care to attend them. And there are likewise Sunday-schools, and big religious "book concerns," and tract societies, and societies for spreading the light of the gospel among the heathen in foreign parts.

Yet, land a heathen on the Battery with money in his pocket, and he will be robbed of the last cent of it before he is a day older. "By their fruits ye shall know them." I wonder whether they who send missionaries to the heathen ever read the daily papers. I think I could take a file of these newspapers, and from their daily chroniclings match anything that could be told in the same period of any heathen community — at least, of any heathen community in a like state of peace and prosperity. I think I could take a file of these papers, and match, horror for horror, all that returning missionaries have to tell — even to the car of Juggernaut or infants tossed from mothers' arms into the sacred river; even to Ashantee "customs" or cannibalistic feasts.

I do not say that such things are because of civilization, or because of Christianity. On the contrary, I point to them as inconsistent with civilization, as incompatible with Christianity. They show that our civilization is one-sided and cannot last as at present based; they show that our so-called Christian communities are not Christian at all. I believe a civilization is possible in which all could be civilized — in which such things would be impossible. But it must be a civilization based on justice and acknowledging the equal rights of all to natural opportunities. I believe that there is in true Christianity a power to regenerate the world. But it must be a Christianity that attacks vested wrongs, not that spurious thing that defends them. The religion which allies itself with injustice to preach down the natural aspirations of the masses is worse than atheism.

XVI. True Conservatism

THERE ARE THOSE who may look on this little book as very radical, in the bad sense they attach to the word. They mistake. This is, in the true sense of the word, a most conservative little book. I do not appeal to prejudice and passion. I appeal to intelligence. I do not incite to strife; I seek to prevent strife.

That the civilized world is on the verge of the most tremendous struggle, which, according to the frankness and sagacity with which it is met, will be a struggle of ideas or a struggle of actual physical force, calling upon all the potent agencies of destruction which modern invention has discovered, every sign of the times portends. The voices that proclaim the eve of revolution are in the air. Steam and electricity are not merely transporting goods and carrying messages. They are everywhere changing social and industrial organization; they are everywhere stimulating thought, and arousing new hopes and fears and desires and passions; they are everywhere breaking down the barriers that have separated men, and integrating nations into one vast organism, through which the same pulses throb and the same nerves tingle.

The present situation in Great Britain is full of dangers, of dangers graver and nearer than those who there are making history are likely to see. Who in France, a century ago, foresaw the drama of blood so soon to open? Who in the United States dreamed of what was coming till the cannon-shot rang and the flag fell on Sumter? How confidently

we said, "The American people are too intelligent, too practical, to go to cutting each other's throats"! How confidently
we relied upon the strong common sense of the great masses,
upon the great business interests, upon the universal desire
to make money! "War does not pay," we said, "therefore
war is impossible." A shot rang over Charleston harbor; a
bit of bunting dropped, and, riven into two hostile camps,
a nation sprang to its feet to close in the death-lock.

And to just such a point are events hurrying in Great
Britain today. History repeats itself, and what happened a
century ago on one side of the English Channel is beginning again on the other. Already has the States General
met, and the Third Estate put on their hats. Already Necker
is in despair. Already has the *lit de justice* been held, and the
Tennis-Court been locked, and ball-cartridge been served
to the Swiss Guard! For the moment the forces of reaction
triumph. Davitt is snatched to prison; a "Liberal" government carries coercion by a tremendous majority, and the
most despotic powers are invoked to make possible the eviction of Irish peasants. The order of Warsaw is to reign in
Ireland, and the upholders of ancient wrong deem it secure
again, as the wave that was mounting seems sweeping back.
Let them wait a little and they will see. For again the wave
will mount, and higher and higher, and soon the white foam
will seethe and hiss on its toppling crest. It is not true conservatism which cries "Peace! peace!" when there is no peace;
which, like the ostrich, sticks its head in the sand and fan-
cies itself secure; which would compromise matters by putting more coal in the furnace, and hanging heavier weights
on the safety-valve! That alone is true conservatism which
would look facts in the face, which would reconcile opposing forces on the only basis on which reconciliation is possible — that of justice.

I speak again of Great Britain, but I speak with reference to the whole modern world. The true nature of the

inevitable conflict with which modern civilization is everywhere beginning to throb, can, it seems to me, best be seen in the United States, and in the newer States even more clearly than in the older States. That intelligent Englishmen imagine that in the democratization of political institutions, in free trade in land, or in peasant proprietorship, can be found any solution of the difficulties which are confronting them, is because they do not see what may be seen in the United States by whoever will look. That intelligent Americans imagine that by these questions which are so menacingly presenting themselves in Europe their peace is to be unvexed, is because they shut their eyes to what is going on around them, because they attribute to themselves and their institutions what is really due to conditions now rapidly passing away — to the sparseness of population and the cheapness of land. Yet it is here, in this American Republic, that the true nature of that inevitable conflict now rapidly approaching which must determine the fate of modern civilization may be most clearly seen.

We have here abolished all hereditary privileges and legal distinctions of class. Monarchy, aristocracy, prelacy, we have swept them all away. We have carried mere political democracy to its ultimate. Every child born in the United States may aspire to be President. Every man, even though he be a tramp or a pauper, has a vote, and one man's vote counts for as much as any other man's vote. Before the law all citizens are absolutely equal. In the name of the people all laws run. They are the source of all power, the fountain of all honor. In their name and by their will all government is carried on; the highest officials are but their servants. Primogeniture and entail we have abolished wherever they existed. We have and have had free trade in land. We started with something infinitely better than any scheme of peasant proprietorship which it is possible to carry into effect in Great Britain. We have had for our public domain the best part of an immense continent. We have had the preemption law and the homestead law. It has been our boast that here every one who wished it could have a farm. We have had full liberty of speech and of the press. We have not merely common schools, but high schools and universities, open to all who may choose to attend. Yet here the same social difficulties apparent on the other side of the Atlantic are beginning to appear. It is already clear that our democracy is a vain pretense, our make-believe of equality a sham and a fraud.

Already are the sovereign people becoming but a *roi fainéant*, like the Merovingian kings of France, like the Mikados of Japan. The shadow of power is theirs; but the substance of power is being grasped and wielded by the bandit chiefs of the stock exchange, the robber leaders who organize politics into machines. In any matter in which they are interested, the little finger of the great corporations is thicker than the loins of the people. Is it sovereign States or is it railroad corporations that are really represented in the elective Senate which we have substituted for an hereditary House of Lords? Where is the count or marquis or duke in Europe who wields such power as is wielded by such simple citizens as our Stanfords, Goulds, and Vanderbilts? What does legal equality amount to, when the fortunes of some citizens can be estimated only in hundreds of millions, and other citizens have nothing? What does the suffrage amount to when, under threat of discharge from employment, citizens can be forced to vote as their employers dictate? When votes can be bought on election day for a few dollars apiece? If there are citizens so dependent that they must vote as their employers wish, so poor that a few dollars on election day seem to them more than any higher consideration, then giving them votes simply adds to the political power of wealth, and universal suffrage becomes the surest basis for the establishment of tyranny. "Tyranny"! There is a lesson in the very word. What are our American bosses but the exact antitypes of the Greek tyrants, from whom the word comes? They who gave the word tyrant its meaning did not claim to rule by right divine. They were simply the Grand Sachems of Greek Tammanys, the organizers of Hellenic "stalwart machines."

Even if universal history did not teach the lesson, it is in the United States already becoming very evident that political equality can continue to exist only upon a basis of social equality; that where the disparity in the distribution of wealth increases, political democracy only makes easier the concentration of power, and must inevitably lead to tyranny and anarchy. And it is already evident that there is nothing in political democracy, nothing in popular education, nothing in any of our American institutions, to prevent the most enormous disparity in the distribution of wealth. Nowhere in the world are such great fortunes growing up as in the United States. Considering that the average income of the working masses of our people is only a few hundred dollars a year, a fortune of a million dollars is a monstrous thing — a more monstrous and dangerous thing under a democratic government than anywhere else. Yet fortunes of ten and twelve million dollars are with us ceasing to be noticeable. We already have citizens whose wealth can be estimated only in hundreds of millions, and before the end of the century, if present tendencies continue, we are likely to have fortunes estimated in thousands of millions — such monstrous fortunes as the world has never seen since the growth of similar fortunes ate out the heart of Rome. And the necessary correlative of the growth of such fortunes is the impoverishment and loss of independence on the part of the masses. These great aggregations of wealth are like great trees, which strike deep roots and spread wide branches, and which, by sucking up the moisture from the soil and intercepting the sunshine, stunt and kill the vegetation around them. When a capital of a million dollars comes into competition with capitals of thousands of dollars, the smaller capitalists must be driven out of the business or destroyed. With great capital nothing can compete save great capital. Hence, every aggregation of wealth increases the tendency to the aggregation of wealth, and decreases the possibility of the employee ever becoming more than an employee, compelling him to compete with his fellows as to who will work cheapest for the great capitalist — a competition that can have but one result, that of forcing wages to the minimum at which the supply of labor can be kept up. Where we are is not so important as in what direction we are going, and in the United States all tendencies are clearly in this direction. A while ago, any journeyman shoemaker could set up in business for himself with the savings of a few months. But now the operative shoemaker could not in a lifetime save enough from his wages to go into business for himself. And, now that great capital has entered agriculture, it must be with the same results. The large farmer, who can buy the latest machinery at the lowest cash prices and use it to the best advantage, who can run a straight furrow for miles, who can make special rates with railroad companies, take advantage of the market, and sell in large lots for the least commission, must drive out the small farmer of the early American type just as the shoe factory has driven out the journeyman shoemaker. And this is going on today.

There is nothing unnatural in this. On the contrary, it is in the highest degree natural. Social development is in accordance with certain immutable laws. And the law of development, whether it be the development of a solar system, of the tiniest organism, or of a human society, is the law of integration. It is in obedience to this law — a law evidently as all-compelling as the law of gravitation — that these new agencies, which so powerfully stimulate social growth, tend to the specialization and interdependence of industry. It is in obedience to this law that the factory is superseding the independent mechanic, the large farm is swallowing up the little one, the big store shutting up the small one, that corporations are arising that dwarf the State, and that population tends more and more to concentrate in cities. Men must work together in larger and in more closely related groups. Production must be on a greater scale. The only question is, whether the relation in which men are thus drawn together and compelled to act together shall be the natural relation of interdependence in equality, or the unnatural relation of dependence upon a master. If the one, then may civilization advance in what is evidently the natural order, each step leading to a higher step. If the other, then what Nature has intended as a blessing becomes a curse, and a condition of inequality is produced which will inevitably destroy civilization. Every new invention but hastens the catastrophe.

Now, all this we may deduce from natural laws as fixed and certain as the law of gravitation. And all this we may see going on today. This is the reason why modern progress, great as it has been, fails to relieve poverty; this is the secret of the increasing discontent which pervades every civilized country. Under present conditions, with land treated as private property, material progress is developing two diverse tendencies, two opposing currents. On the one side, the tendency of increasing population and of all improvement in the arts of production is to build up enormous fortunes, to wipe out the intermediate classes, and to crowd down the masses to a level of lower wages and greater dependence. On the other hand, by bringing men closer together, by stimulating thought, by creating new wants, by arousing new ambitions, the tendency of modern progress is to make the masses discontented with their condition, to feel bitterly its injustice. The result can be predicted just as certainly as the result can be predicted when two trains are rushing toward each other on the same track.

This thing is absolutely certain: Private property in land blocks the way of advancing civilization. The two cannot long coexist. Either private property in land must be abolished, or, as has happened again and again in the history of mankind, civilization must again turn back in anarchy and bloodshed. Let the remaining years of the nineteenth century bear me witness. Even now, I believe, the inevitable struggle has begun. It is not conservatism which would ignore such a tremendous fact. It is the blindness that invites destruction. He that is truly conservative, let him look the facts in the face; let him speak frankly and dispassionately. This is the duty of the hour. For, when a great social question presses for settlement, it is only for a little while that the voice of Reason can be heard. The masses of men hardly think at any time. It is difficult even in sober moments to get them to reason calmly. But when passion is roused, then they are like a herd of stampeded bulls. I do not fear that present social adjustments can continue. That is impossible. What I fear is that the dams may hold till the flood rises to fury. What I fear is that dogged resistance on the one side may kindle a passionate sense of wrong on the other. What I fear are the demagogues and the accidents.

The present condition of all civilized countries is that of increasingly unstable equilibrium. In steam and electricity, and all the countless inventions which they typify, mighty forces have entered the world. If rightly used, they are our servants, more potent to do our bidding than the genii of Arabian story. If wrongly used, they, too, must turn to monsters of destruction. They require and will compel great social changes. That we may already see. Operating under social institutions which are based on natural justice, which acknowledge the equal rights of all to the material and opportunities of nature, their elevating power will be equally exerted, and industrial organization will pass naturally into that of a vast cooperative society. Operating under social institutions which deny natural justice by treating land as private property, their power is unequally exerted, and tends, by producing inequality, to engender forces that will tear and rend and shatter. The old bottles cannot hold the new wine. This is the ferment which throughout the civilized world is everywhere beginning.

XVII *In Hoc Signo Vinces*

LET ME RECAPITULATE.

What I want to impress upon those who may read this book is this:

The land question is nowhere a mere local question; it is a universal question. It involves the great problem of the distribution of wealth, which is everywhere forcing itself upon attention.

It cannot be settled by measures which in their nature can have but local application. It can be settled only by measures which in their nature will apply everywhere.

It cannot be settled by halfway measures. It can be settled only by the acknowledgment of equal rights to land. Upon this basis it can be settled easily and permanently.

If the Irish reformers take this ground, they will make their fight the common fight of all the peoples; they will concentrate strength and divide opposition. They will turn the flank of the system that oppresses them, and awake the struggle in its very intrenchments. They will rouse against it a force that is like the force of rising tides.

What I urge the men of Ireland to do is to proclaim, without limitation or evasion, that the land, of natural right, is the common property of the whole people, and to propose practical measures which will recognize this right in all countries as well as in Ireland.

What I urge the Land Leagues of the United States to do is to announce this great principle as of universal application; to give their movement a reference to America as well as to Ireland; to broaden and deepen and strengthen it by making it a movement for the regeneration of the world — a movement which shall concentrate and give shape to aspirations that are stirring among all nations.

Ask not for Ireland mere charity or sympathy. Let her call be the call of fraternity: "For yourselves, O brothers, as well as for us!" Let her rallying cry awake all who slumber, and rouse to a common struggle all who are oppressed. Let it breathe not old hates; let it ring and echo with the new hope!

In many lands her sons are true to her; under many skies her daughters burn with the love of her. Lo! the ages bring their opportunity. Let those who would honor her bear her banner to the front!

The harp and the shamrock, the golden sunburst on the field of living green! Emblems of a country without nationality; standard of a people downtrodden and oppressed! The hour has come when they may lead the van of the great world-struggle. Types of harmony and of ever-springing hope, of light and of life! The hour has come when they may stand for something higher than local patriotism; something grander than national independence. The hour has come when they may stand forth to speak the world's hope, to lead the world's advance!

Torn away by pirates, tending in a strange land a heathen master's swine, the slave boy, with the spirit of Christ in his heart, praying in the snow for those who had enslaved him, and returning to bring to his oppressors the message of the gospel, returning with good to give where evil had been received, to kindle in the darkness a great light — this is Ireland's patron saint. In his spirit let Ireland's struggle be. Not merely through Irish vales and hamlets, but into England, into Scotland, into Wales, wherever our common tongue is spoken, let the torch be carried and the word be preached. And beyond! The brotherhood of man stops not with differences of speech any more than with seas or mountain-chains. A century ago it was ours to speak the ringing word. Then it was France's. Now it may be Ireland's, if her sons be true.

But wherever, or by whom, the word must be spoken, the standard will be raised. No matter what the Irish leaders do or do not do, it is too late to settle permanently the question on any basis short of the recognition of equal natural right. And, whether the Land Leagues move forward or slink back, the agitation must spread to this side of the Atlantic. The Republic, the true Republic, is not yet here. But her birth-struggle must soon begin. Already, with the hope of her, men's thoughts are stirring.

Not a republic of landlords and peasants; not a republic of millionaires and tramps; not a republic in which some are masters and some serve. But a republic of equal citizens, where competition becomes cooperation, and the interdependence of all gives true independence to each; where moral progress goes hand in hand with intellectual progress, and material progress elevates and enfranchises even the poorest and weakest and lowliest.

And the gospel of deliverance, let us not forget it: it is the gospel of love, not of hate. He whom it emancipates will know neither Jew nor Gentile, nor Irishman nor Englishman, nor German nor Frenchman, nor European nor American, nor difference of color or of race, nor animosities of class or condition. Let us set our feet on old prejudices, let us bury the old hates. There have been "Holy Alliances" of kings. Let us strive for the Holy Alliance of the people.

Liberty, equality, fraternity! Write them on the banners. Let them be our sign and countersign. Without equality, liberty cannot be; without fraternity, neither equality nor liberty can be achieved.

Liberty — the full freedom of each bounded only by the equal freedom of every other!

Equality — the equal right of each to the use and enjoyment of all natural opportunities, to all the essentials of happy, healthful, human life!

Fraternity — that sympathy which links together those who struggle in a noble cause; that would live and let live; that would help as well as be helped; that, in seeking the good of all, finds the highest good of each!

By this sign shall ye conquer!

> *We hold these truths to be self-evident – that all men are created equal; that they are endowed by their Creator with certain unalienable rights; that among these are life, liberty, and the pursuit of happiness!*

It is over a century since these words rang out. It is time to give them their full, true meaning. Let the standard be lifted that all may see it; let the advance be sounded that all may hear it. Let those who would fall back, fall back. Let those who would oppose, oppose. Everywhere are those who will rally. The stars in their courses fight against Sisera!

– Henry George
New York, February 28, 1881

Property in Land

A Passage-at-Arms between the Duke of Argyll and Henry George

Publisher's Note

The literary reputation and the high social and political rank of the Duke of Argyll have attracted unusual attention to his arraignment of Henry George's doctrine as to property in land. Mr. George has made a vigorous and aggressive reply, which is here given in juxtaposition with the Duke's attack. This passage-at-arms triply challenges attention because of the burning interest in the question itself at present, the representative character of the disputants, and the dialectic skill with which the controversy is conducted.   — *Nineteenth Century*, April 1884

I. The Prophet of San Francisco

by the Duke of Argyll

There are some advantages in being a citizen — even a very humble citizen — in the Republic of Letters. If any man has ever written anything on matters of serious concern, which others have read with interest, he will very soon find himself in contact with curious diversities of mind. Subtle sources of sympathy will open up before him in contrast with sources, not less subtle, of antipathy, and both of them are often interesting and instructive in the highest degree.

A good many years ago a friend of mine, whose opinion I greatly value, was kind enough to tell me of his approval of a little book which I had then lately published. As he was a man of pure taste, and naturally much more inclined to criticism than assent, his approval gave me pleasure. But being a man also very honest and outspoken, he took care to explain that his approval was not unqualified. He liked the whole book except one chapter, "in which," he added, "it seems to me there is a good deal of nonsense."

There was no need to ask him what that chapter was. I knew it very well. It could be none other than a chapter called "Law in Politics," which was devoted to the question how far, in human conduct and affairs, we can trace the Reign of Law in the same sense, or in a sense very closely analogous to that in which we can trace it in the physical sciences. There were several things in that chapter which my friend was not predisposed to like. In the first place, he was an active politician, and such men are sure to feel the reasoning to be unnatural and unjust which tends to represent all the activities of their life as more or less the results of circumstance. In the second place, he was above all other things a Free Trader, and the governing idea of that school is that every attempt to interfere by law with anything connected with trade or manufacture is a folly if not a crime. Now, one main object of my "nonsense" chapter was to show that this doctrine is not true as an absolute proposition. It drew a line between two provinces of legislation, in one of which such interference had indeed been proved to be mischievous, but in the other of which interference had been equally proved to be absolutely required. Protection, it was shown, had been found to be wrong in all attempts to regulate the value or the price of anything. But Protection, it was also shown, had been found to be right and necessary in defending the interests of life, health, and morals. As a matter of historical fact, it was pointed out that during the present century there had been two steady movements on the part of Parliament — one a movement of retreat, the other a movement of advance. Step by step legislation had been abandoned in all endeavors to regulate interests purely economic; while, step by step, not less steadily, legislation had been adopted more and more extensively for the regulation of matters in which those higher interests were concerned. Moreover, I had ventured to represent both these movements as equally important — the movement in favor of Protection in one direction being quite as valuable as the movement against Protection in another direction. It was not in the nature of things that my friend should admit this equality, or even any approach to a comparison between the two movements. In promoting one of them he had spent his life, and the truths it represented were to him the subject of passionate conviction. Of the other movement he had been at best only a passive specta-

tor, or had followed its steps with cold and critical tolera-
tion. To place them on anything like the same level as steps
of advance in the science of government, could not but
appear to him as a proposition involving "a good deal of
nonsense." But critics may themselves be criticized; and
sometimes authors are in the happy position of seeing behind both the praise and the blame they get. In this case I
am unrepentant. I am firmly convinced that the social and
political value of the principle which has led to the repeal
of all laws for the regulation of price is not greater than the
value of the principle which has led to the enactment of
many laws for the regulation of labor. If the Factory Acts
and many others of the like kind had not been passed we
should for many years have been hearing a hundred "bitter
cries" for every one which assails us now, and the social
problems which still confront us would have been much
more difficult and dangerous than they are.

Certain it is that if the train of thought which led up
to this conclusion was distasteful to some minds, it turned
out to be eminently attractive to many others. And of this,
some years later, I had a curious proof. From the other
side of the world, and from a perfect stranger, there came
a courteous letter accompanied by the present of a book.
The author had read mine, and he sent his own. In spite
of prepossessions, he had confidence in a candid hearing.
The letter was from Mr. Henry George, and the book was
Progress and Poverty. Both were then unknown to fame; nor
was it possible for me fully to appreciate the compliment
conveyed until I found that the book was directed to prove
that almost all the evils of humanity are to be traced to
the very existence of landowners, and that by divine right
land could only belong to everybody in general and to
nobody in particular.

The credit of being open to conviction is a great credit,
and even the heaviest drafts upon it cannot well be made

the subject of complaint. And so I could not be otherwise than flattered when this appeal in the sphere of politics was followed by another in the sphere of science. Another author was good enough to present me with his book; and I found that it was directed to prove that all the errors of modern physical philosophy arise from the prevalent belief that our planet is a globe. In reality it is flat. Elaborate chapters and equally elaborate diagrams are devoted to the proof. At first I thought that the argument was a joke, like Archbishop Whately's "Historic Doubts." But I soon saw that the author was quite as earnest as Mr. Henry George. Lately I have seen that both these authors have been addressing public meetings with great success; and considering that all obvious appearances and the language of common life are against the accepted doctrine of Copernicus, it is perhaps not surprising that the popular audiences which have listened to the two reformers have evidently been almost as incompetent to detect the blunders of the one as to see through the logical fallacies of the other. But the Californian philosopher has one immense advantage. Nobody has any personal interest in believing that the world is flat. But many persons may have an interest, very personal indeed, in believing that they have a right to appropriate a share in their neighbor's vineyard.

There are, at least, a few axioms in life on which we are entitled to decline discussion. Even the most skeptical minds have done so. The mind of Voltaire was certainly not disposed to accept without question any of the beliefs that underlay the rotten political system which he saw and hated. He was one of those who assailed it with every weapon, and who ultimately overthrew it. Among his fellows in that work there was a perfect revelry of rebellion and of unbelief. In the grotesque procession of new opinions which had begun to pass across the stage while he was still upon it, this particular opinion against property in land had been advocated by the famous "Jean Jacques." Voltaire turned his powerful glance upon it, and this is how he treated it:*

> B. *Avez-vous oublié que Jean-Jacques, un des pères de l'Église Moderne, a dit, que le premier qui osa clore et cultiver un terrain fut l'ennemi du genre humain, qulil fallait l'exterminer, et que les fruits sont à tous, et que la terre n'est à personne? N'avons-nous pas déjà examiné ensemble cette belle proposition si utile à la Société?*

> A. *Quel est ce Jean-Jacques? Il faut que ce soit quelque Hun, bel esprit, qui ait écrit cette impertinence abominable, on quelque manvais plaisant,* buffo magro, *qui ait voulu rire de ce que le monde entier a de plus sérieux....*

For my own part, however, I confess that the mocking spirit of Voltaire is not the spirit in which I am ever tempted to look at the fallacies of Communism. Apart altogether from the appeal which was made to me by this author, I have always felt the high interest which belongs to those fallacies, because of the protean forms in which they tend to revive and reappear, and because of the call they make upon us from time to time to examine and identify the fundamental facts which do really govern the condition of mankind. Never, perhaps, have communistic theories assumed a form more curious, or lent themselves to more fruitful processes of analysis, than in the writings of Mr. Henry George. These writings now include a volume on *Social Problems*, published recently. It represents the same ideas as those which inspire the work on *Progress and Poverty*. They are often expressed in almost the same words, but they exhibit some development and applications which are of high interest and importance. In this paper I shall refer to both, but for the present I can do no more than group together some of the more prominent features of this

_____

*Dictionnaire Philosophique, 1764, art. "Loi Naturelle"

new political philosophy.

In the first place, it is not a little remarkable to find one of the most extreme doctrines of Communism advocated by a man who is a citizen of the United States. We have been accustomed to associate that country with boundless resources and an almost inexhaustible future. It has been for two centuries, and it still is, the land of refuge and the land of promise to millions of the human race. And among all the States which are there "united," those which occupy the Far West are credited with the largest share in this abundant present, and this still more abundant future. Yet it is out of these United States, and out of the one State which, perhaps, above all others, has this fame of opulence, that we have a solitary voice, prophesying a future of intolerable woes. He declares that all the miseries of the Old World are already firmly established in the New. He declares that they are increasing in an ever-accelerating ratio, growing with the growth of the people, and strengthening with its apparent strength. He tells us of crowded cities, of pestilential rooms, of men and women struggling for employments however mean, of the breathlessness of competition, of the extremes of poverty and of wealth — in short, of all the inequalities of condition, of all the pressures and suffocations which accompany the struggle for existence in the oldest and most crowded societies in the world.

I do not pretend to accept this picture as an accurate representation of the truth. At the best it is a picture only of the darkest shadows with a complete omission of the lights. The author is above all things a Pessimist, and he is under obvious temptations to adopt this kind of coloring. He has a theory of his own as to the only remedy for all the evils of humanity; and this remedy he knows to be regarded with aversion both by the intellect and by the conscience of his countrymen. He can only hope for success by trying to convince society that it is in the grasp of some deadly malady.

Large allowance must be made for this temptation. Still, after making every allowance, it remains a most remarkable fact that such a picture can be drawn by a citizen of the United States. There can be no doubt whatever that at least as regards many of the great cities of the Union, it is quite as true a picture of them as it would be of the great cities of Europe. And even as regards the population of the States as a whole, other observers have reported on the feverish atmosphere which accompanies its eager pursuit of wealth, and on the strain which is everywhere manifest for the attainment of standards of living and of enjoyment which are never reached except by a very few. So far, at least, we may accept Mr. George's representations as borne out by independent evidence.

But here we encounter another most remarkable circumstance in Mr. George's books. The man who gives this dark — this almost black — picture of the tendencies of American progress, is the same man who rejects with indignation the doctrine that population does everywhere tend to press in the same way upon the limits of subsistence. This, as is well known, is the general proposition which is historically connected with the name of Malthus, although other writers before him had unconsciously felt and assumed its truth. Since his time it has been almost universally admitted not as a theory but as a fact, and one of the most clearly ascertained of all the facts of economic science. But, like all Communists, Mr. George hates the very name of Malthus. He admits and even exaggerates the fact of pressure as applicable to the people of America. He admits it as applicable to the people of Europe, and of India, and of China. He admits it as a fact as applicable more or less obviously to every existing population of the globe. But he will not allow the fact to be generalized into a law. He will not allow this — because the generalization suggests a cause which he denies, and shuts out another cause which he asserts. But this is not a legitimate reason for refusing to express phenomena in terms as wide and general as their actual occurrence. Never mind causes until we have clearly ascertained facts; but when these are clearly ascertained let us record them fearlessly in terms as wide as the truth demands. If there is not a single population on the globe which does not exhibit the fact of pressure more or less severe on the limits of their actual subsistence, let us at least recognize this fact in all its breadth and sweep. The diversities of laws and institutions, of habits and of manners, are almost infinite. Yet amid all these diversities this one fact is universal. Mr. George himself is the latest witness. He sees it to be a fact — a terrible and alarming fact, in his opinion — as applicable to the young and hopeful society of the New World. In a country where there is no monarch, no aristocracy, no ancient families, no entails of land, no standing armies worthy of the name, no pensions, no courtiers, where all are absolutely equal before the law, there, even there — in this paradise of Democracy, Mr. George tells us that the pressure of the masses upon the means of living and enjoyment which are open to them is becoming more and more severe, and that the inequalities of men are becoming as wide and glaring as in the oldest societies of Asia and of Europe.

The contrast between this wonderful confirmation of Malthusian facts, and the vehement denunciation of Malthusian "law," is surely one of the curiosities of literature. But the explanation is clear enough. Mr. George sees that facts common to so many nations must be due to some cause as common as the result. But, on the other hand, it would not suit his theory to admit that this cause can possibly be anything inherent in the constitution of Man, or in the natural System under which he lives. From this region, therefore, he steadily averts his face. There are a good many other facts in human nature and in human conditions that have this common and universal character. There are a number of such facts connected with the mind, another number connected with the body, and still another number connected with the opportunities of men. But all of these Mr. George passes over — in order that he may fix attention upon one solitary fact — namely, that in all nations individual men, and individual communities of men, have hitherto been allowed to acquire bits of land and to deal with them as their own.

The distinction between Natural Law and Positive Institution is indeed a distinction not to be neglected. But it is one of the very deepest subjects in all philosophy, and there are many indications that Mr. George has dipped into its abysmal waters with the very shortest of sounding lines. Human laws are evolved out of human instincts, and these are among the gifts of nature. Reason may pervert them, and Reason is all the more apt to do so when it begins to spin logical webs out of its own bowels. But it may be safely said that in direct proportion as human laws, and the accepted ideas on which they rest, are really universal, in that same proportion they have a claim to be regarded as really natural, and as the legitimate expression of fundamental truths. Sometimes the very men who set up as reformers against such laws, and denounce as "stupid"* even the greatest nations which have abided by them, are themselves unconsciously subject to the same ideas, and are only working out of them some perverted application.

For here, again, we come upon another wonderful circumstance affecting Mr. George's writings. I have spoken of Mr. George as a citizen of the United States, and also as a citizen of the particular State of California. In this latter

---

* This is the epithet applied by Mr. George to the English people, because they will persist in allowing what all other nations have equally allowed.

capacity, as the citizen of a democratic government, he is a member of that government, which is the government of the whole people. Now, what is the most striking feature about the power claimed by that government, and actually exercised by it every day? It is the power of excluding the whole human race absolutely, except on its own conditions, from a large portion of the earth's surface — a portion so large that it embraces no less than ninety-nine millions of acres, or 156,000 square miles of plain and valley, of mountain and of hill, of lake and river, and of estuaries of the sea. Yet the community which claims and exercises this exclusive ownership over this enormous territory is, as compared with its extent, a mere handful of men. The whole population of the State of California represents only the fractional number of 5.5 to the square mile. It is less than one-quarter of the population of London. If the whole of it could be collected into one place they would hardly make a black spot in the enormous landscape if it were swept by a telescope. Such is the little company of men which claims to own absolutely and exclusively this enormous territory. Yet it is a member of this community who goes about the world preaching the doctrine, as a doctrine of divine right, that land is to be as free as the atmosphere, which is the common property of all, and in which no exclusive ownership can be claimed by any. It is true that Mr. George does denounce the conduct of his own Government in the matter of its disposal of land. But strange to say, he does not denounce it because it claims this exclusive ownership. On the contrary, he denounces it because it ever consents to part with it. Not the land only, but the very atmosphere of California — to use his own phraseology — is to be held so absolutely and so exclusively as the property of this community, that it is never to be parted with except on lease and for such annual rent as the Government may determine. Who gave this exclusive ownership over this immense territory to this particular community? Was it conquest? And if so, may it not be as rightfully acquired by any who are strong enough to seize it? And if exclusive ownership is conferred by conquest, then has it not been open to every conquering army, and to every occupying host in all ages and in all countries of the world, to establish a similar ownership, and to deal with it as they please?

It is at this point that we catch sight of one aspect of Mr. George's theory in which it is capable of at least a rational explanation. The question how a comparatively small community of men like the first gold-diggers of California and their descendants can with best advantage use or employ its exclusive claims of ownership over so vast an area, is clearly quite an open question. It is one thing for any given political society to refuse to divide its vacant territory among individual owners. It is quite another thing for a political society, which for ages has recognized such ownership and encouraged it, to break faith with those who have acquired such ownership and have lived and labored, and bought and sold, and willed upon the faith of it. If Mr. George can persuade the State of which he is a citizen, and the Government of which he is in this sense a member, that it would be best never any more to sell any bit of its unoccupied territory to any individual, by all means let him try to do so, and some plausible arguments might be used in favor of such a course. But there is a strong presumption against it and him. The question of the best method of disposing of such territory has been before every one of our great colonies, and before the United States for several generations; and the universal instinct of them all has been that the individual ownership of land is the one great attraction which they can hold out to the settlers whom it is their highest interest to invite and to establish. They know that the land of a country is never so well "nationalized" as when it is committed to the ownership of men whose interest it is to make the most of it. They know that under no other inducement could men be found to clear the soil from stifling forests, or to water it from arid wastes, or to drain it from pestilential swamps, or to inclose it from the access of wild animals, or to defend it from the assaults of savage tribes. Accordingly their verdict has been unanimous; and it has been given under conditions in which they were free from all traditions except those which they carried with them as parts of their own nature, in harmony and correspondence with the nature of things around them. I do not stop to argue this question here; but I do stop to point out that both solutions of it — the one quite as much as the other — involve the exclusive occupation of land by individuals, and the doctrine of absolute ownership vested in particular communities, as against all the rest of mankind. Both are equally incompatible with the fustian which compares the exclusive occupation of land to exclusive occupation of the atmosphere. Supposing that settlers could be found willing to devote the years of labor and of skill which are necessary to make wild soils productive, under no other tenure than that of a long "improvement lease," paying of course for some long period either no rent at all, or else a rent which must be purely nominal; supposing this to be true, still equally the whole area of any given region would soon be in the exclusive possession for long periods of time of a certain number of individual farmers, and would not be open to the occupation by the poor of all the world. Thus the absolute ownership which Mr. George declares to be blasphemous against God and Nature, is still asserted on behalf of some mere fraction of the human race, and this absolute ownership is again doled out to the members of this small community, and to them alone, in such shares as it considers to be most remunerative to itself.

And here again, for the third time, we come upon a most remarkable testimony to facts in Mr. George's book, the import and bearing of which he does not apparently perceive. Of course the question whether it is most advantageous to any given society of men to own and cultivate its own lands in severalty or in common, is a question largely depending on the conduct and the motives and the character of governments, as compared with the conduct and the character and the motives of individual men. In the disposal and application of wealth, as well as in the acquisition of it, are men more pure and honest when they act in public capacities as members of a Government or of a Legislature, than when they act in private capacities toward their fellow men? Is it not notoriously the reverse? Is it not obvious that men will do, and are constantly seen doing, as politicians, what they would be ashamed to do in private life? And has not this been proved under all the forms which government has taken in the history of political societies? Lastly, I will ask one other question — Is it not true that, to say the very least, this inherent tendency to corruption has received no check from the democratic constitutions of those many "new worlds" in which kings were left behind, and aristocracies have not had time to be established?

These are the very questions which Mr. George answers with no faltering voice; and it is impossible to disregard his evidence. He declares over and over again, in language of virtuous indignation, that government in the United States is everywhere becoming more and more corrupt. Not only are the Legislatures corrupt, but that last refuge of virtue even in the worst societies — the Judiciary — is corrupt also. In none of the old countries of the world has the very name of politician fallen so low as in the democratic communities of America. Nor would it be true to say that it is the wealthy classes who have corrupted the constituencies. These — at least to a very large extent — are themselves corrupt. Probably there is no sample of the *Demos* more infected with corruption than the *Demos* of New York. Its management of the municipal rates is alleged to be a system of scandalous jobbery. Now, the wonderful thing is that of all this Mr. George is thoroughly aware. He sees it, he repeats it in every variety of form. Let us hear a single passage:*

> It behooves us to look facts in the face. The experiment of popular government in the United States is clearly a failure. Not that it is a failure everywhere and in everything. An experiment of this kind does not have to be fully worked out to be proved a failure. But speaking generally of the whole country, from the Atlantic to the Pacific, and from the Lakes to the Gulf, our government by the people has in large degree become, is in larger degree becoming, government by the strong and unscrupulous.

Again, I say that it is fair to remember that Mr. George is a Pessimist. But while remembering this, and making every possible allowance for it, we must not less remember that his evidence does not stand alone. In the United States, from citizens still proud of their country, and out of the United States, from representative Americans, I have been told of transactions from personal knowledge which conclusively indicated a condition of things closely corresponding to the indictment of Mr. George. At all events we cannot be wrong in our conclusion that it is not among the public bodies and Governments of the States of America that we are to look in that country for the best exhibitions of purity or of virtue.

Yet it is to these bodies — legislative, administrative, and judicial, of which he gives us such an account — that Mr. George would confine the rights of absolute ownership in the soil. It is these bodies that he would constitute the sole and universal landlord, and it is to them he would confide the duty of assessing and of spending the rents of everybody all over the area of every State. He tells us that a great

---

* *Social Problems*, Chapter II

revenue, fit for the support of some such great rulers as have been common in the Old World, could be afforded out of one-half the "waste and stealages" of such municipalities as his own at San Francisco. What would be the "waste and stealages" of a governing body having at its disposal the whole agricultural and mining wealth of such States as California and Texas, of Illinois and Colorado?

But this is not all. The testimony which is borne by Mr. George as to what the governing bodies of America now are is as nothing to the testimony of his own writings as to what they would be — if they were ever to adopt his system, and if they were ever to listen to his teaching. Like all Communists, he regards Society not as consisting of individuals whose separate welfare is to be the basis of the welfare of the whole, but as a great abstract Personality, in which all power is to be centered, and to which all separate rights and interests are to be subordinate. If this is to be the doctrine, we might at least have hoped that with such powers committed to Governments, as against the individual, corresponding duties and responsibilities, toward the individual, would have been recognized as an indispensable accompaniment. If, for example, every political society as a whole is an abiding Personality, with a continuity of rights over all its members, we might at least have expected that the continuous obligation of honor and good faith would have been recognized as equally binding on this Personality in all its relations with those who are subject to its rule. But this is not at all Mr. George's view. On the contrary, he preaches systematically not only the high privilege, but the positive duty of repudiation. He is not content with urging that no more bits of unoccupied land should be ever sold, but he insists upon it that the ownership of every bit already sold shall be resumed without compensation to the settler who has bought it, who has spent upon it years of labor, and who from first to last has relied on the security

of the State and on the honor of its Government. There is
no mere practice of corruption which has ever been alleged
against the worst administrative body in any country that
can be compared in corruption with the desolating dishonor
of this teaching. In olden times, under violent and rapacious rulers, the Prophets of Israel and of Judah used to
raise their voices against all forms of wrong and robbery,
and they pronounced a special benediction upon him who
sweareth to his own hurt and changeth not. But the new
Prophet of San Francisco is of a different opinion. Ahab
would have been saved all his trouble, and Jezebel would
have been saved all her tortuous intrigues if only they could
have had beside them the voice of Mr. Henry George. Elijah
was a fool. What right could Naboth have to talk about the
"inheritance of his fathers"* His fathers could have no more
right to acquire the ownership of those acres on the Hill of
Jezreel than he could have to continue in the usurpation of
it. No matter what might be his pretended title, no man
and no body of men could give it: — not Joshua nor the
Judges; not Saul nor David; not Solomon in all his glory —
could "make sure" to Naboth's fathers that portion of God's
earth against the undying claims of the head of the State,
and of the representative of the whole people of Israel.

But now another vista of consequence opens up before
us. If the doctrine be established that no faith is to be kept
with the owners of land, will the same principle not apply
to tenancy as well as ownership? If one generation cannot
bind the next to recognize a purchase, can one generation
bind another to recognize a lease? If the one promise can
be broken and ought to be broken, why should the other be
admitted to be binding? If the accumulated value arising
out of many years, or even generations, of labor, can be and
ought to be appropriated, is there any just impediment

---

* 1 Kings xxi. 3.

against seizing that value every year as it comes to be? If this new gospel be indeed gospel, why should not this Californian form of "faith unfaithful" keep us perennially and forever "falsely true"?

Nay, more, is there any reason why the doctrine of repudiation should be confined to pledges respecting either the tenancy or the ownership of land? This question naturally arose in the minds of all who read with any intelligence *Progress and Poverty* when it first appeared. But the extent to which its immoral doctrines might be applied was then a matter of inference only, however clear that inference might be. If all owners of land, great and small, might be robbed, and ought to be robbed of that which Society had from time immemorial allowed them and encouraged them to acquire and to call their own; if the thousands of men, women, and children who directly and indirectly live on rent, whether in the form of returns to the improver, or of mortgage to the capitalist, or jointure to the widow, or portion to the children, are all equally to be ruined by the confiscation of the fund on which they depend — are there not other funds which would be all swept into the same net of envy and of violence? In particular, what is to become of that great fund on which also thousands and thousands depend — men, women, and children, the aged, the widow, and the orphan — the fund which the State has borrowed and which constitutes the Debt of Nations? Even in *Progress and Poverty* there were dark hints and individual passages which indicated the goal of all its reasoning in this direction. But men's intellects just now are so flabby on these subjects, and they are so fond of shaking their heads when property in land is compared with property in other things, that such suspicions and forebodings as to the issue of Mr. George's arguments would to many have seemed overstrained. Fortunately, in his later book he has had the courage of his opinions, and the logic of false premises has steeled his moral sense against the iniquity of even the most dishonorable conclusions. All National Debts are as unjust as property in land; all such Debts are to be treated with the sponge. As no faith is due to landowners, or to any who depend on their sources of income, so neither is any faith to be kept with bondholders, or with any who depend on the revenues which have been pledged to them. The Jew who may have lent a million, and the small tradesman who may have lent his little savings to the State – the trust funds of children and of widows which have been similarly lent – are all equally to be the victims of repudiation. When we remember the enormous amount of the National Debts of Europe and of the American States, and the vast number of persons of all kinds and degrees of wealth whose property is invested in these "promises to pay," we can perhaps faintly imagine the ruin which would be caused by the gigantic fraud recommended by Mr. George. Take England alone. About seven hundred and fifty millions is the amount of her Public Debt. This great sum is held by about 181,721 persons, of whom the immense majority – about 111,000 – receive dividends amounting to £400 a year and under. Of these, again, by far the greater part enjoy incomes of less than £100 a year. And then the same principle is of course applicable to the debt of all public bodies; those of the Municipalities alone, which are rapidly increasing, would now amount to something like one hundred and fifty millions more.

Everything in America is on a gigantic scale, even its forms of villainy, and the villainy advocated by Mr. George is an illustration of this as striking as the Mammoth Cave of Kentucky, or the frauds of the celebrated "Tammany Ring" in New York. The world has never seen such a Preacher of Unrighteousness as Mr. Henry George. For he goes to the roots of things, and shows us how unfounded are the rules of probity, and what mere senseless superstitions are the obligations which have been only too long acknowledged. Let us hear him on National Debts, for it is an excellent specimen of his childish logic, and of his profligate conclusions:

> *The institution of public debts, like the institution of private property in land, rests upon the preposterous assumption that one generation may bind another generation. If a man were to come to me and say, "Here is a promissory note which your great-grandfather gave to my great-grandfather, and which you will oblige me by paying," I would laugh at him, and tell him that if he wanted to collect his note he had better hunt up the man who made it; that I had nothing to do with my great-grandfather's promises. And if he were to insist upon payment, and to call my attention to the terms of the bond in which my great-grandfather expressly stipulated with his great-grandfather that I should pay him, I would only laugh the more, and be the more certain that he was a lunatic. To such a demand any one of us would reply in effect, "My great-grandfather was evidently a knave or a joker, and your great-grandfather was certainly a fool, which quality you surely have inherited if you expect me to pay you money because my great-grandfather promised that I should do so. He might as well have given your great-grandfather a draft upon Adam or a check upon the First National Bank of the Moon."*
>
> *Yet upon this assumption that ascendants may bind descendants, that one generation may legislate for another generation, rests the assumed validity of our land titles and public debts. **

Yet even in this wonderful passage we have not touched the bottom of Mr. George's lessons in the philosophy of spoliation. If we may take the property of those who have trusted to our honor, surely it must be still more legitimate to take the property of those who have placed in us no such confidence. If we may fleece the public creditor, it must be at least equally open to us to fleece all those who have invested otherwise their private fortunes. All the other accumulations of industry must be as rightfully liable to

---

* *Social Problems*, Chapter XVI.

confiscation. Whenever "the people" see any large handful in the hands of any one, they have a right to have it — in order to save themselves from any necessity of submitting to taxation.

Accordingly we find, as usual, that Mr. George has a wonderful honesty in avowing what hitherto the uninstructed world has been agreed upon considering as dishonesty. But this time the avowal comes out under circumstances which are deserving of special notice. We all know that not many years ago the United States was engaged in a civil war of long duration, at one time apparently of doubtful issue, and on which the national existence hung. I was one of those — not too many in this country — who held from the beginning of that terrible contest that "the North" were right in fighting it. Lord Russell, on a celebrated occasion, said that they were fighting for "dominion." Yes; and for what else have nations ever fought, and by what else than dominion, in one sense or another — have great nations ever come to be? The *Demos* has no greater right to fight for dominion than Kings; but it has the same. But behind and above the existence of the Union as a nation there was the further question involved whether, in this nineteenth century of the Christian era, there was to be established a great dominion of civilized men which was to have negro slavery as its fundamental doctrine and as the cherished basis of its constitution. On both of these great questions the people of the Northern States — in whatever proportions the one or the other issue might affect individual minds — had before them as noble a cause as any which has ever called men to arms. It is a cause which will be forever associated in the memory of mankind with one great figure — the figure of Abraham Lincoln, the best and highest representative of the American people in that tremendous crisis. In nothing has the bearing of that people been more admirable than in the patient and willing submission of the masses, as of one man, not only to the desolating sacrifice of life which it entailed, but to the heavy and lasting burden of taxation which was inseparable from it. It is indeed deplorable – nothing I have ever read in all literature has struck me as so deplorable – that at this time of day, when by patient continuance in well-doing the burden has become comparatively light, and there is a near prospect of its final disappearance, one single American citizen should be found who appreciates so little the glory of his country as to express his regret that they did not begin this great contest by an act of stealing. Yet this is the case with Mr. Henry George. In strict pursuance of his dishonest doctrines of repudiation respecting public debts, and knowing that the war could not have been prosecuted without funds, he speaks with absolute bitterness of the folly which led the Government to "shrink" from at once seizing the whole, or all but a mere fraction, of the property of the few individual citizens who had the reputation of being exceptionally rich. If, for example, it were known that any man had made a fortune of $200,000, the Washington Government ought not to have "shrunk" from taking the whole – except some $2,200, which remainder might, perhaps, by a great favor, be left for such support as it might afford to the former owner. And so by a number of seizures of this kind, all over the States, the war might possibly have been conducted for the benefit of all at the cost of a very few. *

It may be worth while to illustrate how this would have worked in a single instance. When I was in New York, a few years ago, one of the sights which was pointed out to me was a house of great size and of great beauty both in respect to material and to workmanship. In these respects at least, if not in its architecture, it was equal to any of the palaces which are owned by private citizens in any of the richest

---

* Mr. George words are these: "If, when we called on men to die for their country, we had not shrunk from taking, if necessary, nine hundred and ninety-nine thousand dollars from every millionaire, we need not have created any debt " (*Social Problems*, Chapter XVI)

capitals of the Old World. It was built wholly of pure white marble, and the owner, not having been satisfied with any of the marbles of America, had gone to the expense of importing Italian marble for the building. This beautiful and costly house was, I was further told, the property of a Scotchman who had emigrated to America with no other fortune and no other capital than his own good brains. He had begun by selling ribbons. By selling cheap, and for ready money, but always also goods of the best quality, he had soon acquired a reputation for dealings which were eminently advantageous to those who bought. But those who bought were the public, and so a larger and a larger portion of the public became eager to secure the advantages of this exceptionally moderate and honest dealer. With the industry of his race he had also its thrift, and the constant turning of his capital on an ever-increasing scale, coupled with his own limited expenditure, had soon led to larger and larger savings. These, again, had been judiciously invested in promoting every public undertaking which promised advantage to his adopted country, and which, by fulfilling that promise, could alone become remunerative. And so by a process which, in every step of it, was an eminent service to the community of which he was a member, he became what is called a millionaire. Nor in the spending of his wealth had he done otherwise than contribute to the taste and splendor of his country, as well as to the lucrative employment of its people. All Nature is full of the love of ornament, and the habitations of creatures, even the lowest in the scale of being, are rich in coloring and in carving of the most exquisite and elaborate decoration. It is only an ignorant and uncultured spirit which denounces the same love of ornament in Man, and it is a stupid doctrine which sees in it nothing but a waste of means. The great merchant of New York had indeed built his house at great cost; but this is only another form of saying that he had spent among the artificers of that city a great sum of money, and had in the same proportion contributed to the only employment by which they live. In every way, therefore, both as regards the getting and the spending of his wealth, this millionaire was an honor and a benefactor to his country. This is the man on whom that same country would have been incited by Mr. Henry George to turn the big eyes of brutal envy, and to rob of all his earnings. It is not so much the dishonesty or the violence of such teaching that strikes us most, but its unutterable meanness. That a great nation, having a great cause at stake, and representing in the history of the world a life-and-death struggle against barbarous institutions, ought to have begun its memorable war by plundering a few of its own citizens — this is surely the very lowest depth which has ever been reached by any political philosophy.

And not less instructive than the results of this philosophy are the methods of its reasoning, its methods of illustration, and its way of representing facts. Of these we cannot have a better example than the passage before quoted, in which Mr. Henry George explains the right of nations and the right of individuals to repudiate an hereditary debt. It is well to see that the man who defends the most dishonorable conduct on the part of Governments defends it equally on the part of private persons. The passage is a typical specimen of the kind of stuff of which Mr. George's works are full. The element of plausibility in it is the idea that a man should not be held responsible for promises to which he was not himself a consenting party. This idea is presented by itself, with a careful suppression of the conditions which make it inapplicable to the case in hand. Hereditary debts do not attach to persons except in respect to hereditary possessions. Are these possessions to be kept while the corresponding obligations are to be denied? Mr. George is loud on the absurdity of calling upon him to honor any promise which his great-grandfather may have made, but he is si-lent about giving up any resources which his great-grandfather may have left. Possibly he might get out of this difficulty by avowing that he would allow no property to pass from one generation to another — not even from father to son — that upon every death all the savings of every individual should be confiscated by the State. Such a proposal would not be one whit more violent, or more destructive to society, than other proposals which he does avow. But so far as I have observed, this particular consequence of his reasoning is either not seen, or is kept in the dark. With all his apparent and occasional honesty in confronting results however anarchical, there is a good deal of evidence that he knows how to conceal his hand. The prominence given in his agitation to an attack on the particular class of capitalists who are owners of land, and the total or comparative silence which he maintains on his desire to rob fund-holders of all kinds, and especially the public creditor, is a clear indication of a strategy which is more dexterous than honest. And so it may really be true that he repudiates all hereditary debt because he will also destroy all hereditary succession in savings of any kind. But it must be observed that even thus he cannot escape from the inconsistency I have pointed out, as it affects all public debts. These have all been contracted for the purpose of effecting great national objects, such as the preservation of national independence, or the acquisition of national territory, or the preparations needed for national defense. The State cannot be disinherited of the benefits and possessions thus secured, as individuals may be disinherited of their fathers' gains. In the case of National Debts, therefore, it is quite clear that the immorality of Mr. George's argument is as conspicuous as the childishness of its reasoning.

But there are other examples, quite as striking, of the incredible absurdity of his reasoning, which are immediately connected with his dominant idea about property in land. Thus the notion that because all the natural and elementary substances which constitute the raw materials of human wealth are substances derived from the ground, therefore all forms of that wealth must ultimately tend to concentration in the hands of those who own the land; this notion must strike a landowner as one worthy only of Bedlam. He may not be able at a moment's notice to unravel all the fallacies on which it rests, and he may even be able to see in it the mad mimicry of logic which deceives the ignorant. But one does not need to be a landowner to see immediately that the conclusion is an absurdity. We have only to apply this notion in detail in order to see more and more clearly its discrepancy with fact. Thus, for example, we may put one application of it thus: All houses are built of materials derived from the soil, of stone, of lime, of brick, or of wood, or of all four combined. But of these materials three are not only products of the soil, but parts of its very substance and material. Clearly it must follow that the whole value of house property must end in passing into the hands of those who own these materials, quarries of building-stone) beds of brick-earth, beds of lime, and forests. Unfortunately for landowners, this wonderful demonstration does not, somehow, take effect.

But Mr. Henry George's processes in matters of reasoning are not more absurd than his assumptions in matters of fact. The whole tone is based on the assumption that owners of land are not producers, and that rent does not represent, or represents only in a very minor degree, the interest of capital. Even an American ought to know better than this; because, although there are in some parts of the United States immense areas of prairie land which are ready for the plow with almost no preliminary labor, yet even in the New World the areas are still more immense in which the soil can only be made capable of producing human food by the hardest of labor, and the most prolonged. But in the old countries of Europe, and especially in our own, every land-owner knows well, and others ought to know a little, that the present condition of the soil is the result of generations of costly improvements, and of renewed and reiterated out-lays to keep these improvements in effective order. Yet on this subject I fear that many persons are almost as ignorant as Mr. Henry George. My own experience now extends over a period of the best part of forty years. During that time I have built more than fifty homesteads complete for man and beast; I have drained and reclaimed many hundreds, and enclosed some thousands, of acres. In this sense I have "added house to house and field to field," not — as pulpit orators have assumed in similar cases — that I might "dwell alone in the land," but that the cultivating class might live more comfortably, and with better appliances for increas-ing the produce of the soil. I know no more animating scene than that presented to us in the essays and journals which give an account of the agricultural improvements effected in Scotland since the close of the Civil Wars in 1745. Thou-sands and thousands of acres have been reclaimed from bog and waste. Ignorance has given place to science, and barbarous customs of immemorial strength have been re-placed by habits of intelligence and of business. In every county the great landowners, and very often the smaller, were the great pioneers in a process which has transformed the whole face of the country. And this process is still in full career. If I mention again my own case, it is because I know it to be only a specimen, and that others have been working on a still larger scale. During the four years since Mr. George did me the honor of sending to me a book assuming that landowners are not producers, I find that I have spent on one property alone the sum of £40,000 en-tirely on the improvement of the soil. Moreover, I know that this outlay on my own part, and similar outlay on the part of my neighbors, so far from having power to absorb and concentrate in our hands all other forms of wealth, is unable to secure anything like the return which the same capital would have won — and won easily — in many other kinds of enterprise. I am in possession of authentic information that on one great estate in England the outlay on improvements purely agricultural has, for twenty-one years past, been at the rate of £35,000 a year, while including outlay on churches and schools, it has amounted in the last forty years to nearly £2,000,000 sterling. To such outlays landowners are incited very often, and to a great extent, by the mere love of seeing a happier landscape and a more prosperous people. From much of the capital so invested they often seek no return at all, and from very little of it indeed do they ever get a high rate of interest. And yet the whole — every farthing of it goes directly to the public advantage. Production is increased in full proportion, although the profit on that production is small to the owner. There has been grown more corn, more potatoes, more turnips; there has been produced more milk, more butter, more cheese, more beef, more mutton, more pork, more fowls and eggs, and all these articles in direct proportion to their abundance have been sold at lower prices to the people. When a man tells me, and argues on steps of logic which he boasts as irrefutable, that in all this I and others have been serving no interests but our own — nay, more, that we have been but making "the poor poorer" than they were — I know very well that, whether I can unravel his fallacies or not, he is talking the most arrant nonsense, and must have in his composition, however ingenious and however eloquent, a rich combination and a very large percentage of the fanatic and of the goose.

And here, again, we have a new indication of these elements in one great assumption of fact, and that is the assumption that wealth has been becoming less and less diffused — "the rich richer, the poor poorer." It did not require the recent elaborate and able statistical examination of Mr. Giffen to convince me that this assumption is altogether false. It is impossible for any man to have been a considerable employer of labor during a period embracing one full generation, without his seeing and feeling abundant evidence that all classes have partaken in the progress of the country, and no class more extensively than that which lives by labor. He must know that wages have more than doubled — sometimes a great deal more — while the continuous remission of taxes has tended to make, and has actually made almost every article of subsistence a great deal cheaper than it was thirty years ago. And outside the province of mere muscular labor, among all the classes who are concerned in the work of distribution or of manufacture, I have seen around me, and on my own property, the enormous increase of those whose incomes must be comfortable without being large. The houses that are built for their weeks of rest and leisure, the furniture with which these houses are provided, the gardens and shrubberies which are planted for the ornament of them; all of these indications, and a thousand more, tell of increasing comfort far more widely if not universally diffused.

And if personal experience enables me to contradict absolutely one of Mr. George's assumptions, official experience enables me not less certainly to contradict another. Personally I know what private ownership has done for one country. Officially I have had only too good cause to know what State ownership has not done for another country. India is a country in which, theoretically at least, the State is the only and the universal landowner, and over a large part of it the State does actually take to itself a share of the gross produce which fully represents ordinary rent. Yet this is the very country in which the poverty of the masses is so abject that millions live only from hand to mouth, and when there is any — even a partial — failure of the crops, thousands and hundreds of thousands are in danger of actual starvation. The Indian Government is not corrupt – whatever other failings it may have – and the rents of a vast territory can be far more safe if left to its disposal than they could be left at the disposal of such popular Governments as those which Mr. George has denounced on the American Continent. Yet somehow the functions and duties which in more civilized countries are discharged by the institution of private ownership in land are not as adequately discharged by the Indian Administration. Moreover, I could not fail to observe, when I was connected with the Government of India, that the portion of that country which has most grown in wealth is precisely that part of it in which the Government has parted with its power of absorbing rent by having agreed to a Permanent Settlement. Many Anglo-Indian statesmen have looked with envious eyes at the wealth which has been developed in Lower Bengal, and have mourned over the policy by which the State has been withheld from taking it into the hands of Government. There are two questions, however, which have always occurred to me when this mourning has been expressed – the first is whether we are quite sure that the wealth of Lower Bengal would ever have arisen if its sources had not been thus protected; and the second is whether even now it is quite certain that any Governments, even the best, spend wealth better for the public interests than those to whom it belongs by the natural processes of acquisition. These questions have never, I think, been adequately considered. But whatever may be the true answer to either of them, there is at least one question on which all English statesmen have been unanimous – and that is, that promises once given by the Government, however long ago, must be absolutely kept. When landed property has been bought and sold and inherited in Bengal for some three generations – since 1793 – under the guaranty of the Government that the Rent Tax upon it is to remain at a fixed amount, no public man, so far as I know, has ever suggested that the public faith should be violated. And not only so, but there has been a disposition even to put upon the engagement of the Government an overstrained interpretation, and to claim for the landowners who are protected under it an immunity from all other taxes affecting the same sources of income. As Secretary of State for India I had to deal with this question along with my colleagues in the Indian Council, and the result we arrived at was embodied in a dispatch which laid down the principles applicable to the case so clearly that in India it appears to have been accepted as conclusive. The Land Tax was a special impost upon rent. The promise was that this special impost should never be increased; or, in its own words, that there should be no "augmentation of the public assessment in consequence of the improvement of their estates." It was not a promise that no other taxes should ever be raised affecting the same sources of income, provided such taxes were not special, but affected all other sources of income equally. On this interpretation the growing wealth of Bengal accruing under the Permanent Settlement would remain accessible to taxation along with the growing wealth derived from all other kinds of property, but not otherwise. There was to be no confiscation by the State of the increased value of land, any more than of the increased value of other kinds of property, on the pretext that this increase was unearned. On the other hand, the State did not exempt that increased value from any taxation which might be levied also and equally from all the rest of the community. In this way we reconciled and established two great principles which to short-sighted theorists may seem antagonistic. One of these principles is that it is the interest of every community to give equal and absolute security to every one of its members in his pursuit of wealth; the other is that when the public interests demand a public revenue all forms of wealth should be equally accessible to taxation.

It would have saved us all, both in London and in

Calcutta, much anxious and careful reasoning if we could only have persuaded ourselves that the Government of 1793 could not possibly bind the Government of 1870. It would have given us a still wider margin if we had been able to believe that no faith can be pledged to landowners, and that we had a divine right to seize not only all the wealth of the Zemindars of Bengal, but also all the property derived from the same source which had grown up since 1793, and has now become distributed and absorbed among a great number of intermediate sharers, standing between the actual cultivator and the representatives of those to whom the promise was originally given. But one doctrine has been tenaciously held by the "stupid English people" in the government of their Eastern Empire, and that is, that our honor is the greatest of our possessions, and that absolute trust in that honor is one of the strongest foundations of our power.

In this paper it has not been my aim to argue. A simple record and exposure of a few of the results arrived at by Mr. Henry George, has been all that I intended to accomplish. To see what are the practical consequences of any train of reasoning is so much gained. And there are cases in which this gain is everything. In mathematical reasoning the "reduction to absurdity" is one of the most familiar methods of disproof. In political reasoning the "reduction to iniquity" ought to be of equal value. And if it is not found to be so with all minds, this is because of a peculiarity in human character which is the secret of all its corruption, and of the most dreadful forms in which that corruption has been exhibited. In pursuing another investigation I have lately had occasion to observe upon the contrast which, in this respect, exists between our moral and our purely intellectual faculties.* Our Reason is so constituted in respect to certain fundamental truths that those truths are intuitively

---

* *Unity of Nature,* Chapter X., pp. 440-445.

perceived, and any rejection of them is at once seen to be absurd. But in the far higher sphere of Morals and Religion, it would seem that we have no equally secure moorings to duty and to truth. There is no consequence, however hideous or cruel its application may be, that men have been prevented from accepting because of such hideousness or of such cruelty. Nothing, however shocking, is quite sure to shock them. If it follows from some false belief, or from some fallacious verbal proposition, they will entertain it, and sometimes will even rejoice in it with a savage fanaticism. It is a fact that none of us should ever forget that the moral faculties of Man do not as certainly revolt against iniquity as his reasoning faculties do revolt against absurdity. All history is crowded with illustrations of this distinction, and it is the only explanation of a thousand horrors. There has seldom been such a curious example as the immoral teachings of Mr. Henry George. Here we have a man who probably sincerely thinks be is a Christian, and who sets up as a philosopher, but who is not the least shocked by consequences which abolish the Decalogue, and deny the primary obligations both of public and of private honor. This is a very curious phenomenon, and well deserving of some closer investigation. What are the erroneous data — what are the abstract propositions — which so overpower the Moral Sense, and coming from the sphere of Speculation dictate such flagitious recommendations in the sphere of Conduct? To this question I may perhaps return, not with exclusive reference to the writings of one man, but with reference to the writings of many others who have tried to reduce to scientific form the laws which govern the social developments of our race, and who in doing so have forgotten — strangely forgotten — some of the most fundamental facts of Nature.

II. The "Reduction to Iniquity"

by Henry George

"IN THIS PAPER it has not been my aim to argue," says the Duke of Argyll, in concluding his article entitled "The Prophet of San Francisco." It is generally waste of time to reply to those who do not argue. Yet, partly because of my respect for other writings of his, and partly because of the ground to which he invites me, I take the first opportunity I have had to reply to the Duke.

In doing so, let me explain the personal incident to which he refers, and which he has seemingly misunderstood. In sending the Duke of Argyll a copy of *Progress and Poverty,* I intended no impertinence, and was unconscious of any impropriety. Instead, I paid him a high compliment. For, as I stated in an accompanying note, I sent him my book not only to mark my esteem for the author of *The Reign of Law,* but because I thought him a man superior to his accidents.

I am still conscious of the profit I derived from *The Reign of Law,* and can still recall the pleasure it gave me. What attracted me, however, was not, as the Duke seems to think, what he styles his "nonsense chapter." On the con-trary, the notion that it is necessary to impose restrictions upon labor seems to me strangely incongruous, not only with free trade, but with the idea of the dominance and harmony of natural laws, which in preceding chapters he so well develops. Where such restrictions as Factory Acts seem needed in the interests of labor, the seeming need, to my mind, arises from previous restrictions, in the removal of which, and not in further restrictions, the true remedy is to be sought. What attracted me in *The Reign of Law* was the manner in which the Duke points out the existence of physical laws and adaptations which compel the mind that thinks upon them to the recognition of creative purpose. In this way the Duke's book was to me useful and grateful, as I doubt not it has been to many others.

My book, I thought, might, in return, be useful and grateful to the Duke — might give him something of that "immense and instinctive pleasure" of which he had spoken as arising from the recognition of the grand simplicity and unspeakable harmony of universal law. And in the domain in which I had, as I believed, done something to point out the reign of law this pleasure is perhaps even more intense than in that of which he had written. For in physical laws we recognize only intelligence, and can but trust that infinite wisdom implies infinite goodness. But in social laws he who looks may recognize beneficence as well as intelligence; may see that the moral perceptions of men are perceptions of realities; and find ground for an abiding faith that this short life does not bound the destiny of the human soul. I knew the Duke of Argyll then only by his book. I had never been in Scotland, or learned the character as a landlord he bears there. I intended to pay a tribute and give a pleasure to a citizen of the republic of letters, not to irritate a landowner. I did not think a trumpery, title and a patch of ground could fetter a mind that had communed with Nature and busied itself with causes and beginnings. My mistake was that of ignorance. Since the Duke of Argyll has publicly called attention to it, I thus publicly apologize.

The Duke declares it has not been his aim to argue. This is clear. I wish it were as clear it had not been his aim to misrepresent. He seems to have written for those who have never read the books he criticizes. But as those who have done so constitute a very respectable part of the reading world, I can leave his misrepresentations to take care of themselves, confident that the incredible absurdity he attributes to my reasonings will be seen, by whoever reads my books, to belong really to the Duke's distortions. In what I have here to say I prefer to meet him upon his own ground and to hold to the main question.* I accept the "reduction to iniquity."

Strangely enough, the Duke expresses distrust of the very tribunal to which be appeals. "It is a fact," he tells as, "that none of us should ever forget, that the moral faculties do not as certainly revolt against iniquity as the reasoning faculties do against absurdity." If that be the case, why, then, may I ask, is the Duke's whole article addressed to the moral faculties? Why does he talk about right and wrong, about justice and injustice, about honor and dishonor; about my "immoral doctrines" and "profligate conclusions," "the unutterable meanness of the gigantic villainy" I advocate? why style me "such a Preacher of Unrighteousness as the world has never seen," and so on? If the Duke will permit me I will tell him, for in all probability he does not know — he himself, to paraphrase his own words, being a good example of how men who sometimes set up as philosophers and deny laws of the human mind are themselves unconsciously subject to those very laws. The Duke appeals to moral perceptions for the same reason that impels all men, good or bad, learned or simple, to appeal to moral perceptions whenever they become warm in argument; and this reason is, the instinctive feeling that the moral sense is higher

---

* It is unnecessary for me to say anything of India further than to remark that the essence of nationalization of land is not in the collection of rent by government, but in its utilization for the benefit of the people. Nor on the subject of public debts is it worth while here to add anything to what I have said in *Social Problems*.

and truer than the intellectual sense; that the moral faculties do more certainly revolt against iniquity than the intellectual faculties against absurdity. The Duke appeals to the moral sense, because he instinctively feels that with all men its decisions have the highest sanction; and if he afterward seeks to weaken its authority, it is because this very moral sense whispers to him that his case is not a good one.

My opinion as to the relative superiority of the moral and intellectual perceptions is the reverse of that stated by the Duke. It seems to me certain that the moral faculties constitute a truer guide than the intellectual faculties, and that what, in reality, we should never forget, is not that the moral faculties are untrustworthy, but that those faculties may be dulled by refusal to heed them, and distorted by the promptings of selfishness. So true, so ineradicable is the moral sense, that where selfishness or passion would outrage it, the intellectual faculties are always called upon to supply excuse. No unjust war was ever begun without some pretense of asserting right or redressing wrong, or, despite themselves, of doing some good to the conquered. No petty thief but makes for himself some justification. It is doubtful if any deliberate wrong is ever committed, it is certain no wrongful course of action is ever continued, without the framing of some theory which may dull or placate the moral sense.

And while as to things apprehended solely by the intellectual faculties the greatest diversities of perception have obtained and still obtain among men, and those perceptions constantly change with the growth of knowledge, there is a striking consensus of moral perceptions. In all stages of social development, and under all forms of religion, no matter how distorted by selfish motives and intellectual perversions, truth, justice, and benevolence have ever been esteemed, and all our intellectual progress has given us no higher moral ideals than have obtained among primitive peoples. The very distortions of the moral sense, the apparent differences in the moral standards of different times and peoples, do but show essential unity. Wherever moral perceptions have differed or do differ the disturbance may be traced to causes which, originating in selfishness and perpetuated by intellectual perversions, have distorted or dulled the moral faculty. It seems to me that the Creator, whom both the Duke of Argyll and myself recognize behind physical and mental laws, has not left us to grope our way in darkness, but has, indeed, given us a light by which our steps may be safely guided — a compass by which, in all degrees of intellectual development, the way to the highest good way be surely traced. But just as the compass, by which the mariner steers his course over the trackless sea in the blackest night, may be disturbed by other attractions, may be misread or clogged, so is it with the moral sense. This evidently is not a world in which men must be either wise or good, but a world in which they may bring about good or evil as they use the faculties given them.

I speak of this because the recognition of the supremacy and certainty of the moral faculties seems to me to throw light upon problems otherwise dark, rather than because it is necessary here, since I admit even more unreservedly than the Duke the competence of the tribunal before which he cites me. I am willing to submit every question of political economy to the test of ethics. So far as I can see there is no social law which does not conform to moral law, and no social question which cannot be determined more quickly and certainly by appeal to moral perceptions than by appeal to intellectual perceptions. Nor can there be any dispute between us as to the issue to be joined. He charges me with advocating violation of the moral law in proposing robbery. I agree that robbery is a violation of the moral law, and is therefore, without further inquiry, to be condemned.

As to what constitutes robbery, it is, we will both agree,

the taking or withholding from another of that which rightfully belongs to him. That which rightfully belongs to him,
be it observed, not that which legally belongs to him. As to
what extent human law may create rights is beside this
discussion, for what I propose is to change, not to violate
human law. Such change the Duke declares would be un-
righteous. He thus appeals to that moral law which is before and above all human laws, and by which all human
laws are to be judged. Let me insist upon this point. Landholders must elect to try their case either by human law or
by moral law. If they say that land is rightfully property because made so by human law, they cannot charge those who
would change that law with advocating robbery. But if they
charge that such change in human law would be robbery,
then they must show that land is rightfully property irrespective of human law.

For land is not of that species of things to which the
presumption of rightful property attaches. This does attach
to things that are properly termed wealth, and that are the
produce of labor. Such things, in their beginning, must have
an owner, as they originate in human exertion, and the
right of property which attaches to them springs from the
manifest natural right of every individual to himself and to
the benefit of his own exertions. This is the moral basis of
property, which makes certain things rightfully property
totally irrespective of human law. The Eighth Command-
ment does not derive its validity from human enactment. It
is written upon the facts of nature and self-evident to the
perceptions of men. If there were but two men in the world,
the fish which either of them took from the sea, the beast
which he captured in the chase, the fruit which he gath-
ered, or the hut which he erected, would be his rightful
property, which the other could not take from him without
violation of the moral law. But how could either of them
claim the world as his rightful property? Or if they agreed

to divide the world between them, what moral right could their compact give as against the next man who came into the world?

It is needless, however, to insist that property in land rests only on human enactment, which may, at any time, be changed without violation of moral law. No one seriously asserts any other derivation. It is sometimes said that property in land is derived from appropriation. But those who say this do not really mean it. Appropriation can give no right. The man who raises a cupful of water from a river, acquires a right to that cupful, and no one may rightfully snatch it from his hand; but this right is derived from labor, not from appropriation. How could he acquire a right to the river, by merely appropriating it? Columbus did not dream of appropriating the New World to himself and his heirs, and would have been deemed a lunatic had he done so. Nations and princes divided America between them, but by "right of strength." This, and this alone, it is that gives any validity to appropriation. And this, evidently, is what they really mean who talk of the right given by appropriation.

This "right of conquest," this power of the strong, is the only basis of property in land to which the Duke ventures to refer. He does so in asking whether the exclusive right of ownership to the territory of California, which, according to him, I attribute to the existing people of California, does not rest upon conquest, and "if so, may it not be as rightfully acquired by any who are strong enough to seize it?" To this I reply in the affirmative. If exclusive ownership is conferred by conquest, then, not merely, as the Duke says, has it "been open to every conquering army and every occupying host in all ages and in all countries of the world to establish a similar ownership;" but it is now open, and whenever the masses of Scotland, who have the power, choose to take from the Duke the estates he now holds, he cannot, if this be the basis of his claim, consistently complain.

But I have never admitted that conquest or any other exertion of force can give right. Nor have I ever asserted, but on the contrary have expressly denied, that the present population of California, or any other country, have any exclusive right of ownership in the soil, or can in any way acquire such a right. I hold that the present, the past, or the future population of California, or of any other country, have not, have not had, and cannot have, any right save to the use of the soil, and that as to this their rights are equal. I hold with Thomas Jefferson, that "the earth belongs in usufruct to the living, and that the dead have no power or right over it." I hold that the land was not created for one generation to dispose of, but as a dwelling-place for all generations; that the men of the present are not bound by any grants of land the men of the past may have made, and cannot grant away the rights of the men of the future. I hold that if all the people of California, or any other country, were to unite in any disposition of the land which ignored the equal right of one of their number, they would be doing a wrong; and that even if they could grant away their own rights, they are powerless to impair the natural rights of their children. And it is for this reason that I hold that the titles to the ownership of land which the government of the United States is now granting are of no greater moral validity than the land titles of the British Isles, which rest historically upon the forcible spoliation of the masses.

How ownership of land was acquired in the past can have no bearing upon the question of how we should treat land now; yet the inquiry is interesting, as showing the nature of the institution. The Duke of Argyll has written a great deal about the rights of landowners, but has never, I think, told us anything of the historical derivation of these rights. He has spoken of his own estates, but has nowhere told us how they came to be his estates. This, I know, is a delicate question, and on that account I will not press it. But while a man ought not to be taunted with the sins of his ancestors, neither ought he to profit by them. And the general fact is, that the exclusive ownership of land has everywhere had its beginnings in force and fraud, in selfish greed and unscrupulous cunning. It originated, as all evil institutions originate, in the bad passions of men, not in their perceptions of what is right or their experience of what is wise. "Human laws," the Duke tells us, "are evolved out of human instincts, and in direct proportion as the accepted ideas on which they rest are really universal, in that same proportion have they a claim to be regarded as really natural, and as the legitimate expression of fundamental truths." If he would thus found on the widespread existence of exclusive property in land an argument for its righteousness, what, may I ask him, will he say to the much stronger argument that might thus be made for the righteousness of polygamy or chattel slavery? But it is a fact, of which I need hardly more than remind him, though less well informed people may be ignorant of it, that the treatment of land as individual property is comparatively recent, and by at least nine hundred and ninety-nine out of every thousand of those who have lived on this world, has never been dreamed of. It is only within the last two centuries that it has, by the abolition of feudal tenures, and the suppression of tribal customs, fully obtained among our own people. In fact, even among us it has hardly yet reached full development. For not only are we still spreading over land yet unreduced to individual ownership, but in the fragments of common rights which yet remain in Great Britain, as well as in laws and customs, are there survivals of the older system. The first and universal perception of mankind is that declared by the American Indian Chief, Black Hawk: "The Great Spirit has told me that land is not to be made property like other property. The earth is our mother!" And this primitive perception of the right of all men to the soil from which all must live, has never been obscured save by a long course of usurpation and oppression.

But it is needless for me to discuss such questions with the Duke. There is higher ground on which we may meet. He believes in an intelligent Creator; he sees in Nature contrivance and intent; he realizes that it is only by conforming his actions to universal law that man can master his conditions and fulfill his destiny.

Let me, then, ask the Duke to look around him in the richest country of the world, where art, science, and the power that comes from the utilization of physical laws have been carried to the highest point yet attained, and note how few of this population can avail themselves fully of the advantages of civilization. Among the masses the struggle for existence is so intense that the Duke himself declares it necessary by law to restrain parents from working their children to disease and death!

Let him consider the conditions of life involved in such facts as this — conditions, alas, obvious on every side, and then ask himself whether this is in accordance with the intent of Nature?

The Duke of Argyll has explained to me in his *Reign of Law* with what nice adaptations the feathers on a bird's wing are designed to give it the power of flight; he has told me that the claw on the wing of a bat is intended for it to climb by. Will he let me ask him to look in the same way at the human beings around him? Consider, O Duke! The little children growing up in city slums, toiling in mines, working in noisome rooms; the young girls chained to machinery all day or walking the streets by night; the women bending over forges in the Black Country or turned into beasts of burden in the Scottish Highlands; the men who all life long must spend life's energies in the effort to maintain life! Consider them as you have considered the bat and the bird. If the hook of the bat be intended to climb by and the wing of the bird be intended to fly by, with what intent have human creatures been given capabilities of body and mind which under conditions that exist in such countries as Great Britain only a few of them can use and enjoy?

They who see in Nature no evidences of conscious, planning intelligence may think that all this is as it must be; but who that recognizes in his works an infinitely wise Creator can for a moment hesitate to infer that the wide difference between obvious intent and actual accomplishment is due, not to the clash of natural laws, but to our ignoring them? Nor need we go far to confirm this inference. The moment we consider in the largest way what kind of an animal man is, we see in the most important of social adjustments a violation of Nature's intent sufficient to account for want and misery and aborted development.

Given a ship sent to sea with abundant provisions for all her company. What must happen if some of that company take possession of the provisions and deny to the rest any share?

Given a world so made and ordered that intelligent beings placed upon it may draw from its substance an abundant supply for all physical needs. Must there not be want and misery in such a world if some of those beings make its surface and substance their exclusive property and deny the right of the others to its use? Here, as on any other world we can conceive of, two and two make four, and when all is taken from anything nothing remains. What we see clearly would happen on any other world, does happen on this.

The Duke sees intent in Nature. So do I. That which conforms to this intent is natural, wise, and righteous. That which contravenes it is unnatural, foolish, and iniquitous. In this we agree. Let us then bring to this test the institution which I arraign and he defends.

Place, stripped of clothes, a landowner's baby among a dozen workhouse babies, and who that you call in can tell the one from the others? Is the human law which declares the one born to the possession of a hundred thousand acres of land, while the others have no right to a single square inch, conformable to the intent of Nature or not? Is it, judged by this appeal, natural or unnatural, wise or foolish, righteous or iniquitous? Put the bodies of a duke and a peasant on a dissecting-table, and bring, if you can, the surgeon who, by laying bare the brain or examining the viscera, can tell which is duke and which is peasant? Are not both land animals of the same kind, with like organs and like needs? Is it not evidently the intent of Nature that both shall live on land and use land in the same way and to the same degree? Is there not, therefore, a violation of the intent of Nature in human laws which give to one more land than he can possibly use, and deny any land to the other?

Let me ask the Duke to consider, from the point of view of an observer of Nature, a landless man — a being fitted in all his parts and powers for the use of land, compelled by all his needs to the use of land, and yet denied all right to land. Is he not as unnatural as a bird without air, a fish without water? And can anything more clearly violate the intent of Nature than the human laws which produce such anomalies?

I call upon the Duke to observe that what Nature teaches us is not merely that men were equally intended to live on land, and to use land, and therefore had originally equal rights to land, but that they are now equally intended to live on and use land, and, therefore, that present rights to land are equal. It is said that fish deprived of light will, in the course of generations, lose their eyes, and, within certain narrow limits, it is certain that Nature does conform some of her living creatures to conditions imposed by man. In such cases the intent of Nature may be said to have conformed to that of man, or rather to embrace that of man. But there is no such conforming in this case. The intent of Nature, that all human beings should use land, is as clearly seen in the children born today as it could have been seen in any past generation. How foolish, then, are those who say that although the right to land was originally equal, this equality of right has been lost by the action or sufferance of intermediate generations! How illogical those who declare that, while it would be just to assert this equality of right in the laws of a new country where people are now coming to live, it would be unjust to conform to it the laws of a country where people long have lived! Has Nature anywhere or in anything shown any disposition to conform to what we call vested interests? Does the child born in an old country differ from the child born in a new country?

Moral right and wrong, the Duke must agree with me, are not matters of precedent. The repetition of a wrong may dull the moral sense, but will not make it right. A robbery is no less a robbery the thousand-millionth time it is committed than it was the first time. This they forgot who declaring the slave-trade piracy still legalized the enslavement of those already enslaved. This they forget who admitting the equality of natural rights to the soil declare that it would be unjust now to assert them. For, as the keeping of a man in slavery is as much a violation of natural right as the seizure of his remote ancestor, so is the robbery involved in the present denial of natural rights to the soil as much a robbery as was the first act of fraud or force which violated those rights. Those who say it would be unjust for the people to resume their natural rights in the land without compensating present holders, confound right and wrong as flagrantly as did they who held it a crime in the slave to run away without first paying his owner his market value. They have never formed a clear idea of what property in land means. It means not merely a continuous exclusion of some people from the element which it is plainly the intent of Nature that all should enjoy, but it involves a continuous confiscation of labor and the results of labor. The Duke of Argyll has, we say, a large income drawn from land. But is this income really drawn from land? Were there no men on his land, what income could the Duke get from it, save such as his own hands produced? Precisely as if drawn from slaves, this income represents an appropriation of the earnings of labor. The effect of permitting the Duke to treat this land as his property, is to make so many other Scotsmen, in whole or in part, his serfs — to compel them to labor for him without pay, or to enable him to take from them their earnings without return. Surely, if the Duke will look at the matter in this way, he must see that the iniquity is not in abolishing an institution which permits one man to plunder others, but in continuing it. He must see that any claim of landowners to compensation is not a claim to payment for what they have previously taken, but to payment for what they might yet take, precisely as would be the claim of the slaveholder — the true character of which appears in the fact that he would demand more compensation for a strong slave, out of whom he might yet get much work, than for a decrepit one, out of whom he had already forced nearly all the labor he could yield.

In assuming that denial of the justice of property in land is the prelude to an attack upon all rights of property, the Duke ignores the essential distinction between land and things rightfully property. The things which constitute wealth, or capital (which is wealth used in production), and to which the right of property justly attaches, are produced by human exertion. Their substance is matter, which existed before man, and which man can neither create nor destroy; but their essence — that which gives them the character of wealth — is labor impressed upon or modifying the conditions of matter. Their existence is due to the physical exertion of man and, like his physical frame, they tend constantly to return again to Nature's reservoirs of matter and force. Land, on the contrary, is that part of the external universe on which and from which alone man can live; that reservoir of matter and force on which he must draw for all his needs. Its existence is not due to man, but is referable only to that Power from which man himself proceeds. It continues while he comes and goes, and will continue, so far as we can see, after he and his works shall disappear. Both species of things have value, but the value of the one species depends upon the amount of labor required for their production; the value of the other upon the power which its reduction to ownership gives of commanding labor or the results of labor without paying any equivalent. The recognition of the right of property in wealth, or things produced by labor, is thus but a recognition of the right of each human being to himself and to the results of his own exertions; but the recognition of a similar right of property in land is necessarily the impairment and denial of this true right of property.

Turn from principles to facts. Whether as to national strength or national character, whether as to the number of people or as to their physical and moral health, whether as to the production of wealth or as to its equitable distribution, the fruits of the primary injustice involved in making the land, on which and from which a whole people must live, the property of but a portion of their number, are everywhere evil and nothing but evil.

If this seems to any too strong a statement, it is only because they associate individual ownership of land with permanence of possession and security of improvements. These are necessary to the proper use of land, but so far from being dependent upon individual ownership of land, they can be secured without it in greater degree than with it. This will be evident upon reflection. That the existing

system does not secure permanence of possession and security of improvements in anything like the degree necessary
to the best use of land, is obvious everywhere, but especially
obvious in Great Britain, where the owners of land and the
users of land are for the most part distinct persons. In many
cases the users of land have no security from year to year, a
logical development of individual ownership in land so flagrantly unjust to the user and so manifestly detrimental to
the community, that in Ireland, where this system most
largely prevailed, it has been deemed necessary for the State
to interfere in the most arbitrary manner. In other cases,
where land is let for years, the user is often hampered with
restrictions that prevent improvement and interfere with
use, and at the expiration of the lease he is not merely deprived of his improvements, but is frequently subjected to a
blackmail calculated upon the inconvenience and loss which
removal would cost him. Wherever I have been in Great
Britain, from Land's End to John O'Groat's, and from
Liverpool to Hull, I have heard of improvements prevented
and production curtailed from this cause — in instances
which run from the prevention of the building of an out-
house, the painting of a dwelling, the enlargement of a
chapel, the widening of a street, or the excavation of a dock,
to the shutting up of a mine, the demolition of a village,
the tearing up of a railway track, or the turning of land
from the support of men to the breeding of wild beasts. I
could cite case after case, each typical of a class, but it is
unnecessary. How largely use and improvement are restricted
and prevented by private ownership of land may be appreciated only by a few, but specific cases are known to all.
How insecurity of improvement and possession prevents
the proper maintenance of dwellings in the cities, how it
hampers the farmer, how it fills the shopkeeper with dread
as the expiration of his lease draws nigh, have been, to some
extent at least, brought out by recent discussions, and in all

these directions propositions are being made for State interference more or less violent, arbitrary, and destructive of the sound principle that men should be left free to manage their own property as they deem best.

Does not all this interference and demand for interference show that private property in land does not produce good results, that it does not give the necessary permanence of possession and security of improvements? Is not an institution that needs such tinkering fundamentally wrong? That property in land must have different treatment from other property, all, or nearly all, are now agreed. Does not this prove that land ought not to be made individual property at all; that to treat it as individual property is to weaken and endanger the true rights of property?

The Duke of Argyll asserts that in the United States we have made land private property because we have found it necessary to secure settlement and improvement. Nothing could be further from the truth. The Duke might as well urge that our protective tariff is a proof of the necessity of "protection." We have made land private property because we are but transplanted Europeans, wedded to custom, and have followed it in this matter more readily, because in a new country the evils that at length spring from private property in land are less obvious, while a much larger portion of the people seemingly profit by it — those on the ground gaining at the expense of those who come afterward. But so far from this treatment of land in the United States having promoted settlement and reclamation, the very reverse is true. What it has promoted is the scattering of population in the country and its undue concentration in cities, to the disadvantage of production and the lessening of comfort. It has forced into the wilderness families for whom there was plenty of room in well-settled neighborhoods, and raised tenement-houses amid vacant lots, led to waste of labor and capital in roads and railways not really needed, locked up natural opportunities that otherwise would have been improved, made tramps and idlers of men who, had they found it in time, would gladly have been at work, and given to our agriculture a character that is rapidly and steadily decreasing the productiveness of the soil.

As to political corruption in the United States, of which I have spoken in *Social Problems,* and to which the Duke refers, it springs, as I have shown in that book, not from excess but from deficiency of democracy, and mainly from our failure to recognize the equality of natural rights as well as of political rights. In comparing the two countries, it may be well to note that the exposure of abuses is quicker and sharper in the United States than in England, and that to some extent abuses which in the one country appear in naked deformity, are in the other hidden by the ivy of custom and respectability. But be this as it may, the reforms I propose, instead of adding to corruptive forces, would destroy prolific sources of corruption. Our "protective" tariff, our excise taxes, and demoralizing system of local taxation, would, in their direct and indirect effects, corrupt any government, even if not aided by the corrupting effects of the grabbing for public lands. But the first step I propose would sweep away these corruptive influences, and it is to governments thus reformed, in a state of society in which the reckless struggle for wealth would be lessened by the elimination of the fear of want, that I would give, not the management of land or the direction of enterprise, but the administration of the funds arising from the appropriation of economic rent.

The Duke styles me a Pessimist. But, however pessimistic I may be as to present social tendencies, I have a firm faith in human nature. I am convinced that the attainment of pure government is merely a matter of conforming social institutions to moral law. If we do this, there is, to my mind, no reason why in the proper sphere of public administration we should not find men as honest and as faithful as when acting in private capacities.

But to return to the "reduction to iniquity." Test the institution of private property in land by its fruits in any country where it exists. Take Scotland. What, there, are its results? That wild beasts have supplanted human beings; that glens which once sent forth their thousand fighting men are now tenanted by a couple of gamekeepers; that there is destitution and degradation that would shame savages; that little children are stunted and starved for want of proper nourishment; that women are compelled to do the work of animals; that young girls who ought to be fitting themselves for wifehood and motherhood are held to the monotonous toil of factories, while others, whose fate is sadder still, prowl the streets; that while a few Scotsmen have castles and palaces, more than a third of Scottish families live in one room each, and more than two-thirds in not more than two rooms each; that thousands of acres are kept as playgrounds for strangers, while the masses have not enough of their native soil to grow a flower, are shut out even from moor and mountain; dare not take a trout from a loch or a salmon from the sea!

If the Duke thinks all classes have gained by the advance in civilization, let him go into the huts of the Highlands. There he may find countrymen of his, men and women the equals in natural ability and in moral character of any peer or peeress in the land, to whom the advance of our wondrous age has brought no gain. He may find them tilling the ground with the crooked spade, cutting grain with the sickle, threshing it with the flail, winnowing it by tossing it in the air, grinding it as their forefathers did a thousand years ago. He may see spinning-wheel and distaff yet in use, and the smoke from the fire in the center of the hut ascending as it can through the thatch, that the precious heat, which costs so much labor to procure, may be economized to the utmost. These human beings are in natural parts and powers just such human beings as may be met at a royal levee, at a gathering of scientists, or inventors, or captains of industry. That they so live and so work, is not because of their stupidity, but because of their poverty — the direct and indisputable result of the denial of their natural rights. They have not merely been prevented from participating in the "general advance," but are positively worse off than were their ancestors before commerce had penetrated the Highlands or the modern era of labor-saving inventions had begun. They have been driven from the good land to the poor land. While their rents have been increased, their holdings have been diminished, and their pasturage cut off. Where they once had beasts, they cannot now eat a chicken or keep a donkey, and their women must do work once done by animals. With the same thoughtful attention he has given to "the way of an eagle in the air," let the Duke consider a sight he must have seen many times — a Scottish woman toiling uphill with a load of manure on her back. Then let him apply the "reduction to iniquity."

Let the Duke not be content with feasting his eyes upon those comfortable houses of the large farmers which so excite his admiration. Let him visit the bothies in which farm-servants are herded together like cattle, and learn, as he may learn, that the lot of the Scottish farm servant — a lot from which no industry or thrift can release him — is to die in the workhouse or in the receipt of a parish dole if he be so unfortunate as to outlive his ability to work. Or let him visit those poor broken-down creatures who, enduring everything rather than accept the humiliation of the workhouse, are eking out their last days upon a few shillings from the parish, supplemented by the charity of people nearly as poor as themselves. Let him consider them, and if he has imagination enough, put himself in their place. Then let him try the "reduction to iniquity."

Let the Duke go to Glasgow, the metropolis of Scotland, where in underground cellars and miserable rooms, he will find crowded together families who (some of them, lest they might offend the deer) have been driven from their native soil into the great city to compete with each other for employment at any price, to have their children debauched by daily contact with all that is vile. Let him some Saturday evening leave the districts where the richer classes live, wander for a while through the streets tenanted by working-people, and note the stunted forms, the pinched features. Vice, drunkenness, the recklessness that comes when hope goes, he will see too. How should not such conditions produce such effects? But he will also see, if he chooses to look, hard, brave, stubborn struggling — the workman, who, do his best, cannot find steady employment; the breadwinner stricken with illness; the widow straining to keep her children from the workhouse. Let the Duke observe and reflect upon these things, and then apply the "reduction to iniquity."

Or, let him go to Edinburgh, the "modern Athens," of which Scotsmen speak with pride, and in buildings from whose roofs a bowman might strike the spires of twenty churches, he will find human beings living as he would not keep his meanest dog. Let him toil up the stairs of one of those monstrous buildings, let him enter one of those "dark houses," let him close the door, and in the blackness think what life must be in such a place. Then let him try the "reduction to iniquity." And if he go to that good charity (but, alas, how futile is Charity without Justice!) where little children are kept while their mothers are at work, and children are fed who would otherwise go hungry, he may see infants whose limbs are shrunken from want of nourishment. Perhaps they may tell him, as they told me, of that little girl, barefooted, ragged, and hungry, who, when they gave her bread, raised her eyes and clasped her hands, and thanked our Father in Heaven for his bounty to her. They who told me that never dreamed, I think, of its terrible meaning. But I ask the Duke of Argyll, did that little child, thankful for that poor dole, get what our Father provided for her? Is He so niggard? If not, what is it, who is it, that stands between such children and our Father's bounty? If it be an institution, is it not our duty to God and to our neighbor to rest not till we destroy it? If it be a man, were it not better for him that a millstone were hanged about his neck and he were cast into the depths of the sea?

There can be no question of overpopulation — no pretense that Nature has brought more men into being than she has made provision for. Scotland surely is not overpopulated. Much land is unused; much land is devoted to lower uses, such as the breeding of game and the raising of cattle, that might be devoted to higher uses; there are mineral resources untouched; the wealth drawn from the sea is but a small part of what might be drawn. But it is idle to argue this point. Neither in Scotland, nor in any other country, can any excess of population over the power of Nature to provide for them be shown. The poverty so painful in Scotland is manifestly no more due to overpopulation than the crowding of two-thirds of the families into houses of one or two rooms is due to want of space to build houses upon. And just as the crowding of people into insufficient lodgings is directly due to institutions which permit men to hold vacant land needed for buildings until they can force a monopoly price from those wishing to build, so is the poverty of the masses due to the fact that they are in like manner shut out from the opportunities Nature has provided for the employment of their labor in the satisfaction of their wants.

Take the Island of Skye as illustrating on a small scale the cause of poverty throughout Scotland. The people of Skye are poor — very poor. Is it because there are too many of them? An explanation lies nearer — an explanation which would account for poverty no matter how small the population. If there were but one man in Skye, and if all that he produced, save enough to give him a bare living, were periodically taken from him and carried off, he would necessarily be poor. That is the condition of the people of Skye. With a population of some seventeen thousand there are, if my memory serves me, twenty-four landowners. The few proprietors who live upon the island, though they do nothing to produce wealth, have fine houses, and live luxuriously, while the greater portion of the rents are carried off to be spent abroad. It is not merely that there is thus a constant drain upon the wealth produced; but that the power of producing wealth is enormously lessened. As the people are deprived of the power to accumulate capital, production is carried on in the most primitive style, and at the greatest disadvantage.

If there are really too many people in Scotland, why not have the landlords emigrate? They are not merely best fitted to emigrate, but would give the greatest relief. They consume most, waste most, carry off most, while they produce least. As landlords, in fact, they produce nothing. They merely consume and destroy. Economically considered, they have the same effect upon production as bands of robbers or pirate fleets. To national wealth they are as weevils in the grain, as rats in the storehouse, as ferrets in the poultry-yard.

The Duke of Argyll complains of what he calls my assumption that owners of land are not producers, and that rent does not represent, or represents in a very minor degree, the interest of capital. The Duke will justify his complaint if he will show how the owning of land can produce anything. Failing in this, he must admit that though the same person may be a laborer, capitalist, and landowner, the owner of land, as an owner of land, is not a producer.

And surely he knows that the term "rent" as used in political economy, and as I use it in the books he criticizes, never represents the interest on capital, but refers alone to the sum paid for the use of the inherent capabilities of the soil.

As illustrating the usefulness of landlords, the Duke says:

> My own experience now extends over a period of the best part of forty years. During that time I have built more than fifty homesteads complete for man and beast; I have drained and reclaimed many hundreds, and inclosed some thousands, of acres. In this sense I have "added house to house and field to field," not – as pulpit orators have assumed in similar cases – that I might "dwell alone in the land," but that the cultivating class might live more comfortably, and with better appliances for increasing the produce of the soil.

And again he says that during the last four years he has spent on one property £40,000 in the improvement of the soil.

I fear that in Scotland the Duke of Argyll has been "hiding his light under a bushel," for his version of the way in which he has "added house to house and field to field" differs much from that which common Scotsmen give. But this is a matter into which I do not wish to enter. What I would like to ask the Duke is, how he built the fifty homesteads and reclaimed the thousands of acres? Not with his own hands, of course; but with his money. Where, then, did he get that money? Was it not taken as rent from the cultivators of the soil? And might not they, had it been left to them, have devoted it to the building of homesteads and the improvement of the soil as well as he? Suppose the Duke spends on such improvements all he draws in rent, minus what it costs him to live, is not the cost of his living so much waste so far as the improvement of the land is concerned? Would there not be a considerably greater fund to devote to this purpose if the Duke got no rent, and had to work for a living?

But all Scottish landholders are not even such improvers as the Duke. There are landlords who spend their incomes in racing, in profligacy, in doing things which when not injurious are quite as useless to man or beast as the works of that English Duke, recently dead, who spent millions in burrowing underground like a mole. What the Scottish landlords call their "improvements" have, for the most part, consisted in building castles, laying out pleasure-grounds, raising rents, and evicting their kinsmen. But the encouragement given to agriculture, by even such improving owners as the Duke of Argyll, is very much like the encouragement given to traffic by the Duke of Bedford, who keeps two or three old men and women to open and shut gates he has erected across the streets of London. That much the greater part of the incomes drawn by landlords is as completely lost for all productive purposes as though it were thrown into the sea, there can be no doubt. But that even the small part which is devoted to reproductive improvement is largely wasted, the Duke of Argyll himself clearly shows in stating, what I have learned from other sources, that the large outlays of the great landholders yield little interest, and in many cases no interest at all. Clearly, the stock of wealth would have been much greater had this capital been left in the hands of the cultivators, who, in most cases, suffer from lack of capital, and in many cases have to pay the most usurious interest.

In fact, the plea of the landlords that they, as landlords, assist in production, is very much like the plea of the slaveholders that they gave a living to the slaves. And I am convinced that if the Duke of Argyll will consider the matter as a philosopher rather than as a landlord, he will see the gross inconsistency between the views he expresses as to negro slavery and the position he assumes as to property in land.

In principle the two systems of appropriating the labor of other men are essentially the same. Since it is from land

and on land that man must live, if he is to live at all, a human being is as completely enslaved when the land on which he must live is made the property of another as when his own flesh and blood are made the property of that other. And at least, after a certain point in social development is reached, the slavery that results from depriving men of all legal right to land is, for the very reason that the relation between master and slave is not so direct and obvious, more cruel and more demoralizing than that which makes property of their bodies.

And turning to facts, the Duke must see, if he will look, that the effects of the two systems are substantially the same. He is, for instance, an hereditary legislator, with power in making laws which other Scotsmen, who have little or no voice in making laws, must obey under penalty of being fined, imprisoned, or hanged. He has this power, which is essentially that of the master to compel the slave, not because any one thinks that Nature gives wisdom and patriotism to eldest sons more than to younger sons, or to some families more than to other families, but because as the legal owner of a considerable part of Scotland, he is deemed to have greater rights in making laws than other Scotsmen, who can live in their native land only by paying some of the legal owners of Scotland for the privilege.

That power over men arises from ownership of land as well as from ownership of their bodies the Duke may see in varied manifestations if he will look. The power of the Scottish landlords over even the large farmers, and, in the smaller towns, over even the well-to-do shopkeepers the tyranny they feared. If this be the condition of the well-to-do, the condition of the crofters can be imagined. One of them said to me, "We have feared the landlord more than we have feared God Almighty; we have feared the factor more than the landlord, and the ground officer more than the factor." But there is a class lower still even than the crofters — the cotters —

who, on forty-eight hours' notice, can be turned out of what by courtesy are called their homes, and who are at the mercy of the large farmers or tacksmen, who in turn fear the landlord or agent. Take this class, or the class of farm-servants who are kept in bothies. Can the Duke tell me of any American slaves who were lodged and fed as these white slaves are lodged and fed, or who had less of all the comforts and enjoyments of life?

The slaveholders of the South never, in any case that I have heard of, interfered with the religion of the slaves, and the Duke of Argyll will doubtless admit that this is a power which one man ought not to have over another. Yet he must know that at the disruption of the Scottish Church, some forty years ago, Scottish proprietors not merely evicted tenants who joined the Free Church (and in many cases eviction meant ruin and death), but absolutely refused sites for churches and even permission for the people to stand upon the land and worship God according to the dictates of their conscience. Hugh Miller has told, in *The Cruise of the Betsy*, how one minister, denied permission to live on the land, had to make his home on the sea in a small boat. Large congregations had to worship on mountain roadsides without shelter from storm and sleet, and even on the seashore, where the tide flowed around their knees as they took the communion. But perhaps the slavishness which has been engendered in Scotland by land monopoly is not better illustrated than in the case where, after keeping them off his land for more than six years, a Scottish duke allowed a congregation the use of a gravel-pit for purposes of worship, whereupon they sent him a resolution of thanks!

In the large cities tyranny of this kind cannot, of course, be exercised, but it is in the large cities that the slavery resulting from the reduction of land to private ownership assumes the darkest shades. Negro slavery had its horrors, but they were not so many or so black as those constantly occurring in such cities. Their own selfish interests, if not their human sympathies or the restraint of public opinion, would have prevented the owners of negro slaves from lodging and feeding and working them as many of the so-called free people in the centers of civilization are lodged and fed and worked.

With all allowance for the prepossessions of a great landlord, it is difficult to understand how the Duke of Argyll can regard as an animating scene the history of agricultural improvement in Scotland since 1745. From the date mentioned, and the fact that he is a Highlander, I presume that he refers mainly to the Highlands. But as a parallel to calling this history "animating," I can think of nothing so close as the observation of an economist of the Duke's school, who, in an account of a visit to Scotland, a generation or so ago, spoke of the pleasure with which, in a workhouse, he had seen "both sexes and all ages, even to infants of two and three years, earning their living by picking oakum," or as the expression of pride with which a Polish noble, in the last century, pointed out to an English visitor some miserable-looking creatures who, he said, were samples of the serfs, any one of whom he could kick as he pleased!

"Thousands and thousands of acres," says the Duke, "have been reclaimed from barren wastes; ignorance has given place to science, and barbarous customs of immemorial strength have been replaced by habits of intelligence and business." This is one side of the picture, but unfortunately there is another side — chieftains taking advantage of the reverential affection of their clansmen, and their ignorance of a foreign language and a foreign law, to reduce those clansmen to a condition of virtual slavery; to rob them of the land which by immemorial custom they had enjoyed; to substitute for the mutual tie that bound chief to vassal and vassal to chief, the cold maxims of money-making greed; to drive them from their homes that sheep might have place, or to hand them over to the tender mercies of a great farmer.

"There has been grown," says the Duke, "more corn, more potatoes, more turnips; there has been produced more milk, more butter, more cheese, more beef, more mutton, more pork, more fowls and eggs." But what becomes of them? The Duke must know that the ordinary food of the common people is meal and potatoes; that of these many do not get enough; that many would starve outright if they were not kept alive by charity. Even the wild meat which their fathers took freely, the common people cannot now touch. A Highland poor-law physician, whose district is on the estate of a prominent member of the Liberal party, was telling me recently of the miserable poverty of the people among whom his official duties lie, and how insufficient and monotonous food was beginning to produce among them diseases like the pellagra in Italy. When I asked him if they could not, despite the gamekeepers, take for themselves enough fish and game to vary their diet, "They never think of it," he replied; "they are too cowed. Why, the moment any one of them was even suspected of cultivating a taste for trout or grouse, he would be driven off the estate like a mad dog."

Besides the essays and journals referred to by the Duke of Argyll, there is another publication, which anyone wishing to be informed on the subject may read with advantage, though not with pleasure. It is entitled *Highland Clearances,* and is published in Inverness by A. McKenzie. There is nothing in savage life more cold-bloodedly atrocious than the warfare here recorded as carried on against the clansmen by those who were their hereditary protectors. The burning of houses; the ejection of old and young; the tearing down of shelters put up to shield women with child and tender infants from the bitter night blast; the threats of similar treatment against all who should give them hospitality; the forcing of poor helpless creatures into emigrant

ships which carried them to strange lands and among a
people of whose tongue they were utterly ignorant, to die
in many cases like rotten sheep or to be reduced to utter
degradation. An animating scene truly! Great districts once
peopled with a race, rude it may be and slavish to their
chiefs, but still a race of manly virtues, brave, kind, and
hospitable – now tenanted only by sheep or cattle, by grouse
or deer! No one can read of the atrocities perpetrated upon
the Scottish people, during what is called "the improvement
of the Highlands," without feeling something like utter contempt for men who, lions abroad, were such sheep at home
that they suffered these outrages without striking a blow,
even if an ineffectual one. But the explanation of this re-
veals a lower depth in the "reduction to iniquity." The reason of the tame submission of the Highland people to
outrages which should have nerved the most timid is to be
found in the prostitution of their religion. The Highland
people are a deeply religious people, and during these evictions their preachers preached to them that their trials were
the visitations of the Almighty and must be submitted to
under the penalty of eternal damnation!

I met accidentally in Scotland, recently, a lady of the
small landlord class, and the conversation turned upon the
poverty of the Highland people. "Yes, they are poor," she
said, "but they deserve to be poor; they are so dirty. I have
no sympathy with women who won't keep their houses neat
and their children tidy."

I suggested that neatness could hardly be expected from
women who every day had to trudge for miles with creels of
peat and seaweed on their backs.

"Yes," she said, "they do have to work hard. But that is
not so sad as the hard lives of the horses. Did you ever
think of the horses? They have to work all their lives – till
they can't work any longer. It makes me sad to think of it.
There ought to be big farms where horses should be turned

out after they had worked some years, so that they might have time to enjoy themselves before they died."

"But the people?" I interposed. "They, too, have to work till they can't work longer."

"Oh, yes!" she replied, "but the people have souls, and even if they do have a hard time of it here, they will, if they are good, go to heaven when they die, and be happy hereafter. But the poor beasts have no souls, and if they don't enjoy themselves here, they have no chance of enjoying themselves at all. It is too bad!"

The woman was in sober earnest. And I question if she did not fairly represent much that has been taught in Scotland as Christianity. But at last, thank God! the day is breaking, and the blasphemy that has been preached as religion will not be heard much longer. The manifesto of the Scottish Land Restoration League, calling upon the Scottish people to bind themselves together in solemn league and covenant for the extirpation of the sin and shame of landlordism is a lark's note in the dawn.

As in Scotland so elsewhere. I have spoken particularly of Scotland only because the Duke does so. But everywhere that our civilization extends the same primary injustice is bearing the same evil fruits. And everywhere the same spirit is rising, the same truth is beginning to force its way.

Encyclical Letter of Pope Leo XIII
On the Condition of Labor

To our Venerable Brethren, all Patriarchs, Primates, Archbishops, and Bishops of the Catholic World, in grace and communion with the Apostolic See, Pope Leo XIII.

Venerable Brethren, Health and Apostolic Benediction.

1. It is not surprising that the spirit of revolutionary change, which has so long been predominant in the nations of the world, should have passed beyond politics and made its influence felt in the cognate field of practical economy. The elements of a conflict are unmistakable: the growth of industry, and the surprising discoveries of science; the changed relations of masters and workmen; the enormous fortunes of individuals, and the poverty of the masses; the increased self-reliance and the closer mutual combination of the working population; and, finally, a general moral deterioration. The momentous seriousness of the present state of things just now fills every mind with painful apprehension; wise men discuss it; practical men propose schemes; popular meetings, legislatures, and sovereign princes, all are occupied with it — and there is nothing which has a deeper hold on public attention.

2. Therefore, Venerable Brethren, as on former occasions, when it seemed opportune to refute false teaching, We have addressed you in the interest of the Church and

of the commonweal, and have issued Letters on Political
Power, on Human Liberty, on the Christian Constitution
of the State, and on similar subjects, so now We have
thought it useful to speak on the *condition of labor*. It is a
matter on which We have touched once or twice already.
But in this Letter the responsibility of the Apostolic office
urges Us to treat the question expressly and at length, in
order that there may be no mistake as to the principles
which truth and justice dictate for its settlement. The discussion is not easy, nor is it free from danger. It is not easy
to define the relative rights and the mutual duties of the
wealthy and of the poor, of capital and of labor. And the
danger lies in this, that crafty agitators constantly make
use of these disputes to pervert men's judgments and to
stir up the people to sedition.

3. But all agree, and there can be no question whatever,
that some remedy must be found, and quickly found, for
the misery and wretchedness which press so heavily at this
moment on the large majority of the very poor. The ancient workmen's Guilds were destroyed in the last century,
and no other organization took their place. Public institutions and the laws have repudiated the ancient religion.
Hence by degrees it has come to pass that working men
have been given over, isolated and defenseless, to the cal-
lousness of employers, and the greed of unrestrained competition. The evil has been increased by rapacious usury,
which, although more than once condemned by the Church,
is nevertheless, under a different form but with the same
guilt, still practiced by avaricious and grasping men. And to
this must be added the custom of working by contract, and
the concentration of so many branches of trade in the hands
of a few individuals, so that a small number of very rich
men have been able to lay upon the masses of the poor a
yoke little better than slavery itself.

4. To remedy these evils the Socialists, working on the

poor man's envy of the rich, endeavor to destroy private property, and maintain that individual possessions should become the common property of all, to be administered by the State or by municipal bodies. They hold that, by thus transferring property from private persons to the community, the present evil state of things will be set to rights, because each citizen will then have his equal share of whatever there is to enjoy. But their proposals are so clearly futile for all practical purposes, that if they were carried out the working man himself would be among the first to suffer. Moreover they are emphatically unjust, because they would rob the lawful possessor, bring the State into a sphere that is not its own, and cause complete confusion in the community.

5. It is surely undeniable that, when a man engages in remunerative labor, the very reason and motive of his work is to obtain property, and to hold it as his own private possession. If one man hires out to another his strength or his industry, he does this for the purpose of receiving in return what is necessary for food and living; he thereby expressly proposes to acquire a full and real right, not only to the remuneration, but also to the disposal of that remuneration as he pleases. Thus, if he lives sparingly, saves money, and invests his savings, for greater security, in land, the land in such a case is only his wages in another form; and consequently, a workingman's little estate thus purchased should be as completely at his own disposal as the wages he receives for his labor. But it is precisely in this power of disposal that ownership consists, whether the property be land or movable goods. The Socialists, therefore, in endeavoring to transfer the possessions of individuals to the community, strike at the interests of every wage-earner, for they deprive him of the liberty of disposing of his wages, and thus of all hope and possibility of increasing his stock and of bettering his condition in life.

6. What is of still greater importance, however, is that the remedy they propose is manifestly against justice. For every man has by nature the right to possess property as his own. This is one of the chief points of distinction between man and the animal creation. For the brute has no power of self-direction, but is governed by two chief instincts, which keep his powers alert, move him to use his strength, and determine him to action without the power of choice. These instincts are self preservation and the propagation of the species. Both can attain their purpose by means of things which are close at hand; beyond their surroundings the brute creation cannot go, for they are moved to action by sensibility alone, and by the things which sense perceives. But with man it is different indeed. He possesses, on the one hand, the full perfection of animal nature, and therefore he enjoys, at least as much as the rest of the animal race, the fruition of the things of the body. But animality, however perfect, is far from being the whole of humanity, and is indeed humanity's humble handmaid, made to serve and obey. It is the mind, or the reason, which is the chief thing in us who are human beings; it is this which makes a human being human, and distinguishes him essentially and completely from the brute. And on this account — viz., that man alone among animals possesses reason — it must be within his right to have things not merely for temporary and momentary use, as other living beings have them, but in stable and permanent possession; he must have not only things which perish in the using, but also those which, though used, remain for use in the future.

7. This becomes still more clearly evident if we consider man's nature a little more deeply. For man, comprehending by the power of his reason things innumerable, and joining the future with the present — being, moreover, the master of his own acts — governs himself by the foresight of his counsel, under the eternal law and the power of God,

Whose providence governs all things; wherefore it is in his power to exercise his choice not only on things which regard his present welfare, but also on those which will be for his advantage in time to come. Hence man not only can possess the fruits of the earth, but also the earth itself; for of the products of the earth he can make provision for the future. Man's needs do not die out, but recur; satisfied today, they demand new supplies tomorrow. Nature, therefore, owes to man a storehouse that shall never fail, the daily supply of his daily wants. And this he finds only in the inexhaustible fertility of the earth.

8. Nor must we, at this stage, have recourse to the State. Man is older than the State; and he holds the right of providing for the life of his body prior to the formation of any State. And to say that God has given the earth to the use and enjoyment of the universal human race is not to deny that there can be private property. For God has granted the earth to mankind in general; not in the sense that all without distinction can deal with it as they please, but rather that no part of it has been assigned to any one in particular, and that the limits of private possession have been left to be fixed by man's own industry and the laws of individual peoples. Moreover the earth, though divided among private owners, ceases not thereby to minister to the needs of all; for there is no one who does not live on what the land brings forth. Those who do not possess the soil, contribute their labor; so that it may be truly said that all human subsistence is derived either from labor on one's own land, or from some laborious industry which is paid for either in the produce of the land itself or in that which is exchanged for what the land brings forth.

9. Here, again, we have another proof that private ownership is according to nature's law. For that which is required for the preservation of life, and for life's well-being, is produced in great abundance by the earth, but not until

man has brought it into cultivation and lavished upon it
his care and skill. Now, when man thus spends the industry
of his mind and the strength of his body in procuring the
fruits of nature, by that act he makes his own that portion
of nature's field which he cultivates — that portion on which
he leaves, as it were, the impress of his own personality; and
it cannot but be just that he should possess that portion as
his own, and should have a right to keep it without moles-
tation.

10. These arguments are so strong and convincing that
it seems surprising that certain obsolete opinions should
now be revived in opposition to what is here laid down. We
are told that it is right for private persons to have the use of
the soil and the fruits of their land, but that it is unjust for
any one to possess as owner either the land on which he
has built or the estate which he has cultivated. But those
who assert this do not perceive that they are robbing man
of what his own labor has produced. For the soil which is
tilled and cultivated with toil and skill utterly changes its
condition; it was wild before, it is now fruitful; it was barren, and now it brings forth in abundance. That which has
thus altered and improved it becomes so truly part of itself
as to be in great measure indistinguishable and inseparable
from it. Is it just that the fruit of a man's sweat and labor
should be enjoyed by another? As effects follow their cause,
so it is just and right that the results of labor should belong
to him who has labored.

11. With reason, therefore, the common opinion of
mankind, little affected by the few dissentients who have
maintained the opposite view, has found in the study of
nature, and in the law of Nature herself, the foundation of
the division of property, and has consecrated by the practice of all ages the principle of private ownership, as being
preeminently in conformity with human nature, and as con-
ducing in the most unmistakable manner to the peace and

tranquillity of human life. The same principle is confirmed and enforced by the civil laws — laws which, as long as they are just, derive their binding force from the law of nature. The authority of the Divine Law adds its sanction, forbidding us in the gravest terms even to covet that which is another's: *Thou shalt not covet thy neighbor's wife; nor his house, nor his field, nor his man-servant, nor his maid-servant, nor his ox, nor his ass, nor anything which is his.*[1]

12. The rights here spoken of, belonging to each individual man, are seen in a much stronger light if they are considered in relation to man's social and domestic obligations.

13. In choosing a state of life, it is indisputable that all are at full liberty either to follow the counsel of Jesus Christ as to the virginity, or to enter into the bonds of marriage. No human law can abolish the natural and primitive right of marriage, or in any way limit the chief and principal purpose of marriage, ordained by God's authority from the beginning: *Increase and multiply.*[2] Thus we have the Family; the "society" of a man's own household; a society limited indeed in numbers, but a true "society," anterior to every kind of State or nation, with rights and duties of its own, totally independent of the commonwealth.

14. That right of property, therefore, which has been proved to belong naturally to individual persons, must also belong to a man in his capacity of head of a family; nay, such a person must possess this right so much the more clearly in proportion as his position multiplies his duties. For it is a most sacred law of nature that a father must provide food and all necessaries for those whom he has begotten; and, similarly, nature dictates that a man's children, who carry on, as it were, and continue his own personality,

---

1. Deuteronomy v. 21
2. Genesis i. 28

should be provided by him with all that is needful to enable them honorably to keep themselves from want and misery in the uncertainties of this mortal life. Now, in no other way can a father effect this except by the ownership of profitable property, which he can transmit to his children by inheritance. A family, no less than a State, is, as We have said, a true society, governed by a power within itself, that is to say by the father. Wherefore, provided the limits be not transgressed which are prescribed by the very purposes for which it exists, the Family has at least equal rights with the State in the choice and pursuit of those things which are needful to its preservation and its just liberty.

15. We say, at least equal rights; for since the domestic household is anterior both in idea and in fact to the gathering of men into a commonwealth, the former must necessarily have rights and duties which are prior to those of the latter, and which rest more immediately on nature. If the citizens of a State — that is to say, the Families — on entering into association and fellowship, experienced at the hands of the State hindrance instead of help, and found their rights attacked instead of being protected, such association were rather to be repudiated than sought after.

16. The idea, then, that the civil government should, at its own discretion, penetrate and pervade the family and the household, is a great and pernicious mistake. True, if a family finds itself in great difficulty, utterly friendless, and without prospect of help, it is right that extreme necessity be met by public aid; for each family is a part of the commonwealth. In like manner, if within the walls of the household there occur grave disturbance of mutual rights, the public power must interfere to force each party to give the other what is due; for this is not to rob citizens of their rights, but justly and properly to safeguard and strengthen them. But the rulers of the State must go no further: nature bids them stop here. Paternal authority can neither be abol-

ished by the State, nor absorbed; for it has the same source as human life itself. "The child belongs to the father," and is, as it were, the continuation of the father's personality; and, to speak with strictness, the child takes its place in civil society not in its own right, but in its quality as a member of the family in which it is begotten. And it is for the very reason that "the child belongs to the father" that, as St. Thomas of Aquin says, "before it attains the use of free will, it is in the power and care of its parents."[1] The Socialists, therefore, in setting aside the parent and introducing the providence of the State, act against natural justice, and threaten the very existence of family life.

17. And such interference is not only unjust, but it is quite certain to harass and disturb all classes of citizens and to subject them to odious and intolerable slavery. It would open the door to envy, to evil speaking, and to quarreling; the sources of wealth would themselves run dry, for no one would have any interest in exerting his talents or his industry; and that ideal equality of which so much is said would in reality be the leveling down of all to the same condition of misery and dishonor.

18. Thus it is clear that the main tenet of Socialism, the community of goods, must be utterly rejected; for it would injure those whom it is intended to benefit, it would be contrary to the natural rights of mankind, and it would introduce confusion and disorder into the commonwealth. Our first and most fundamental principle, therefore, when we undertake to alleviate the condition of the masses, must be the inviolability of private property. This laid down, We go on to show where We must find the remedy that We seek.

19. We approach the subject with confidence, and in the exercise of the rights which belong to Us. For no practi-

---

1. St. Thomas, *Summa Theologica*, 2a 2æ Q. x. Art. 12.

cal solution of this question will ever be found without the assistance of Religion and of the Church. It is We who are the chief guardian of Religion and the chief dispenser of what belongs to the Church, and We must not by silence neglect the duty which lies upon Us. Doubtless this most serious question demands the attention and the efforts of others besides Ourselves — of the rulers of States, of employers of labor, of the wealthy, and of the working population themselves for whom We plead. But We affirm without hesitation, that all the striving of men will be vain if they leave out the Church. It is the Church that proclaims from the Gospel those teachings by which the conflict can be put an end to, or at the least made far less bitter; the Church uses its efforts not only to enlighten the mind, but to direct by its precepts the life and conduct of men; the Church improves and ameliorates the condition of the workingman by numerous useful organizations; does its best to enlist the services of all ranks in discussing and endeavoring to meet, in the most practical way, the claims of the working-classes; and acts on the decided view that for these purposes recourse should be had, in due measure and degree, to the help of the law and of State authority.

20. Let it be laid down, in the first place, that humanity must remain as it is. It is impossible to reduce human society to a level. The Socialists may do their utmost, but all striving against nature is vain. There naturally exist among mankind innumerable differences of the most important kind; people differ in capability, in diligence, in health, and in strength; and unequal fortune is a necessary result of inequality in condition. Such inequality is far from being disadvantageous either to individuals or to the community; social and public life can only go on by the help of various kinds of capacity and the playing of many parts; and each man, as a rule, chooses the part which peculiarly suits his case. As regards bodily labor, even had man never fallen

from the state of innocence, he would not have been wholly unoccupied; but that which would then have been his free choice and his delight, became afterwards compulsory, and the painful expiation of his sin. *Cursed be the earth in thy work; in thy labor thou shalt eat of it all the days of thy life.*[1] In like manner, the other pains and hardships of life will have no end or cessation on this earth; for the consequences of sin are bitter and hard to bear, and they must be with man as long as life lasts. To suffer and to endure, therefore, is the lot of humanity; let men try as they may, no strength and no artifice will ever succeed in banishing from human life the ills and troubles which beset it. If any there are who pretend differently — who hold out to a hard-pressed people freedom from pain and trouble, undisturbed repose, and constant enjoyment — they cheat the people and impose upon them, and their lying promises will only make the evil worse than before. There is nothing more useful than to look at the world as it really is — and at the same time to look elsewhere for a remedy to its troubles.

21. The great mistake that is made in the matter now under consideration is to possess one's self of the idea that class is naturally hostile to class; that rich and poor are intended by nature to live at war with one another. So irrational and so false is this view, that the exact contrary is the truth. Just as the symmetry of the human body is the result of the disposition of the members of the body, so in a State it is ordained by nature that these two classes should exist in harmony and agreement, and should, as it were, fit into one another, so as to maintain the equilibrium of the body politic. Each requires the other; capital cannot do without labor, nor labor without capital. Mutual agreement results in pleasantness and good order; perpetual conflict necessarily produces confusion and outrage. Now, in preventing

---

1. Genesis iii. 17.

such strife as this, and in making it impossible, the efficacy of Christianity is marvelous and manifold. First of all, there is nothing more powerful than Religion (of which the Church is the interpreter and guardian) in drawing rich and poor together, by reminding each class of its duties to the other, and especially of the duties of justice. Thus Religion teaches the laboring-man and the workman to carry out honestly and well all equitable agreements freely made; never to injure capital, or to outrage the person of an employer; never to employ violence in representing his own cause, or to engage in riot or disorder; and to have nothing to do with men of evil principles, who work upon the people with artful promises, and raise foolish hopes which usually end in disaster and in repentance when too late. Religion teaches the rich man and the employer that their workpeople are not their slaves; that they must respect in every man his dignity as a man and as a Christian; that labor is nothing to be ashamed of, if we listen to right reason and to Christian philosophy, but is an honorable employment, enabling a man to sustain his life in an upright and creditable way; and that it is shameful and inhuman to treat men like chattels to make money by, or to look upon them merely as so much muscle or physical power. Thus, again, Religion teaches that, as among the workman's concerns are Religion herself and things spiritual and mental, the employer is bound to see that he has time for the duties of piety; that he be not exposed to corrupting influences and dangerous occasions; and that he be not led away to neglect his home and family or to squander his wages. Then, again, the employer must never tax his work-people beyond their strength, nor employ them in work unsuited to their sex or age. His great and principal obligation is to give to every one that which is just. Doubtless before we can decide whether wages are adequate, many things have to be considered; but rich men and masters should remember this — that to exercise pressure for the sake of gain upon the indigent and the destitute, and to make one's profit out of the need of another is condemned by all laws, human and divine. To defraud any one of wages that are his due is a crime which cries to the avenging anger of Heaven. *Behold, the hire of the laborers... which by fraud hath been kept back by you, crieth; and the cry of them hath entered into the ears of the Lord of Sabaoth.*[1] Finally, the rich must religiously refrain from cutting down the workman's earnings, either by force, by fraud, or by usurious dealing; and with the more reason because the poor man is weak and unprotected, and because his slender means should be sacred in proportion to their scantiness.

22. Were these prospects carefully obeyed and followed, would not strife die out and cease?

23. But the Church, with Jesus Christ for its Master and Guide, aims higher still. It lays down precepts yet more perfect, and tries to bind class to class in friendliness and good understanding. The things of this earth cannot be understood or valued rightly without taking into consideration the life to come, the life that will last forever. Exclude the idea of futurity, and the very notion of what is good and right would perish; nay, the whole system of the universe would become a dark and unfathomable mystery. The great truth which we learn from Nature herself is also the grand Christian dogma on which Religion rests as on its base — that when we have done with this present life then shall we really begin to live. God has not created us for the perishable and transitory things of earth, but for things heavenly and everlasting; He has given us this world as a place of exile, and not as our true country. Money, and the other things which men call good and desirable — we may have them in abundance, or we may want them altogether; as far as eternal happiness is concerned, it is no matter; the

---

1. St. James v. 4.

only thing that is important is to use them aright. Jesus Christ, when He redeemed us with plentiful redemption, took not away the pains and sorrows which in such large proportion make up the texture of our mortal life; He transformed them into motives of virtue and occasions of merit; and no man can hope for eternal reward unless he follow in the blood-stained footprints of his Saviour. *If we suffer with Him, we shall also reign with Him.*[1] His labors and His sufferings, accepted by His own free will, have marvelously sweetened all suffering and all labor. And not only by His example, but by His grace and by the hope of everlasting recompense, He has made pain and grief more easy to endure; *for that which is at present momentary and light of our tribulation, worketh for us above measure exceedingly an eternal weight of glory.* [2]

24. Therefore those whom fortune favors are warned that freedom from sorrow and abundance of earthly riches are no guaranty of the beatitude that shall never end, but rather the contrary;[3] that the rich should tremble at the threatenings of Jesus Christ — threatenings so strange in the mouth of Our Lord;[4] and that a most strict account must be given to the Supreme Judge for all that we possess. The chiefest and most excellent rule for the right use of money is one which the heathen philosophers indicated, but which the Church has traced out clearly, and has not only made known to men's minds, but has impressed upon their lives. It rests on the principle that it is one thing to have a right to the possession of money, and another to have a right to use money as one pleases. Private ownership, as we have seen, is the natural right of man; and to exercise that right, especially as members of society, is not only lawful, but absolutely necessary. *It is lawful,* says St.

---

1. Timothy ii 12.   4. St. Luke vi. 24, 25.
2. 2 Corinthians iv. 17.
3. St. Matthew xix. 23, 24.

Thomas of Aquin, *for a man to hold private property; and it is also necessary for the carrying on of human life.*[1] But if the question be asked, How must one's possessions be used? the Church replies without hesitation in the words of the same holy Doctor: *Man should not consider his outward possessions as his own, but as common to all, so as to share them without difficulty when others are in need. Whence the Apostle saith, Command the rich of this world... to give with ease, to communicate.*[2] True, no one is commanded to distribute to others that which is required for his own necessities and those of his household; nor even to give away what is reasonably required to keep up becomingly his condition in life; *for no one ought to live unbecomingly.*[3] But when necessity has been supplied, and one's position fairly considered, it is a duty to give to the indigent out of that which is over. *That which remaineth, give alms.*[4] It is a duty, not of justice (except in extreme cases), but of Christian charity — a duty which is not enforced by human law. But the laws and judgments of men must give place to the laws and judgments of Christ the true God, Who in many ways urges on His followers the practice of almsgiving — *It is more blessed to give than to receive;*[5] and Who will count a kindness done or refused to the poor as done or refused to Himself — *as long as you did it to one of My least brethren, you did it to Me.*[6] Thus, to sum up what has been said: Whoever has received from the Divine bounty a large share of blessings, whether they be external and corporeal or gifts of the mind, has received them for the purpose of using them for the perfecting of his own nature, and, at the same time, that he may employ them, as the minister of God's Providence, for the benefit of others. *He that hath a talent,* says St. Gregory the Great, *let him see that*

---

1. 2a 2æ Q. lxvi. Art. 2.

2. 2a 2æ Q. lxv. Art. 2.

3. Ibid. Q. xxxii. Art. 6.

4. St. Luke xi. 41.

5. Acts xx. 35.

6. St. Matthew xxv. 40.

he hide it not; he that hath abundance, let him arouse himself to mercy and generosity; he that hath art and skill, let him do his best to share the use and utility thereof with his neighbor.[1]

25. As for those who do not possess the gifts of fortune, they are taught by the Church that, in God's sight, poverty is no disgrace, and that there is nothing to be ashamed of in seeking one's bread by labor. This is strengthened by what we see in Christ Himself, Who *whereas He was rich, for our sakes became poor;*[2] and Who, being the Son of God, and God Himself, chose to seem and to be considered the son of a carpenter — nay, did not disdain to spend a great part of His life as a carpenter Himself. *Is not this the carpenter, the Son of Mary?*[3] From the contemplation of this Divine example it is easy to understand that the true dignity and excellence of man lies in his moral qualities, that is, in virtue; that virtue is the common inheritance of all, equally within the reach of high and low, rich and poor; and that virtue, and virtue alone, wherever found, will be followed by the rewards of everlasting happiness. Nay, God Himself seems to incline more to those who suffer evil; for Jesus Christ calls the poor blessed;[4] He lovingly invites those in labor and grief to come to Him for solace;[5] and He displays the tenderest charity to the lowly and the oppressed. These reflections cannot fail to keep down the pride of those who are well off, and to cheer the spirit of the afflicted; to incline the former to generosity and the latter to tranquil resignation. Thus the separation which pride would make tends to disappear, nor will it be difficult to make rich and

---

1. St. Gregory the Great, Hom. ix. in Evangel. n. 7.
2. Corinthians viii. 9.
3. St. Mark vi. 3.
4. St. Matthew v. 3: "Blessed are the poor in spirit."
5. Ibid. xi. 28: "Come to Me, all you that labor and are burdened, and I will refresh you."

poor join hands in friendly concord.

26. But, if Christian precepts prevail, the two classes will not only be united in the bonds of friendship but also in those of brotherly love. For they will understand and feel that all men are the children of the common Father, that is, of God; that all have the same last end, which is God Himself, Who alone can make either men or angels absolutely and perfectly happy; that all and each are redeemed by Jesus Christ and raised to the dignity of children of God, and are thus united in brotherly ties both with each other and with Jesus Christ, the first-born among many brethren; that the blessings of nature and the gifts of grace belong in common to the whole human race, and that to all, except to those that are unworthy, is promised the inheritance of the Kingdom of Heaven. If sons, heirs also; heirs indeed of God, and co-heirs of Christ.[1]

27. Such is the scheme of duties and of rights which is put forth to the world by the Gospel. Would it not seem that strife must quickly cease were society penetrated with ideas like these?

28. But the Church, not content with pointing out the remedy, also applies it. For the Church does its utmost to teach and to train men, and to educate them; and by means of its Bishops and Clergy it diffuses its salutary teachings far and wide. It strives to influence the mind and heart so that all may willingly yield themselves to be formed and guided by the commandments of God. It is precisely in this fundamental and principal matter, on which everything depends, that the Church has a power peculiar to itself. The agencies which it employs are given it for the very purpose of reaching the hearts of men, by Jesus Christ Himself, and derive their efficiency from God. They alone can touch the innermost heart and conscience, and bring

---

1. Romans viii. 17.

men to act from a motive of duty, to resist their passions
and appetites, to love God and their fellow men with a love
that is unique and supreme, and courageously to break down
every barrier which stands in the way of a virtuous life.

29. On this subject We need only recall for one moment the examples written down in history. Of these things
there cannot be the shadow of doubt; for instance, that
civil society was renovated in every part by the teachings of
Christianity; that in the strength of that renewal the human race was lifted up to better things — nay, that it was
brought back from death to life, and to so excellent a life
that nothing more perfect had been known before, or will
come to pass in the ages that have yet to be. Of this beneficent transformation Jesus Christ was at once the first cause
and the final purpose; as from Him all came, so to Him all
was to be referred. For when, by the light of the Gospel
message, the human race came to know the grand mystery
of the Incarnation of the Word and the redemption of man,
the life of Jesus Christ, God and Man, penetrated every
race and nation, and impregnated them with His faith, His
precepts, and His laws. And if Society is to be cured now, in
no other way can it be cured but by a return to the Christian life and Christian institutions. When a society is perishing, the true advice to give to those who would restore it
is, to recall it to the principles from which it sprang; for the
purpose and perfection of an association is to aim at and to
attain that for which it was formed; and its operation should
be put in motion and inspired by the end and object which
originally gave it its being. So that to fall away from its pri-
mal constitution is disease; to go back to it is recovery. And
this may be asserted with the utmost truth both of the State
in general and of that body of its citizens — by far the greater
number — who sustain life by labor.

30. Neither must it be supposed that the solicitude of
the Church is so occupied with the spiritual concerns of its

children as to neglect their interests temporal and earthly. Its desire is that the poor, for example, should rise above poverty and wretchedness, and should better their condition in life; and for this it strives. By the very fact that it calls men to virtue and forms them to its practice, it promotes this in no slight degree. Christian morality, when it is adequately and completely practiced, conduces of itself to temporal prosperity, for it merits the blessing of that God Who is the source of all blessings; it powerfully restrains the lust of possession and the lust of pleasure — twin plagues, which too often make a man without self-restraint miserable in the midst of abundance;[1] it makes men supply by economy for the want of means, teaching them to be content with frugal living, and keeping them out of the reach of those vices which eat up not merely small incomes, but large fortunes, and dissipate many a goodly inheritance.

31. Moreover, the Church intervenes directly in the interest of the poor, by setting on foot and keeping up many things which it sees to be efficacious in the relief of poverty. Here again it has always succeeded so well that it has even extorted the praise of its enemies. Such was the ardor of brotherly love among the earliest Christians that numbers of those who were better off deprived themselves of their possessions in order to relieve their brethren; whence *neither was there any one needy among them.*[2] To the order of Deacons, instituted for that very purpose, was committed by the Apostles the charge of the daily distributions; and the Apostle Paul, though burdened with the solicitude of all the churches, hesitated not to undertake laborious journeys in order to carry the alms of the faithful to the poorer Christians. Tertullian calls these contributions, given voluntarily by Christians in their assemblies, deposits of piety; because, to cite his words, they were

---

1. "The root of all evils is cupidity." — 1 Tim. vi. 10.
2. Acts iv. 34.

employed in feeding the needy, in burying them, in the support of boys and girls destitute of means and deprived of their parents, in the care of the aged and in the relief of the shipwrecked.[1]

32. Thus by degrees came into existence the patrimony which the Church has guarded with religious care as the inheritance of the poor. Nay, to spare them the shame of begging, the common Mother of rich and poor has exerted herself to gather together funds for the support of the needy. The Church has stirred up everywhere the heroism of charity, and has established Congregations of Religious and many other useful institutions for help and mercy, so that there might be hardly any kind of suffering which was not visited and relieved. At the present day there are many who, like the heathen of old, blame and condemn the Church for this beautiful charity. They would substitute in its place a system of State-organized relief. But no human methods will ever supply for the devotion and self-sacrifice of Christian charity. Charity, as a virtue, belongs to the Church; for it is no virtue unless it is drawn from the Sacred Heart of Jesus Christ; and he who turns his back on the Church cannot be near to Christ.

33. It cannot, however, be doubted that to attain the purpose of which We treat, not only the Church, but all human means must conspire. All who are concerned in the matter must be of one mind and must act together. It is in this, as in the Providence which governs the world; results do not happen save where all the causes cooperate.

34. Let us now, therefore, inquire what part the State should play in the work of remedy and relief.

35. By the State We here understand, not the particular form of government which prevails in this or that nation, but the State as rightly understood; that is to say, any

---

1. *Apologia Secunda*, xxxix.

government conformable in its institutions to right reason and natural law, and to those dictates of the Divine wisdom which We have expounded in the Encyclical on the Christian Constitution of the State. The first duty, therefore, of the rulers of the State should be to make sure that the laws and institutions, the general character and administration of the commonwealth, shall be such as to produce of themselves public well-being and private prosperity. This is the proper office of wise statesmanship and the work of the heads of the State. Now, a State chiefly prospers and flourishes by morality, by well-regulated family life, by respect for religion and justice, by the moderation and equal distribution of public burdens, by the progress of the arts and of trade, by the abundant yield of the land — by everything which makes the citizens better and happier. Here, then, it is in the power of a ruler to benefit every order of the State, and amongst the rest to promote in the highest degree the interests of the poor; and this by virtue of his office, and without being exposed to any suspicion of undue interference — for it is the province of the commonwealth to consult for the common good. And the more that is done for the working population by the general laws of the country, the less need will there be to seek for particular means to relieve them.

36. There is another and a deeper consideration which must not be lost sight of. To the State the interests of all are equal, whether high or low. The poor are members of the national community equally with the rich; they are real component parts, living parts, which make up, through the family, the living body; and it need hardly be said that they are by far the majority. It would be irrational to neglect one portion of the citizens and to favor another; and therefore the public administration must duly and solicitously provide for the welfare and the comfort of the working people, or else that law of justice will be violated which ordains that each shall

have his due. To cite the wise words of St. Thomas of Aquin: *As the part and the whole are in a certain sense identical, the part may in some sense claim what belongs to the whole.*[1] Among the many and grave duties of rulers who would do their best for the people, the first and chief is to act with strict justice — with that justice which is called in the Schools distributive — toward each and every class.

37. But although all citizens, without exception, can and ought to contribute to that common good in which individuals share so profitably to themselves, yet it is not to be supposed that all can contribute in the same way and to the same extent. No matter what changes may be made in forms of government, there will always be differences and inequalities of condition in the State: Society cannot exist or be conceived without them. Some there must be who dedicate themselves to the work of the commonwealth, who make the laws, who administer justice, whose advice and authority govern the nation in times of peace, and defend it in war. Such men clearly occupy the foremost place in the State, and should be held in the foremost estimation, for their work touches most nearly and effectively the general interests of the community. Those who labor at a trade or calling do not promote the general welfare in such a fashion as this; but they do in the most important way benefit the nation, though less directly. We have insisted that, since it is the end of Society to make men better, the chief good that Society can be possessed of is Virtue. Nevertheless, in all well-constituted States it is a by no means unimportant matter to provide those bodily and external commodities, *the use of which is necessary to virtuous action.*[2] And in the provision of material well-being, the labor of the poor — the exercise of their skill and the employment of their strength

---

1. 2a 2æ Q. lxi. Art. 1 ad 2.
2. St. Thomas of Aquin, *De Begimine Principium*, I. cap. 15.

in the culture of the land and the workshops of trade — is most efficacious and altogether indispensable. Indeed, their cooperation in this respect is so important that it may be truly said that it is only by the labor of the working man that States grow rich. Justice, therefore, demands that the interests of the poorer population be carefully watched over by the Administration, so that they who contribute so largely to the advantage of the community may themselves share in the benefits they create — that being housed, clothed, and enabled to support life, they may find their existence less hard and more endurable. It follows that whatever shall appear to be conducive to the well-being of those who work should receive favorable consideration. Let it not be feared that solicitude of this kind will injure any interest; on the contrary, it will be to the advantage of all; for it cannot but be good for the commonwealth to secure from misery those on whom it so largely depends.

38. We have said that the State must not absorb the individual or the family; both should be allowed free and untrammeled action as far as is consistent with the common good and the interest of others. Nevertheless, rulers should anxiously safeguard the community and all its parts; the community, because the conservation of the community is so emphatically the business of the supreme power that the safety of the commonwealth is not only the first law, but it is a Government's whole reason of existence; and the parts, because both philosophy and the Gospel agree in laying down that the object of the administration of the State should be, not the advantage of the ruler but the benefit of those over whom he rules. The gift of authority is from God, and is, as it were, a participation of the highest of all sorereignties; and it should be exercised as the power of God is exercised — with a fatherly solicitude which not only guides the whole, but reaches to details as well.

39. Whenever the general interest of any particular class

suffers, or is threatened with, evils which can in no other way be met, the public authority must step in to meet them. Now, among the interests of the public, as of private individuals, are these: that peace and good order should be maintained; that family life should be carried on in accordance with God's laws and those of nature; that Religion should be reverenced and obeyed; that a high standard of morality should prevail in public and private life; that sanctity of justice should be respected, and that no one should injure another with impunity; that the members of the commonwealth should grow up to man's estate strong and robust, and capable, if need be, of guarding and defending their country. If by a strike, or other combination of workmen, there should be imminent danger of disturbance to the public peace; or if circumstances were such that among the laboring population the ties of family life were relaxed; if Religion were found to suffer through the workmen not having time and opportunity to practice it; if in workshops and factories there were danger to morals through the mixing of the sexes or from any occasion of evil; or if employers laid burdens upon the workmen which were unjust, or degraded them with conditions that were repugnant to their dignity as human beings; finally, if health were endangered by excessive labor, or by work unsuited to sex or age — in these cases, there can be no question that, within certain limits, it would be right to call in the help and authority of the law. The limits must be determined by the nature of the occasion which calls for the law's interference — the principle being this, that the law must not undertake more, or go further, than is required for the remedy of the evil or the removal of the danger.

40. Rights must be religiously respected wherever they are found; and it is the duty of the public authority to prevent and punish injury, and to protect each one in the possession of his own. Still, when there is question of protecting

the rights of individuals, the poor and helpless have a claim to special consideration. The richer population have many ways of protecting themselves, and stand less in need of help from the State; those who are badly off have no resources of their own to fall back upon, and must chiefly rely upon the assistance of the State. And it is for this reason that wage-earners, who are undoubtedly among the weak and necessitous, should be specially cared for and protected by the commonwealth.

41. Here, however, it will be advisable to advert expressly to one or two of the more important details. It must be borne in mind that the chief thing to be secured is the safeguarding, by legal enactment and policy, of private property. Most of all is it essential in these times of covetous greed, to keep the multitude within the line of duty; for if all may justly strive to better their condition, yet neither justice nor the common good allows any one to seize that which belongs to another, or, under the pretext of futile and ridiculous equality, to lay hands on other people's fortunes. It is most true that by far the larger part of the people who work prefer to improve themselves by honest labor rather than by doing wrong to others. But there are not a few who are imbued with bad principles and are anxious for revolutionary change, and whose great purpose it is to stir up tumult and bring about a policy of violence. The authority of the State should intervene to put restraint upon these disturbers, to save the workmen from their seditious arts, and to protect lawful owners from spoliation.

42. When work-people have recourse to a strike, it is frequently because the hours of labor are too long, or the work too hard, or because they consider their wages insufficient. The grave inconvenience of this not uncommon occurrence should be obviated by public remedial measures; for such paralysis of labor not only affects the masters and their work-people, but is extremely injurious to trade, and

to the general interests of the public; moreover, on such occasions, violence and disorder are generally not far off, and thus it frequently happens that the public peace is threatened. The laws should be beforehand, and prevent these troubles from arising; they should lend their influence and authority to the removal in good time of the causes which lead to conflicts between masters and those whom they employ.

43. But if the owners of property must be made secure, the Workman, too, has property and possessions in which he must be protected; and, first of all, there are his spiritual and mental interests. Life on earth, however good and desirable in itself, is not the final purpose for which man is created; it is only the way and the means to that attainment of truth, and that practice of goodness in which the full life of the soul consists. It is the soul which is made after the image and likeness of God; it is in the soul that sovereignty resides, in virtue of which man is commanded to rule the creatures below him, and to use all the earth and the ocean for his profit and advantage. *Fill the earth and subdue it; and rule over the fishes of the sea, and the fowls of the air, and all living creatures which move upon the earth.*[1] In this respect all men are equal; there is no difference between rich and poor, master and servant, ruler and ruled, *for the same is lord over all.*[2] No man may outrage with impunity that human dignity which God Himself treats with reverence, nor stand in the way of that higher life which is the preparation for the eternal life of Heaven. Nay, more; a man has here no power over himself. To consent to any treatment which is calculated to defeat the end and purpose of his being is beyond his right; he cannot give up his soul to servitude; for it is not man's own rights which are here in question, but the

---

1. Genesis i. 28.
2. Romans x. 12.

rights of God, most sacred and inviolable.

44. From this follows the obligation of the cessation of work and labor on Sundays and certain festivals. This rest from labor is not to be understood as mere idleness; much less must it be an occasion of spending money and of vicious excess, as many would desire it to be; but it should be rest from labor consecrated by religion. Repose united with religious observance disposes man to forget for a while the business of this daily life, and to turn his thoughts to heavenly things and to the worship which he so strictly owes to the Eternal Deity. It is this, above all, which is the reason and motive of the Sunday rest; a rest sanctioned by God's great law of the ancient covenant, *Remember thou keep holy the Sabbath Day,*[1] and taught to the world by His own mysterious "rest" after the creation of man; *He rested on the seventh day from all His work which He had done.*[2]

45. If we turn now to things exterior and corporeal, the first concern of all is to save the poor workers from the cruelty of grasping speculators, who use human beings as mere instruments for making money. It is neither justice nor humanity so to grind men down with excessive labor as to stupefy their minds and wear out their bodies. Man's powers, like his general nature, are limited, and beyond these limits he cannot go. His strength is developed and increased by use and exercise, but only on condition of due intermission and proper rest. Daily labor, therefore, must be so regulated that it may not be protracted during longer hours than strength admits. How many and how long the intervals of rest should be, will depend on the nature of the work, on circumstances of time and place, and on the health and strength of the workman. Those who labor in mines and quarries, and in work within the bowels of the earth, should

---

1. Genesis ii. 2.
2. Exodus xx. 8.

have shorter hours in proportion as their labor is more severe and more trying to health. Then, again, the season of
the year must be taken into account; for not unfrequently a
kind of labor is easy at one time which at another is intolerable or very difficult. Finally, work which is suitable for a
strong man cannot reasonably be required from a woman
or a child. And, in regard to children, great care should be
taken not to place them in workshops and factories until
their bodies and minds are sufficiently mature. For just as
rough weather destroys the buds of Spring, so too early an
experience of life's hard work blights the young promise of
a child's powers, and makes any real education impossible.
Women, again, are not suited to certain trades; for a woman
is by nature fitted for home-work, and it is that which is
best adapted at once to preserve her modesty and to promote the good bringing up of children and the well-being
of the family. As a general principle it may be laid down
that a workman ought to have leisure and rest in proportion to the wear and tear of his strength; for the waste of
strength must be repaired by the cessation of work.

46. In all agreements between masters and work-people
there is always the condition, expressed or understood, that
there be allowed proper rest for soul and body. To agree in
any other sense would be against what is right and just; for
it can never be right or just to require on the one side, or to
promise on the other, the giving up of those duties which a
man owes to his God and to himself.

47. We now approach a subject of very great importance,
and one on which, if extremes are to be avoided, right ideas
are absolutely necessary. Wages, we are told, are fixed by
free consent; and, therefore, the employer, when he pays
what was agreed upon, has done his part and is not called
upon for anything further. The only way, it is said, in which
injustice could happen would be if the master refused to
pay the whole of the wages, or the workman would not

complete the work undertaken; when this happens the State should intervene, to see that each obtains his own — but not under any other circumstances.

48. This mode of reasoning is by no means convincing to a fair-minded man, for there are important considerations which it leaves out of view altogether. To labor is to exert one's self for the sake of procuring what is necessary for the purposes of life, and most of all for self-preservation. *In the sweat of thy brow thou shalt eat bread.*[1] Therefore a man's labor has two notes or characters. First of all, it is personal, for the exertion of individual power belongs to the individual who puts it forth, employing this power for that personal profit for which it was given. Secondly, man's labor is necessary, for without the results of labor a man cannot live; and self-conservation is a law of Nature, which it is wrong to disobey. Now, if we were to consider labor merely so far as it is personal doubtless it would be within the workman's right to accept any rate of wages whatever; for in the same way as he is free to work or not, so he is free to accept a small remuneration or even none at all. But this is a mere abstract supposition; the labor of the working man is not only his personal attribute, but it is necessary; and this makes all the difference. The preservation of life is the bounden duty of each and all, and to fail therein is a crime. It follows that each one has a right to procure what is required in order to live, and the poor can procure it in no other way than by work and wages.

49. Let it be granted then that, as a rule, workman and employer should make free agreements, and in particular should freely agree as to wages; nevertheless, there is a dictate of nature more imperious and more ancient than any bargain between man and man, that the remuneration must be enough to support the wage-earner in reasonable and

---

1. Genesis iii. 19.

frugal comfort. If through necessity or fear of a worse evil the workman accepts harder conditions because an employer or a contractor will give him no better, he is the victim of force and injustice. In these and similar questions, however — such as, for example, the hours of labor in different trades, the sanitary precautions to be observed in factories and workshops, etc. — in order to supersede undue interference on the part of the State, especially as circumstances, times, and localities differ so widely, it is advisable that recourse be had to Societies or Boards such as We shall mention presently, or to some other method of safeguarding the interests of wage-earners; the State to be asked for approval and protection.

50. If a workman's wages be sufficient to enable him to maintain himself, his wife, and his children in reasonable comfort, he will not find it difficult, if he is a sensible man, to study economy; and he will not fail, by cutting down expenses, to put by a little property; nature and reason would urge him to this. We have seen that this great Labor question cannot be solved except by assuming as a principle that private ownership must be held sacred and inviolable. The law, therefore, should favor ownership, and its policy should be to induce as many of the people as possible to become owners.

51. Many excellent results will follow from this; and first of all, property will certainly become more equitably divided. For the effect of civil change and revolution has been to divide society into two widely differing castes. On the one side there is the party which holds the power because it holds the wealth; which has in its grasp all labor and all trade, which manipulates for its own benefit and its own purposes all the sources of supply, and which is powerfully represented in the councils of the State itself. On the other side there is the needy and powerless multitude, sore and suffering, and always ready for disturbance. If working-people

can be encouraged to look forward to obtaining a share in the land, the result will be that the gulf between vast wealth and deep poverty will be bridged over, and the two orders will be brought nearer together. Another consequence will be the greater abundance of the fruits of the earth. Men always work harder and more readily when they work on that which is their own; nay, they learn to love the very soil which yields in response to the labor of their hands, not only food to eat, but an abundance of good things for themselves and those that are dear to them. It is evident how such a spirit of willing labor would add to the produce of the earth and to the wealth of the community. And a third advantage would arise from this: men would cling to the country in which they were born; for no one would exchange his country for a foreign land if his own afforded him the means of living a tolerable and happy life. These three important benefits, however, can only be expected on the condition that a man's means be not drained and exhausted by excessive taxation. The right to possess private property is from nature, not from man; and the State has only the right to regulate its use in the interests of the public good, but by no means to abolish it altogether. The State is therefore unjust and cruel if, in the name of taxation, it deprives the private owner of more than is just.

52. In the last place — employers and workmen may themselves effect much in the matter of which We treat, by means of those institutions and organizations which afford opportune assistance to those in need, and which draw the two orders more closely together. Among these may be enumerated: Societies for mutual help; various foundations established by private persons for providing for the workman, and for his widow or his orphans, in sudden calamity, in sickness, and in the event of death; and what are called "patronages" or institutions for the care of boys and girls, for young people and also for those of more mature age.

53. The most important of all are Workmen's Associations; for these virtually include all the rest. History attests what excellent results were effected by the Artificers' Guilds of a former day. They were the means not only of many advantages to the workmen, but in no small degree of the advancement of art, as numerous monuments remain to prove. Such associations should be adapted to the requirements of the age in which we live — an age of greater instruction, of different customs, and of more numerous requirements in daily life. It is gratifying to know that there are actually in existence not a few Societies of this nature, consisting either of workmen alone or of workmen and employers together; but it were greatly to be desired that they should multiply and become more effective. We have spoken of them more than once; but it will be well to explain here how much they are needed, to show that they exist by their own right, and to enter into their organization and their work.

54. The experience of his own weakness urges man to call in help from without. We read in the pages of Holy Writ: *It is better that two should be together than one; for they have the advantage of their society. If one fall he shall be supported by the other. Woe to him that is alone, for when he falleth he hath none to lift him up.*[1] And further: *A brother that is helped by his brother is like a strong city.*[2] It is this natural impulse which unites men in civil society; and it is this also which makes them band themselves together in associations of citizen with citizen; associations which, it is true, cannot be called societies in the complete sense of the word, but which are societies nevertheless.

55. These lesser societies and the society which constitutes the State differ in many things, because their immedi-

---

1. Ecclesiastes iv. 9, 10.
2. Proverbs xviii. 19.

ate purpose and end is different. Civil society exists for the common good, and therefore is concerned with the interests of all in general, and with individual interests in their due place and proportion. Hence it is called public society, because by its means, as St. Thomas of Aquin says, *Men communicate with one another in the setting up of a commonwealth.*[1] But the societies which are formed in the bosom of the State are called private, and justly so, because their immediate purpose is the private advantage of the associates. *Now a private society*, says St. Thomas again, *is one which is formed for the purpose of carrying out private business; as when two or three enter into a partnership with the view of trading in conjunction.*[2] Particular societies, then, although they exist within the State, and are each a part of the State, nevertheless cannot be prohibited by the State absolutely and as such. For to enter into "society" of this kind is the natural right of man; and the State must protect natural rights, not destroy them; and if it forbids its citizens to form associations, it contradicts the very principle of its own existence; for both they and it exist in virtue of the same principle, viz., the natural propensity of man to live in society.

56. There are times, no doubt, when it is right that the law should interfere to prevent association; as when men join together for purposes which are evidently bad, unjust, or dangerous to the State. In such cases the public authority may justly forbid the formation of associations, and may dissolve them when they already exist. But every precaution should be taken not to violate the rights of individuals and not to make unreasonable regulations under the pretense of public benefit. For laws only bind when they are in accordance with right reason, and therefore with the eternal law of God.[1]

---

1. *Contra impugnantes Dei cultum et religionem*, Cap. II.
2. Ibid.

57. And here we are reminded of the Confraternities, Societies, and Religious Orders, which have arisen by the Church's authority and the piety of the Christian people.

The annals of every nation down to our own times testify to what they have done for the human race. It is indisputable, on grounds of reason alone, that such associations, being perfectly blameless in their objects, have the sanction of the law of nature. On their religious side they rightly claim to be responsible to the Church alone. The administrators of the State, therefore, have no rights over them, nor can they claim any share in their management; on the contrary, it is the State's duty to respect and cherish them, and, if necessary, to defend them from attack. It is notorious that a very different course has been followed, more especially in our own times. In many places the State has laid violent hands on these communities, and committed manifold injustice against them; it has placed them under the civil law, taken away their rights as corporate bodies, and robbed them of their property. In such property the Church had her rights, each member of the body had his or her rights, and there were also the rights of those who had founded or endowed them for a definite purpose, and of those for whose benefit and assistance they existed. Wherefore We cannot refrain from complaining of such spoliation as unjust and fraught with evil results; and with the more reason because, at the very time when the law proclaims that association is free to all, We see that Catholic societies, however peaceable and useful, are hindered in every way, whilst the utmost freedom is given to men whose

---

1. "Human law is law only in virtue of its accordance with right reason: and thus it is manifest that it flows from the eternal law. And in so far as it deviates from right reason it is called an unjust law; in such case it is not law at all, but rather a species of violence." — St. Thomas of Aquin, *Summa Theologica*, 1a 2æ Q. xeiii. Art. 3.

objects are at once hurtful to Religion and dangerous to the State.

58. Associations of every kind, and especially those of working men, are now far more common than formerly. In regard to many of these there is no need at present to inquire whence they spring, what are their objects, or what means they use. But there is a good deal of evidence which goes to prove that many of these societies are in the hands of invisible leaders, and are managed on principles far from compatible with Christianity and the public well-being; and that they do their best to get into their hands the whole field of labor and to force workmen either to join them or to starve. Under these circumstances Christian workmen must do one of two things: either join Associations in which their religion will be exposed to peril, or form associations among themselves — unite their forces and courageously shake off the yoke of an unjust and intolerable oppression. No one who does not wish to expose man's chief good to extreme danger will hesitate to say that the second alternative must by all means be adopted.

59. Those Catholics are worthy of all praise — and there are not a few — who, understanding what the times require, have, by various enterprises and experiments, endeavored to better the condition of the working-people without any sacrifice of principle. They have taken up the cause of the working man, and have striven to make both families and individuals better off; to infuse the spirit of justice into the mutual relations of employer and employed; to keep before the eyes of both classes the precepts of duty and the laws of the Gospel — that Gospel which, by inculcating self-restraint, keeps men within the bounds of moderation, and tends to establish harmony among the divergent interests and various classes which compose the State. It is with such ends in view that We see men of eminence meeting together for discussion, for the promotion of united action, and for prac-

tical work. Others, again, strive to unite working people of various kinds into associations, help them with their advice and their means, and enable them to obtain honest and profitable work. The Bishops, on their part, bestow their ready good will and support; and with their approval and guidance many members of the clergy, both secular and regular, labor assiduously on behalf of the spiritual and mental interests of the members of Associations. And there are not wanting Catholics possessed of affluence who have, as it were, cast in their lot with the wage-earners, and who have spent large sums in founding and widely spreading Benefit and Insurance Societies; by means of which the working man may without difficulty acquire by his labor not only many present advantages, but also the certainty of honorable support in time to come. How much this multiplied and earnest activity has benefited the community at large is too well known to require Us to dwell upon it. We find in it the grounds of the most cheering hope for the future; provided that the Associations We have described continue to grow and spread, and are well and wisely administered. Let the State watch over these Societies of citizens united together in the exercise of their right; but let it not thrust itself into their peculiar concerns and their organization; for things move and live by the soul within them, and they may be killed by the grasp of a hand from without.

60. In order that an Association may be carried on with unity of purpose and harmony of action, its organization and government must be firm and wise. All such Societies, being free to exist, have the further right to adopt such rules and organization as may best conduce to the attainment of their objects. We do not deem it possible to enter into definite details on the subject of organization: this must depend on national character, on practice and experience, on the nature and scope of the work to be done, on the magnitude of the various trades and employments, and on other

circumstances of fact and of time — all of which must be carefully weighed.

61. Speaking summarily, we may lay it down as a general and perpetual law, that Workmen's Associations should be so organized and governed as to furnish the best and most suitable means for attaining what is aimed at, that is to say, for helping each individual member to better his condition to the utmost in body, mind, and property. It is clear that they must pay special and principal attention to piety and morality, and that their internal discipline must be directed precisely by these considerations; otherwise they entirely lose their special character, and come to be very little better than those Societies which take no account of Religion at all. What advantage can it be to a Workman to obtain by means of a Society all that he requires, and to endanger his soul for want of spiritual food? *What doth it profit a man if he gain the whole world and suffer the loss of his own soul?* [1] This, as Our Lord teaches, is the note or character that distinguishes the Christian from the heathen. *After all these things do the heathens seek.... Seek ye first the Kingdom of God and His justice, and all these things shall be added unto you.* [2] Let our associations, then, look first and before all to God; let religious instruction have therein a foremost place, each one being carefully taught what is his duty to God, what to believe, what to hope for, and how to work out his salvation; and let all be warned and fortified with especial solicitude against wrong opinions and false teaching. Let the working man be urged and led to the worship of God, to the earnest practice of religion, and, among other things, to the sanctification of Sundays and festivals. Let him learn to reverence and love the Holy Church, the common Mother of us all; and so to obey the precepts and to frequent the

---

1. St. Matthew xvi. 26.
2. St. Matthew vi. 32, 33.

Sacraments of the Church, those Sacraments being the means ordained by God for obtaining forgiveness of sin and for leading a holy life.

62. The foundations of the organization being laid in Religion, We next go on to determine the relations of the members one to another, in order that they may live together in concord and go on prosperously and successfully. The offices and charges of the Society should be distributed for the good of the Society itself, and in such manner that difference in degree or position should not interfere with unanimity and good will. Office-bearers should be appointed with prudence and discretion, and each one's charge should be carefully marked out; thus no member will suffer wrong. Let the common funds be administered with the strictest honesty, in such way that a member receive assistance in proportion to his necessities. The rights and duties of employers should be the subject of careful consideration as compared with the rights and duties of the employed. If it should happen that either a master or a workman deemed himself injured, nothing would be more desirable than that there should be a committee composed of honest and capable men of the Association itself, whose duty it should be, by the laws of the Association, to decide the dispute. Among the purposes of a Society should be to try to arrange for a continuous supply of work at all times and seasons; and to create a fund from which the members may be helped in their necessities, not only in cases of accident, but also in sickness, old age, and misfortune.

63. Such rules and regulations, if obeyed willingly by all, will sufficiently insure the well-being of poor people; whilst such mutual Associations among Catholics are certain to be productive, in no small degree, of prosperity to the State. It is not rash to conjecture the future from the past. Age gives way to age, but the events of one century are wonderfully like those of another; for they are directed by

the Providence of God, Who overrules the course of history in accordance with His purposes in creating the race of man. We are told that it was cast as a reproach on the Christians of the early ages of the Church, that the greater number of them had to live by begging or by labor. Yet, destitute as they were of wealth and influence, they ended by winning over to their side the favor of the rich and the good will of the powerful. They showed themselves industrious, laborious, and peaceful, men of justice, and, above all, men of brotherly love. In the presence of such a life and such an example prejudice disappeared, the tongue of malevolence was silenced, and the lying traditions of ancient superstition yielded little by little to Christian truth.

64. At this moment the condition of the working population is the question of the hour; and nothing can be of higher interest to all classes of the State than that it should be rightly and reasonably decided. But it will be easy for Christian working men to decide it right if they form Associations, choose wise guides, and follow the same path which with so much advantage to themselves and the commonwealth was trod by their fathers before them. Prejudice, it is true, is mighty, and so is the love of money; but if the sense of what is just and right be not destroyed by depravity of heart, their fellow-citizens are sure to be won over to a kindly feeling toward men whom they see to be so industrious and so modest, who so unmistakably prefer honesty to lucre, and the sacredness of duty to all other considerations.

65. And another great advantage would result from the state of things We are describing: there would be so much more hope and possibility of recalling to a sense of their duty those working men who have either given up their faith altogether, or whose lives are at variance with its precepts. These men, in most cases, feel that they have been fooled by empty promises and deceived by false appearances. They cannot but perceive that their grasping employers too

often treat them with the greatest inhumanity and hardly care for them beyond the profit their labor brings; and if they belong to an Association, it is probably one in which there exists, in place of charity and love, that intestine strife which always accompanies unresigned and irreligious poverty. Broken in spirit and worn down in body, how many of them would gladly free themselves from this galling slavery! But human respect, or the dread of starvation, makes them afraid to take the step. To such as these Catholic Associations are of incalculable service, helping them out of their difficulties, inviting them to companionship, and receiving the repentant to a shelter in which they may securely trust.

66. We have now laid before you, Venerable Brethren, who are the persons, and what are the means, by which this most difficult question must be solved. Every one must put his hand to the work which falls to his share, and that at once and immediately, lest the evil which is already so great may by delay become absolutely beyond remedy. Those who rule the State must use the law and the institutions of the country; masters and rich men must remember their duty; the poor whose interests are at stake, must make every lawful and proper effort; and since Religion alone, as We said at the beginning, can destroy the evil at its root, all men must be persuaded that the primary thing needful is to return to real Christianity, in the absence of which all the plans and devices of the wisest will be of little avail.

67. As far as regards the Church, its assistance will never be wanting, be the time or the occasion what it may; and it will intervene with the greater effect in proportion as its liberty of action is the more unfettered: let this be carefully noted by those whose office it is to provide for the public welfare. Every minister of holy Religion must throw into the conflict all the energy of his mind and all the strength of his endurance; with your authority, Venerable Brethren, and by your example, they must never cease to urge upon

all men of every class, upon the high as well as the lowly, the Gospel doctrines of Christian life; by every means in their power they must strive for the good of the people; and above all they must earnestly cherish in themselves, and try to arouse in others, Charity, the mistress and queen of virtues. For the happy results we all long for must be chiefly brought about by the plenteous outpouring of Charity; of that true Christian Charity which is the fulfilling of the whole Gospel law, which is always ready to sacrifice itself for others' sake, and which is man's surest antidote against worldly pride and immoderate love of self; that Charity whose office is described and whose Godlike features are drawn by the Apostle St. Paul in these words: *Charity is patient, is kind... seeketh not her own... suffereth all things... endureth all things.*[1]

68. On each one of you, Venerable Brethren, and on your Clergy and people, as an earnest of God's mercy and a mark of Our affection, We lovingly in the Lord bestow the Apostolic Benediction.

Given at St. Peter's, in Rome, the fifteenth day of May, 1891, the fourteenth year of Our Pontificate.

Leo XIII., Pope.

---

1. 1 Corinthians xiii. 4-7.

The Condition of Labor
An Open Letter to Pope Leo XIII

YOUR HOLINESS: I have read with care your Encyclical letter on the condition of labor, addressed, through the Patriarchs, Primates, Archbishops and Bishops of your faith, to the Christian World.

Since its most strikingly pronounced condemnations are directed against a theory that we who hold it know to be deserving of your support, I ask permission to lay before your Holiness the grounds of our belief, and to set forth some considerations that you have unfortunately overlooked. The momentous seriousness of the facts you refer to, the poverty, suffering and seething discontent that pervade the Christian world, the danger that passion may lead ignorance in a blind struggle against social conditions rapidly becoming intolerable, are my justification.

I.

Our postulates are all stated or implied in your Encyclical. They are the primary perceptions of human reason, the fundamental teachings of the Christian faith: We hold: That —

This world is the creation of God. The men brought into it for the brief period of their earthly lives are the equal creatures of his bounty, the equal subjects of His provident care.

By his constitution man is beset by physical wants, on the satisfaction of which depend not only the maintenance of his physical life but also the development of his intellectual and spiritual life.

God has made the satisfaction of these wants dependent on man's own exertions, giving him the power and laying on him the injunction to labor — a power that of itself raises him far above the brute, since we may reverently say that it enables him to become as it were a helper in the creative work.

God has not put on man the task of making bricks without straw. With the need for labor and the power to labor he has also given to man the material for labor. This material is land — man physically being a land animal, who can live only on and from land, and can use other elements, such as air, sunshine and water, only by the use of land.

Being the equal creatures of the Creator, equally entitled under his providence to live their lives and satisfy their needs, men are equally entitled to the use of land, and any adjustment that denies this equal use of land is morally wrong.

As to the right of ownership, we hold: That —

Being created individuals, with individual wants and powers, men are individually entitled (subject of course to the moral obligations that arise from such relations as that of the family) to the use of their own powers and the enjoyment of the results.

There thus arises, anterior to human law, and deriving its validity from the law of God, a right of private ownership in things produced by labor — a right that the possessor may transfer, but of which to deprive him without his will is theft.

This right of property, originating in the right of the individual to himself, is the only full and complete right of property. It attaches to things produced by labor, but cannot attach to things created by God.

Thus, if a man take a fish from the ocean he acquires a right of property in that fish, which exclusive right he may transfer by sale or gift. But he cannot obtain a similar right of property in the ocean, so that he may sell it or give it or forbid others to use it.

Or, if he set up a windmill he acquires a right of property in the things such use of wind enables him to produce. But he cannot claim a right of property in the wind itself, so that he may sell it or forbid others to use it.

Or, if he cultivate grain he acquires a right of property in the grain his labor brings forth. But he cannot obtain a similar right of property in the sun which ripened it or the soil on which it grew. For these things are of the continuing gifts of God to all generations of men, which all may use, but none may claim as his alone.

To attach to things created by God the same right of private ownership that justly attaches to things produced by labor is to impair and deny the true rights of property. For a man who out of the proceeds of his labor is obliged to pay another man for the use of ocean or air or sunshine or soil, all of which are to men involved in the single term land, is in this deprived of his rightful property and thus robbed.

As to the use of land, we hold: That —

While the right of ownership that justly attaches to things produced by labor cannot attach to land, there may attach to land a right of possession. As your Holiness says, "God has not granted the earth to mankind in general in the sense that all without distinction can deal with it as they please," and regulations necessary for its best use may be fixed by human laws. But such regulations must conform to the moral law — must secure to all equal participation in the advantages of God's general bounty. The principle is the same as where a human father leaves property equally to a number of children. Some of the things thus left may be incapable of common use or of specific division. Such things may properly be assigned to some of the children, but only under condition that the equality of benefit among them all be preserved.

In the rudest social state, while industry consists in hunting, fishing, and gathering the spontaneous fruits of the earth, private possession of land is not necessary. But as men begin to cultivate the ground and expend their labor in permanent works, private possession of the land on which labor is thus expended is needed to secure the right of property in the products of labor. For who would sow if not assured of the exclusive possession needed to enable him to reap? Who would attach costly works to the soil without such exclusive possession of the soil as would enable him to secure the benefit?

This right of private possession in things created by God is however very different from the right of private ownership in things produced by labor. The one is limited, the other unlimited, save in cases when the dictate of self-preservation terminates all other rights. The purpose of the one, the exclusive possession of land, is merely to secure the other, the exclusive ownership of the products of labor; and it can never rightfully be carried so far as to impair or deny this. While anyone may hold exclusive possession of land so far as it does not interfere with the equal rights of others, he can rightfully hold it no further.

Thus Cain and Abel, were there only two men on earth, might by agreement divide the earth between them. Under this compact each might claim exclusive right to his share as against the other. But neither could rightfully continue such claim against the next man born. For since no one comes into the world without God's permission, his presence attests his equal right to the use of God's bounty. For them to refuse him any use of the earth which they had divided between them would therefore be for them to commit murder. And for them to refuse him any use of the earth, unless by laboring for them or by giving them part of the products of his labor he bought it of them, would be for them to commit theft.

God's laws do not change. Though their applications may alter with altering conditions, the same principles of right and wrong that hold when men are few and industry is rude also hold amid teeming populations and complex industries. In our cities of millions and our states of scores of millions, in a civilization where the division of labor has gone so far that large numbers are hardly conscious that they are land-users, it still remains true that we are all land animals and can live only on land, and that land is God's bounty to all, of which no one can be deprived without being murdered, and for which no one can be compelled to pay another without being robbed. But even in a state of society where the elaboration of industry and the increase of permanent improvements have made the need for private possession of land widespread, there is no difficulty in conforming individual possession with the equal right to land. For as soon as any piece of land will yield to the possessor a larger return than is had by similar labor on other land a value attaches to it which is shown when it is sold or rented. Thus, the value of the land itself, irrespective of the value of any improvements in or on it, always indicates the precise value of the benefit to which all are entitled in its use, as distinguished from the value which, as producer or successor of a producer, belongs to the possessor in individual right.

To combine the advantages of private possession with the justice of common ownership it is only necessary therefore to take for common uses what value attaches to land irrespective of any exertion of labor on it. The principle is the same as in the case referred to, where a human father leaves equally to his children things not susceptible of specific division or common use. In that case such things would be sold or rented and the value equally applied.

It is on this common-sense principle that we, who term ourselves single tax men, would have the community act.

We do not propose to assert equal rights to land by keeping land common, letting any one use any part of it at any time. We do not propose the task, impossible in the present state of society, of dividing land in equal shares; still less the yet more impossible task of keeping it so divided.

We propose — leaving land in the private possession of individuals, with full liberty on their part to give, sell or bequeath it — simply to levy on it for public uses a tax that shall equal the annual value of the land itself, irrespective of the use made of it or the improvements on it. And since this would provide amply for the need of public revenues, we would accompany this tax on land values with the repeal of all taxes now levied on the products and processes of industry — which taxes, since they take from the earnings of labor, we hold to be infringements of the right of property.

This we propose, not as a cunning device of human ingenuity, but as a conforming of human regulations to the will of God.

God cannot contradict Himself nor impose on His creatures laws that clash.

If it be God's command to men that they should not steal — that is to say, that they should respect the right of property which each one has in the fruits of his labor;

And if he be also the Father of all men, who in His common bounty has intended all to have equal opportunities for sharing;

Then, in any possible stage of civilization, however elaborate, there must be some way in which the exclusive right to the products of industry may be reconciled with the equal right to land.

If the Almighty be consistent with Himself, it cannot be, as say those socialists referred to by you, that in order to secure the equal participation of men in the opportunities of life and labor we must ignore the right of private property. Nor yet can it be, as you yourself in the Encyclical seem to argue, that to secure the right of private property we must ignore the equality of right in the opportunities of life and labor. To say the one thing or the other is equally to deny the harmony of God's laws.

But, the private possession of land, subject to the payment to the community of the value of any special advantage thus given to the individual, satisfies both laws, securing to all equal participation in the bounty of the Creator and to each the full ownership of the products of his labor.

Nor do we hesitate to say that this way of securing the equal right to the bounty of the Creator and the exclusive right to the products of labor is the way intended by God for raising public revenues. For we are not atheists, who deny God; nor semi-atheists, who deny that he has any concern in politics and legislation.

It is true as you say — a salutary truth too often forgotten — that "man is older than the state, and he holds the right of providing for the life of his body prior to the formation of any state." Yet, as you too perceive, it is also true that the state is in the divinely appointed order. For He who foresaw all things and provided for all things, foresaw and provided that with the increase of population and the development of industry the organization of human society into states or governments would become both expedient and necessary.

No sooner does the state arise than, as we all know, it needs revenues. This need for revenues is small at first, while population is sparse, industry rude and the functions of the state few and simple. But with growth of population and advance of civilization the functions of the state increase and larger and larger revenues are needed.

Now, He that made the world and placed man in it, He that preordained civilization as the means whereby man might rise to higher powers and become more and more conscious of the works of his Creator, must have foreseen this increasing need for state revenues and have made provision for it. That is to say: The increasing need for public revenues with social advance, being a natural, God-ordained need, there must be a right way of raising them — some way that we can truly say is the way intended by God. It is clear that this right way of raising public revenues must accord with the moral law.

Hence: It must not take from individuals what rightfully belongs to individuals.

It must not give some an advantage over others, as by increasing the prices of what some have to sell and others must buy. It must not lead men into temptation, by requiring trivial oaths, by making it profitable to lie, to swear falsely, to bribe or to take bribes.

It must not confuse the distinctions of right and wrong, and weaken the sanctions of religion and the state by creating crimes that are not sins, and punishing men for doing what in itself they have an undoubted right to do.

It must not repress industry. It must not check commerce. It must not punish thrift. It must offer no impediment to the largest production and the fairest division of wealth.

Let me ask your Holiness to consider the taxes on the processes and products of industry by which through the civilized world public revenues are collected — the *octroi* duties that surround Italian cities with barriers; the monstrous customs duties that hamper intercourse between so-called Christian states; the taxes on occupations, on earnings, on investments, on the building of houses, on the cultivation of fields, on industry and thrift in all forms. Can these be the ways God has intended that governments should raise the means they need? Have any of them the characteristics indispensable in any plan we can deem a right one?

All these taxes violate the moral law. They take by force what belongs to the individual alone; they give to the unscrupulous an advantage over the scrupulous; they have the effect, nay are largely intended, to increase the price of what some have to sell and others must buy; they corrupt government; they make oaths a mockery; they shackle commerce; they fine industry and thrift; they lessen the wealth that men might enjoy, and enrich some by impoverishing others.

Yet what most strikingly shows how opposed to Christianity is this system of raising public revenues is its influence on thought.

Christianity teaches us that all men are brethren; that their true interests are harmonious, not antagonistic. It gives us, as the golden rule of life, that we should do to others as we would have others do to us. But out of the system of taxing the products and processes of labor, and out of its effects in increasing the price of what some have to sell and others must buy, has grown the theory of "protection," which denies this gospel, which holds Christ ignorant of political economy and proclaims laws of national well-being utterly at variance with his teaching. This theory sanctifies national hatreds; it inculcates a universal war of hostile tariffs; it teaches peoples that their prosperity lies in imposing on the productions of other peoples restrictions they do not wish imposed on their own; and instead of the Christian doctrine of man's brotherhood it makes injury of foreigners a civic virtue.

"By their fruits ye shall know them." Can anything more clearly show that to tax the products and processes of industry is not the way God intended public revenues to be raised?

But to consider what we propose — the raising of public revenues by a single tax on the value of land irrespective of improvements — is to see that in all respects this does conform to the moral law.

Let me ask your Holiness to keep in mind that the value we propose to tax, the value of land irrespective of improvements, does not come from any exertion of labor or investment of capital on or in it — the values produced in this way being values of improvement which we would exempt. The value of land irrespective of improvement is the value that attaches to land by reason of increasing population and social progress. This is a value that always goes to the owner as owner, and never does and never can go to the user; for if the user be a different person from the owner he must always pay the owner for it in rent or in purchase-money; while if the user be also the owner, it is as owner, not as user, that he receives it, and by selling or renting the land he can, as owner, continue to receive it after he ceases to be a user.

Thus, taxes on land irrespective of improvement cannot lessen the rewards of industry, nor add to prices,* nor

---

* As to this point it may be well to add that all economists are agreed that taxes on land values irrespective of improvement or use — or what in the terminology of political economy is styled rent, a term distinguished from the ordinary use of the word rent by being applied solely to payments for the use of land itself — must be paid by the owner and cannot be shifted by him on the user. To explain in another way the reason given in the text: Price is not determined by the will of the seller or the will of the buyer, but by the equation of demand and supply, and therefore as to things constantly demanded and constantly produced rests at a point determined by the cost of

in any way take from the individual what belongs to the individual. They can take only the value that attaches to land by the growth of the community, and which therefore belongs to the community as a whole.

To take land values for the state, abolishing all taxes on the products of labor, would therefore leave to the laborer the full produce of labor; to the individual all that rightfully belongs to the individual. It would impose no burden on industry, no check on commerce, no punishment on thrift; it would secure the largest production and the fairest distribution of wealth, by leaving men free to produce and to exchange as they please, without any artificial enhancement of prices; and by taking for public purposes a value that cannot be carried off, that cannot be hidden, that of all values is most easily ascertained and most certainly and cheaply collected, it would enormously lessen the number

---

production — whatever tends to increase the cost of bringing fresh quantities of such articles to the consumer increasing price by checking supply, and whatever tends to reduce such cost decreasing price by increasing supply. Thus taxes on wheat or tobacco or cloth add to the price that the consumer must pay, and thus the cheapening in the cost of producing steel which improved processes have made in recent years has greatly reduced the price of steel. But land has no cost of production, since it is created by God, not produced by man. Its price therefore is fixed: 1 (monopoly rent), where land is held in close monopoly, by what the owners can extract from the users under penalty of deprivation and consequently of starvation, and amounts to all that common labor can earn on it beyond what is necessary to life; 2 (economic rent proper), where there is no special monopoly, by what the particular land will yield to common labor over and above what may be had by like expenditure and exertion on land having no special advantage and for which no rent is paid; and, 3 (speculative rent, which is a species of monopoly rent, telling particularly in selling price), by the expectation of future increase of value from social growth and improvement, which expectation causing landowners to withhold land at present prices has the same effect as combination.

Taxes on land values or economic rent can therefore never

of officials, dispense with oaths, do away with temptations to bribery and evasion, and abolish man-made crimes in themselves innocent.

But, further: That God has intended the state to obtain the revenues it needs by the taxation of land values is shown by the same order and degree of evidence that shows that God has intended the milk of the mother for the nourishment of the babe.

See how close is the analogy. In that primitive condition ere the need for the state arises there are no land values. The products of labor have value, but in the sparsity of population no value as yet attaches to land itself. But as increasing density of population and increasing elaboration of industry necessitate the organization of the state, with its need for revenues, value begins to attach to land. As population still increases and industry grows more elaborate, so the needs for public revenues increase. And at the same time and from the same causes land values increase. The connection is invariable. The value of things produced by labor tends to decline with social development, since the larger scale of production and the improvement of processes

---

be shifted by the landowner to the land-user, since they in no wise increase the demand for land or enable landowners to check supply by withholding land from use. Where rent depends on mere monopolization, a case I mention because rent may in this way be demanded for the use of land even before economic or natural rent arises, the taking by taxation of what the landowners were able to extort from labor could not enable them to extort any more, since laborers, if not left enough to live on, will die. So, in the case of economic rent proper, to take from the landowners the premiums they receive, would in no way increase the superiority of their land and the demand for it. While, so far as price is affected by speculative rent, to compel the landowners to pay taxes on the value of land whether they were getting any income from it or not, would make it more difficult for them to withhold land from use; and to tax the full value would not merely destroy the power but the desire to do so.

tend steadily to reduce their cost. But the value of land on which population centers goes up and up. Take Rome or Paris or London or New York or Melbourne. Consider the enormous value of land in such cities as compared with the value of land in sparsely settled parts of the same countries. To what is this due? Is it not due to the density and activity of the populations of those cities — to the very causes that require great public expenditure for streets, drains, public buildings, and all the many things needed for the health, convenience and safety of such great cities? See how with the growth of such cities the one thing that steadily increases in value is land; how the opening of roads, the building of railways, the making of any public improvement, adds to the value of land. Is it not clear that here is a natural law — that is to say a tendency willed by the Creator? Can it mean anything else than that He who ordained the state with its needs has in the values which attach to land provided the means to meet those needs?

That it does mean this and nothing else is confirmed if we look deeper still, and inquire not merely as to the intent, but as to the purpose of the intent. If we do so we may see in this natural law by which land values increase with the growth of society not only such a perfectly adapted provision for the needs of society as gratifies our intellectual perceptions by showing us the wisdom of the Creator, but a purpose with regard to the individual that gratifies our moral perceptions by opening to us a glimpse of His beneficence.

Consider: Here is a natural law by which as society advances the one thing that increases in value is land — a natural law by virtue of which all growth of population, all advance of the arts, all general improvements of whatever kind, add to a fund that both the commands of justice and the dictates of expediency prompt us to take for the common uses of society. Now, since increase in the fund available for the common uses of society is increase in the gain that goes equally to each member of society, is it not clear that the law by which land values increase with social advance while the value of the products of labor does not increase, tends with the advance of civilization to make the share that goes equally to each member of society more and more important as compared with what goes to him from his individual earnings, and thus to make the advance of civilization lessen relatively the differences that in a ruder social state must exist between the strong and the weak, the fortunate and the unfortunate? Does it not show the purpose of the Creator to be that the advance of man in civilization should be an advance not merely to larger powers but to a greater and greater equality, instead of what we, by our ignoring of his intent, are making it, an advance toward a more and more monstrous inequality?

That the value attaching to land with social growth is intended for social needs is shown by the final proof. God is indeed a jealous God in the sense that nothing but injury and disaster can attend the effort of men to do things other than in the way he has intended; in the sense that where the blessings he proffers to men are refused or misused they turn to evils that scourge us. And just as for the mother to withhold the provision that fills her breast with the birth of the child is to endanger physical health, so for society to refuse to take for social uses the provision intended for them is to breed social disease.

For refusal to take for public purposes the increasing values that attach to land with social growth is to necessitate the getting of public revenues by taxes that lessen production, distort distribution and corrupt society. It is to leave some to take what justly belongs to all; it is to forego the only means by which it is possible in an advanced civilization to combine the security of possession that is necessary to improvement with the equality of natural opportunity that is the most important of all natural rights. It is thus at the basis of all social life to set up an unjust inequality between man and man, compelling some to pay others for the privilege of living, for the chance of working, for the advantages of civilization, for the gifts of their God. But it is even more than this. The very robbery that the masses of men thus suffer gives rise in advancing communities to a new robbery. For the value that with the increase of population and social advance attaches to land being suffered to go to individuals who have secured ownership of the land, it prompts to a forestalling of and speculation in land wherever there is any prospect of advancing population or of coming improvement, thus producing an artificial scarcity of the natural elements of life and labor, and a strangulation of production that shows itself in recurring spasms of industrial depression as disastrous to the world as destructive wars. It is this that is driving men from the old countries to the new countries, only to bring there the same curses. It is this that causes our material advance not merely to fail to improve the condition of the mere worker, but to make the condition of large classes positively worse. It is this that in our richest Christian countries is giving us a large population whose lives are harder, more hopeless, more degraded than those of the veriest savages. It is this that leads so many men to think that God is a bungler and is constantly bringing more people into his world than he has made provision for; or that there is no God, and that belief in him is a superstition which the facts of life and the advance of science are dispelling.

The darkness in light, the weakness in strength, the poverty amid wealth, the seething discontent foreboding civil strife, that characterize our civilization of today, are the natural, the inevitable results of our rejection of God's beneficence, of our ignoring of his intent. Were we on the other hand to follow His clear, simple rule of right, leaving scrupulously to the individual all that individual labor produces, and taking for the community the value that attaches to land by the growth of the community itself, not merely could evil modes of raising public revenues be dispensed with, but all men would be placed on an equal level of opportunity with regard to the bounty of their Creator, on an equal level of opportunity to exert their labor and to enjoy its fruits. And then, without drastic or restrictive measures, the forestalling of land would cease. For then the possession of land would mean only security for the permanence of its use, and there would be no object for any one to get land or to keep land except for use; nor would his possession of better land than others had confer any unjust advantage on him, or unjust deprivation on them, since the equivalent of the advantage would be taken by the state for the benefit of all.

The Right Reverend Dr. Thomas Nulty, Bishop of Meath, who sees all this as clearly as we do, in pointing out to the clergy and laity of his diocese* the design of Divine Providence that the rent of land should be taken for the community, says:

> I think, therefore, that I may fairly infer, on the strength of authority as well as of reason, that the people are and always must be the real owners of the land of their country. This great social fact appears to me to be of incalculable importance, and it is fortunate, indeed, that on the strictest principles of justice it is not clouded even by a shadow of uncertainty or doubt. There is, moreover, a charm and a peculiar beauty in the clearness with which it reveals the wisdom and the benevolence of the designs of Providence in the admirable provision he has made for the wants and the necessities of that state of social existence of which he is

---

* Letter addressed to the Clergy and Laity of the Diocese of Meath, Ireland, April 2, 1881.

author, and in which the very instincts of nature tell us we are to spend our lives. A vast public property, a great national fund, has been placed under the dominion and at the disposal of the nation to supply itself abundantly with resources necessary to liquidate the expenses of its government, the administration of its laws and the education of its youth, and to enable it to provide for the suitable sustentation and support of its criminal and pauper population. One of the most interesting peculiarities of this property is that its value is never stationary; it is constantly progressive and increasing in a direct ratio to the growth of the population, and the very causes that increase and multiply the demands made on it increase proportionately its ability to meet them.

There is, indeed, as Bishop Nulty says, a peculiar beauty in the clearness with which the wisdom and benevolence of Providence are revealed in this great social fact, the provision made for the common needs of society in what economists call the law of rent. Of all the evidence that natural religion gives, it is this that most clearly shows the existence of a beneficent God, and most conclusively silences the doubts that in our days lead so many to materialism.

For in this beautiful provision made by natural law for the social needs of civilization we see that God has intended civilization; that all our discoveries and inventions do not and cannot outrun his forethought, and that steam, electricity and labor-saving appliances only make the great moral laws clearer and more important. In the growth of this great fund, increasing with social advance — a fund that accrues from the growth of the community and belongs therefore to the community — we see not only that there is no need for the taxes that lessen wealth, that engender corruption that promote inequality and teach men to deny the gospel; but that to take this fund for the purpose for which it was evidently intended would in the highest civilization secure to all the equal enjoyment of God's bounty, the abundant opportunity to satisfy their wants, and would provide amply for every legitimate need of the state. We see that God in His dealings with men has not been a bungler or a niggard; that He has not brought too many men into the world; that He has not neglected abundantly to supply them; that He has not intended that bitter competition of the masses for a mere animal existence and that monstrous aggregation of wealth which characterize our civilization; but that these evils which lead so many to say there is no God, or yet more impiously to say that they are of God's ordering, are due to our denial of his moral law. We see that the law of justice, the law of the Golden Rule, is not a mere counsel of perfection, but indeed the law of social life. We see that if we were only to observe it there would be work for all, leisure for all, abundance for all; and that civilization would tend to give to the poorest not only necessaries, but all comforts and reasonable luxuries as well. We see that Christ was not a mere dreamer when he told men that if they would seek the kingdom of God and its right-doing they might no more worry about material things than do the lilies of the field about their raiment; but that he was only declaring what political economy in the light of modern discovery shows to be a sober truth.

Your Holiness, even to see this is deep and lasting joy. For it is to see for one's self that there is a God who lives and reigns, and that He is a God of justice and love — Our Father who art in Heaven. It is to open a rift of sunlight through the clouds of our darker questionings, and to make the faith that trusts where it cannot see a living thing.

II.

YOUR HOLINESS will see from the explanation I have given that the reform we propose, like all true reforms, has both an ethical and an economic side. By ignoring the ethical side, and pushing our proposal merely as a reform of taxation, we could avoid the objections that arise from confounding ownership with possession and attributing to private property in land that security of use and improvement that can be had even better without it. All that we seek practically is the legal abolition, as fast as possible, of taxes on the products and processes of labor, and the consequent concentration of taxation on land values irrespective of improvements. To put our proposals in this way would be to urge them merely as a matter of wise public expediency.

There are indeed many single-tax men who do put our proposals in this way; who seeing the beauty of our plan from a fiscal standpoint do not concern themselves further. But to those who think as I do, the ethical is the more important side. Not only do we not wish to evade the question of private property in land, but to us it seems that the beneficent and far-reaching revolution we aim at is too great a thing to be accomplished by "intelligent self-interest," and can be carried by nothing less than the religious conscience.

Hence we earnestly seek the judgment of religion. This is the tribunal of which your Holiness as the head of the largest body of Christians is the most august representative.

It therefore behooves us to examine the reasons you urge in support of private property in land — if they be sound to accept them, and if they be not sound respectfully to point out to you wherein is their error.

To your proposition that "Our first and most fundamental principle when we undertake to alleviate the condition of the masses must be the inviolability of private property" we would joyfully agree if we could only understand you to have in mind the moral element, and to mean rightful private property, as when you speak of marriage as ordained by God's authority we may understand an implied exclusion of improper marriages. Unfortunately, however, other expressions show that you mean private property in general and have expressly in mind private property in land. This confusion of thought, this non-distribution of terms, runs through your whole argument, leading you to conclusions so unwarranted by your premises as to be utterly repugnant to them, as when from the moral sanction of private property in the things produced by labor you infer something entirely different and utterly opposed, a similar right of property in the land created by God.

Private property is not of one species, and moral sanction can no more be asserted universally of it than of marriage. That proper marriage conforms to the law of God does not justify the polygamic or polyandric or incestuous marriages that are in some countries permitted by the civil law. And as there may be immoral marriage so may there be immoral private property. Private property is that which may be held in ownership by an individual, or that which may be held in ownership by an individual with the sanction of the state. The mere lawyer, the mere servant of the state, may rest here, refusing to distinguish between what the state holds equally lawful. Your Holiness, however, is not a servant of the state, but a servant of God, a guardian of morals. You know, as said by St. Thomas of Aquin, that—

> *Human law is law only in virtue of its accordance with right reason and it is thus manifest that it flows from the eternal law. And in so far as it deviates from right reason it is called an unjust law.* IN SUCH CASE IT IS NOT LAW AT ALL, BUT RATHER A SPECIES OF VIOLENCE.

Thus, that any species of property is permitted by the state does not of itself give it moral sanction. The state has often made things property that are not justly property, but involve violence and robbery. For instance, the things of religion, the dignity and authority of offices of the church, the power of administering her sacraments and controlling her temporalities, have often by profligate princes been given as salable property to courtiers and concubines. At this very day in England an atheist or a heathen may buy in open market, and hold as legal property, to be sold, given or bequeathed as he pleases, the power of appointing to the cure of souls, and the value of these legal rights of presentation is said to be no less than £17,000,000.

Or again: Slaves were universally treated as property by the customs and laws of the classical nations, and were so acknowledged in Europe long after the acceptance of Christianity. At the beginning of this century there was no Christian nation that did not, in her colonies at least, recognize property in slaves, and slave ships crossed the seas under Christian flags. In the United States, little more than thirty years ago, to buy a man gave the same legal ownership as to buy a horse, and in Mohammedan countries law and custom yet make the slave the property of his captor or purchaser.

Yet your Holiness, one of the glories of whose pontificate is the attempt to break up slavery in its last strongholds, will not contend that the moral sanction that attaches to property in things produced by labor can, or ever could, apply to property in slaves.

Your use, in so many passages of your Encyclical, of the inclusive term "property" or "private" property, of which in morals nothing can be either affirmed or denied, makes your meaning, if we take isolated sentences, in many places ambiguous. But reading it as a whole, there can be no doubt of your intention that private property in land shall be understood when you speak merely of private property. With this interpretation, I find that the reasons you urge for private property in land are eight. Let us consider them in order of presentation. You urge:

1. *That what is bought with rightful property is rightful property.* (5.)*

Clearly, purchase and sale cannot give, but can only transfer ownership. Property that in itself has no moral sanction does not obtain moral sanction by passing from seller to buyer.

If right reason does not make the slave the property of the slave-hunter it does not make him the property of the slave-buyer. Yet your reasoning as to private property in land would as well justify property in slaves. To show this it is only needful to change in your argument the word land to the word slave. It would then read:

> *It is surely undeniable that, when a man engages in remunerative labor, the very reason and motive of his work is to obtain property, and to hold it as his own private possession.*
>
> *If one man hires out to another his strength or his industry, he does this for the purpose of receiving in return what is necessary for food and living; he thereby expressly proposes to acquire a full and legal right, not only to the remuneration, but also to the disposal of that remuneration as he pleases.*
>
> *Thus, if he lives sparingly, saves money, and invests his savings, for greater security, in a slave, the slave in such a case is only his wages in another form; and consequently, a workingman's slave thus purchased should be as completely at his own disposal as the wages he receives for his labor.*

Nor in turning your argument for private property in land into an argument for private property in men am I doing a new thing. In my own country, in my own time, this very argument, that purchase gave ownership, was the common defense of slavery. It was made by statesmen, by

---

* To facilitate references the paragraphs of the Encyclical are indicated by number.

jurists, by clergymen, by bishops; it was accepted over the whole country by the great mass of the people. By it was justified the separation of wives from husbands, of children from parents, the compelling of labor, the appropriation of its fruits, the buying and selling of Christians by Christians. In language almost identical with yours it was asked, "Here is a poor man who has worked hard, lived sparingly, and invested his savings in a few slaves. Would you rob him of his earnings by liberating those slaves?" Or it was said: "Here is a poor widow; all her husband has been able to leave her is a few negroes, the earnings of his hard toil. Would you rob the widow and the orphan by freeing these negroes?" And because of this perversion of reason, this confounding of unjust property rights with just property rights, this acceptance of man's law as though it were God's law, there came on our nation a judgment of fire and blood.

The error of our people in thinking that what in itself was not rightfully property could become rightful property by purchase and sale is the same error into which your Holiness falls. It is not merely formally the same; it is essentially the same. Private property in land, no less than private property in slaves, is a violation of the true rights of property. They are different forms of the same robbery; twin devices by which the perverted ingenuity of man has sought to enable the strong and the cunning to escape God's requirement of labor by forcing it on others.

What difference does it make whether I merely own the land on which another man must live or own the man himself? Am I not in the one case as much his master as in the other? Can I not compel him to work for me? Can I not take to myself as much of the fruits of his labor; as fully dictate his actions? Have I not over him the power of life and death? For to deprive a man of land is as certainly to kill him as to deprive him of blood by opening his veins, or of air by tightening a halter around his neck.

The essence of slavery is in empowering one man to obtain the labor of another without recompense. Private property in land does this as fully as chattel slavery. The slave-owner must leave to the slave enough of his earnings to enable him to live. Are there not in so-called free countries great bodies of working men who get no more? How much more of the fruits of their toil do the agricultural laborers of Italy and England get than did the slaves of our Southern States? Did not private property in land permit the landowner of Europe in ruder times to demand the *jus primæ noctis?* Does not the same last outrage exist today in diffused form in the immorality born of monstrous wealth on the one hand and ghastly poverty on the other?

In what did the slavery of Russia consist but in giving to the master land on which the serf was forced to live? When an Ivan or a Catherine enriched their favorites with the labor of others they did not give men, they gave land. And when the appropriation of land has gone so far that no free land remains to which the landless man may turn, then without further violence the more insidious form of labor robbery involved in private property in land takes the place of chattel slavery, because more economical and convenient. For under it the slave does not have to be caught or held, or to be fed when not needed. He comes of himself, begging the privilege of serving, and when no longer wanted can be discharged. The lash is unnecessary; hunger is as efficacious. This is why the Norman conquerors of England and the English conquerors of Ireland did not divide up the people, but divided the land. This is why European slave-ships took their cargoes to the New World, not to Europe.

Slavery is not yet abolished. Though in all Christian countries its ruder form has now gone, it still exists in the heart of our civilization in more insidious form, and is increasing. There is work to be done for the glory of God and the liberty of man by other soldiers of the cross than those warrior monks whom, with the blessing of your Holiness, Cardinal Lavigerie is sending into the Sahara. Yet, your Encyclical employs in defense of one form of slavery the same fallacies that the apologists for chattel slavery used in defense of the other!

The Arabs are not wanting in acumen. Your Encyclical reaches far. What shall your warrior monks say, if when at the muzzle of their rifles they demand of some Arab slave-merchant his miserable caravan, he shall declare that he bought them with his savings, and producing a copy of your Encyclical, shall prove by your reasoning that his slaves are consequently "only his wages in another form," and ask if they who bear your blessing and own your authority propose to "deprive him of the liberty of disposing of his wages and thus of all hope and possibility of increasing his stock and bettering his condition in life"?

2. *That private property in land proceeds from man's gift of reason.* (6-7.)

In the second place your Holiness argues that man possessing reason and forethought may not only acquire ownership of the fruits of the earth, but also of the earth itself, so that out of its products he may make provision for the future.

Reason, with its attendant forethought, is indeed the distinguishing attribute of man; that which raises him above the brute, and shows, as the Scriptures declare, that he is created in the likeness of God. And this gift of reason does, as your Holiness points out, involve the need and right of private property in whatever is produced by the exertion of reason and its attendant forethought, as well as in what is produced by physical labor. In truth, these elements of man's production are inseparable, and labor involves the use of reason. It is by his reason that man differs from the animals in being a producer, and in this sense a maker. Of themselves his physical powers are slight, forming as it were but the connection by which the mind takes hold of material things, so as to utilize to its will the matter and forces of nature. It is mind, the intelligent reason, that is the prime mover in labor, the essential agent in production.

The right of private ownership does therefore indisputably attach to things provided by man's reason and forethought. But it cannot attach to things provided by the reason and forethought of God!

To illustrate: Let us suppose a company traveling through the desert as the Israelites traveled from Egypt. Such of them as had the forethought to provide themselves with vessels of water would acquire a just right of property in the water so carried, and in the thirst of the waterless desert those who had neglected to provide themselves, though they might ask water from the provident in charity, could not demand it in right. For while water itself is of the providence of God, the presence of this water in such vessels, at such place, results from the providence of the men who carried it. Thus they have to it an exclusive right.

But suppose others use their forethought in pushing ahead and appropriating the springs, refusing when their fellows come up to let them drink of the water save as they buy it of them. Would such forethought give any right?

Your Holiness, it is not the forethought of carrying water where it is needed, but the forethought of seizing springs, that you seek to defend in defending the private ownership of land!

Let me show this more fully, since it may be worth while to meet those who say that if private property in land be not just, then private property in the products of labor is not just, as the material of these products is taken from land. It will be seen on consideration that all of man's production is analogous to such transportation of water as we have supposed. In growing grain, or smelting metals, or building houses, or weaving cloth, or doing any of the things that constitute producing, all that man does is to change in place or form preexisting matter. As a producer man is merely a changer, not a creator; God alone creates. And since the changes in which man's production consists inhere in matter so long as they persist, the right of private ownership attaches the accident to the essence, and gives the right of ownership in that natural material in which the labor of production is embodied. Thus water, which in its original form and place is the common gift of God to all men, when drawn from its natural reservoir and brought into the desert, passes rightfully into the ownership of the individual who by changing its place has produced it there.

But such right of ownership is in reality a mere right of temporary possession. For though man may take material from the storehouse of nature and change it in place or form to suit his desires, yet from the moment he takes it, it tends back to that storehouse again. Wood decays, iron rusts, stone disintegrates and is displaced, while of more perishable products, some will last for only a few months, others for only a few days, and some disappear immediately on use. Though, so far as we can see, matter is eternal and force forever persists; though we can neither annihilate nor create the tiniest mote that floats in a sunbeam or the faintest impulse that stirs a leaf, yet in the ceaseless flux of nature, man's work of moving and combining constantly passes away. Thus the recognition of the ownership of what natural material is embodied in the products of man never constitutes more than temporary possession — never interferes with the reservoir provided for all. As taking water from one place and carrying it to another place by no means lessens the store of water, since whether it is drunk or spilled or left to evaporate, it must return again to the natural reservoirs — so is it with all things on which man in production can lay the impress of his labor.

Hence, when you say that man's reason puts it within his right to have in stable and permanent possession not only things that perish in the using, but also those that remain for use in the future, you are right in so far as you may include such things as buildings, which with repair will last for generations, with such things as food or firewood, which are destroyed in the use. But when you infer that man can have private ownership in those permanent things of nature that are the reservoirs from which all must draw, you are clearly wrong. Man may indeed hold in private ownership the fruits of the earth produced by his labor, since they lose in time the impress of that labor, and pass again into the natural reservoirs from which they were taken, and thus the ownership of them by one works no injury to others. But he cannot so own the earth itself, for that is the reservoir from which must constantly be drawn not only the material with which alone men can produce, but even their very bodies.

The conclusive reason why man cannot claim ownership in the earth itself as he can in the fruits that he by labor brings forth from it, is in the facts stated by you in the very next paragraph (7), when you truly say:

> Man's needs do not die out, but recur; satisfied today, they demand new supplies tomorrow. Nature, therefore, owes to man a storehouse that shall never fail, the daily supply of his daily wants. And this he finds only in the inexhaustible fertility of the earth.

By man you mean all men. Can what nature owes to all men be made the private property of some men, from which they may debar all other men?

Let me dwell on the words of your Holiness, "Nature, therefore, owes to man a storehouse that shall never fail." By Nature you mean God. Thus your thought, that in creating us, God himself has incurred an obligation to provide us with a storehouse that shall never fail, is the same as is thus expressed and carried to its irresistible conclusion by the Bishop of Meath:

> God was perfectly free in the act by which He created us; but having created us he bound himself by that act to provide us with the means necessary for our subsistence. The land is the only source of this kind now known to us. The land, therefore, of every country is the common property of the people of that country, because its real owner, the Creator who made it, has transferred it as a voluntary gift to them. "Terram autem dedit filiis hominum." Now, as every individual in that country is a creature and child of God, and as all his creatures are equal in his sight, any settlement of the land of a country that would exclude the humblest man in that country from his share of the common inheritance would be not only an injustice and a wrong to that man, but, moreover, be AN IMPIOUS RESISTANCE TO THE BENEVOLEBT INTENTIONS OF HIS CREATOR.

3. *That private property in land deprives no one of the use of land.* (8.)

Your own statement that land is the inexhaustible storehouse that God owes to man must have aroused in your Holiness's mind an uneasy questioning of its appropriation as private property, for, as though to reassure yourself, you proceed to argue that its ownership by some will not injure others. You say in substance, that even though divided among private owners the earth does not cease to minister to the needs of all, since those who do not possess the soil can by selling their labor obtain in payment the produce of the land.

Suppose that to your Holiness as a judge of morals one should put this case of conscience:

I am one of several children to whom our father left a field abundant for our support. As he assigned no part of it to any one of us in particular, leaving the limits of our separate possession to be fixed by ourselves, I being the eldest took the whole field in exclusive ownership. But in doing so I have not deprived my brothers of their support from it, for I have let them work for me on it, paying them from the produce as much wages as I would have had to pay strangers. Is there any reason why my conscience should not be clear?

What would be your answer? Would you not tell him that he was in mortal sin, and that his excuse added to his guilt? Would you not call on him to make restitution and to do penance?

Or, suppose that as a temporal prince your Holiness were ruler of a rainless land, such as Egypt, where there were no springs or brooks, their want being supplied by a bountiful river like the Nile. Supposing that having sent a number of your subjects to make fruitful this land, bidding them do justly and prosper, you were told that some of them had set up a claim of ownership in the river, refusing the others a drop of water, except as they bought it of them; and that thus they had become rich without work, while the others, though working hard, were so impoverished by paying for water as to be hardly able to exist?

Would not your indignation wax hot when this was told?

Suppose that then the river-owners should send to you and thus excuse their action: The river, though divided among private owners, ceases not thereby to minister to the needs of all, for there is no one who drinks who does not drink of the water of the river. Those who do not possess the water of the river contribute their labor to get it; so that it may be truly said that all water is supplied either from one's own river, or from some laborious industry which is paid for either in the water, or in that which is exchanged for the water.

Would the indignation of your Holiness be abated? Would it not wax fiercer yet for the insult to your intelligence of this excuse?

I do not need more formally to show your Holiness

that between utterly depriving a man of God's gifts and
depriving him of God's gifts unless he will buy them, is
merely the difference between the robber who leaves his
victim to die and the robber who puts him to ransom. But
I would like to point out how your statement that "the earth,
though divided among private owners, ceases not thereby
to minister to the needs of all" overlooks the largest facts.

From your palace of the Vatican the eye may rest on the
expanse of the *Campagna*, where the pious toil of religious
congregations and the efforts of the state are only now beginning to make it possible for men to live. Once that expanse was tilled by thriving husbandmen and dotted with
smiling hamlets. What for centuries has condemned it to
desertion? History tells us. It was private property in land;
the growth of the great estates of which Pliny saw that ancient Italy was perishing; the cause that, by bringing failure
to the crop of men, let in the Goths and Vandals, gave Roman Britain to the worship of Odin and Thor, and in what
were once the rich and populous provinces of the East shiv-
ered the thinned ranks and palsied arms of the legions on
the scimitars of Mohammedan hordes, and in the sepul-
cher of our Lord and in the Church of St. Sophia trampled
the cross to rear the crescent!

If you will go to Scotland, you may see great tracts that
under the Gaelic tenure, which recognized the right of each
to a foothold in the soil, bred sturdy men, but that now,
under the recognition of private property in land, are given
up to wild animals. If you go to Ireland, your Bishops will
show you, on lands where now only beasts graze, the traces
of hamlets that, when they were young priests, were filled
with honest, kindly, religious people.*

---

* "Let any one who wishes visit this diocese and see with his own
eyes the vast and boundless extent of the fairest land in Europe that
has been ruthlessly depopulated since the commencement of the

If you will come to the United States, you will find in a land wide enough and rich enough to support in comfort the whole population of Europe, the growth of a sentiment that looks with evil eye on immigration, because the artificial scarcity that results from private property in land makes it seem as if there is not room enough and work enough for those already here.

Or go to the Antipodes, and in Australia, as in England, you may see that private property in land is operating to leave the land barren and to crowd the bulk of the population into great cities. Go wherever you please where the forces loosed by modern invention are beginning to be felt and you may see that private property in land is the curse, denounced by the prophet, that prompts men to lay field to field till they "alone dwell in the midst of the earth."

To the mere materialist this is sin and shame. Shall we to whom this world is God's world — we who hold that man is called to this life only as a prelude to a higher life — shall we defend it?

4. *That Industry expended on land gives ownership in the land itself.* (9-10.)

Your Holiness next contends that industry expended on land gives a right to ownership of the land, and that the improvement of land creates benefits indistinguishable and inseparable from the land itself.

This contention, if valid, could only justify the ownership of land by those who expend industry on it. It would not justify private property in land as it exists. On the con-

---

present century, and which is now abandoned to a loneliness and solitude more depressing than that of the prairie or the wilderness. Thus has this land system actually exercised the power of life and death on a vast scale, for which there is no parallel even in the dark records of slavery." — *Bishop Nulty's Letter to the Clergy and Laity of the Diocese of Meath.*

trary, it would justify a gigantic no-rent declaration that would take land from those who now legally own it, the landlords, and turn it over to the tenants and laborers. And if it also be that improvements cannot be distinguished and separated from the land itself, how could the landlords claim consideration even for improvements they had made?

But your Holiness cannot mean what your words imply. What you really mean, I take it, is that the original justification and title of landownership is in the expenditure of labor on it. But neither can this justify private property in land as it exists. For is it not all but universally true that existing land titles do not come from use, but from force or fraud?

Take Italy! Is it not true that the greater part of the land of Italy is held by those who so far from ever having expended industry on it have been mere appropriators of the industry of those who have? Is this not also true of Great Britain and of other countries? Even in the United States, where the forces of concentration have not yet had time fully to operate and there has been some attempt to give land to users, it is probably true today that the greater part of the land is held by those who neither use it nor propose to use it themselves, but merely hold it to compel others to pay them for permission to use it.

And if industry give ownership to land what are the limits of this ownership? If a man may acquire the ownership of several square miles of land by grazing sheep on it, does this give to him and his heirs the ownership of the same land when it is found to contain rich mines, or when by the growth of population and the progress of society it is needed for farming, for gardening, for the close occupation of a great city? Is it on the rights given by the industry of those who first used it for grazing cows or growing potatoes that you would found the title to the land now covered by the city of New York and having a value of thousands of millions of dollars?

But your contention is not valid. Industry expended on land gives ownership in the fruits of that industry, but not in the land itself, just as industry expended on the ocean would give a right of ownership to the fish taken by it, but not a right of ownership in the ocean. Nor yet is it true that private ownership of land is necessary to secure the fruits of labor on land; nor does the improvement of land create benefits indistinguishable and inseparable from the land itself. That secure possession is necessary to the use and improvement of land I have already explained, but that ownership is not necessary is shown by the fact that in all civilized countries land owned by one person is cultivated and improved by other persons. Most of the cultivated land in the British Islands, as in Italy and other countries, is cultivated not by owners but by tenants. And so the costliest buildings are erected by those who are not owners of the land, but who have from the owner a mere right of possession for a time on condition of certain payments. Nearly the whole of London has been built in this way, and in New York, Chicago, Denver, San Francisco, Sydney and Melbourne, as well as in continental cities, the owners of many of the largest edifices will be found to be different persons from the owners of the ground. So far from the value of improvements being inseparable from the value of land, it is in individual transactions constantly separated. For instance, one-half of the land on which the immense Grand Pacific Hotel in Chicago stands was recently separately sold, and in Ceylon it is a not infrequent occurrence for one person to own a fruit-tree and another to own the ground in which it is planted.

There is, indeed, no improvement of land, whether it be clearing, plowing, manuring, cultivating, the digging of cellars, the opening of wells or the building of houses, that so long as its usefulness continues does not have a value clearly distinguishable from the value of the land. For land having such improvements will always sell or rent for more than similar land without them.

If, therefore, the state levy a tax equal to what the land irrespective of improvement would bring, it will take the benefits of mere ownership, but will leave the full benefits of use and improvement, which the prevailing system does not do. And since the holder, who would still in form continue to be the owner, could at any time give or sell both possession and improvements, subject to future assessment by the state on the value of the land alone, he will be perfectly free to retain or dispose of the full amount of property that the exertion of his labor or the investment of his capital has attached to or stored up in the land.

Thus, what we propose would secure, as it is impossible in any other way to secure, what you properly say is just and right — "that the results of labor should belong to him who has labored." But private property in land — to allow the holder without adequate payment to the state to take for himself the benefit of the value that attaches to land with social growth and improvement — does take the results of labor from him who has labored, does turn over the fruits of one man's labor to be enjoyed by another. For labor, as the active factor, is the producer of all wealth. Mere ownership produces nothing. A man might own a world, but so sure is the decree that "by the sweat of thy brow shalt thou eat bread," that without labor he could not get a meal or provide himself a garment. Hence, when the owners of land, by virtue of their ownership, and without laboring themselves, get the products of labor in abundance, these things must come from the labor of others, must be the fruits of others' sweat, taken from those who have a right to them and enjoyed by those who have no right to them.

The only utility of private ownership of land as distinguished from possession is the evil utility of giving to the owner products of labor he does not earn. For until land will yield to its owner some return beyond that of the labor and capital he expends on it — that is to say, until by sale or rental he can without expenditure of labor obtain from it products of labor, ownership amounts to no more than security of possession, and has no value. Its importance and value begin only when, either in the present or prospectively, it will yield a revenue — that is to say, will enable the owner, as owner, to obtain products of labor without exertion on his part, and thus to enjoy the results of others' labor.

What largely keeps men from realizing the robbery involved in private property in land is that in the most striking cases the robbery is not of individuals, but of the community. For, as I have before explained, it is impossible for rent in the economic sense — that value which attaches to land by reason of social growth and improvement — to go to the user. It can go only to the owner or to the community. Thus those who pay enormous rents for the use of land in such centers as London or New York are not individually injured. Individually they get a return for what they pay, and must feel that they have no better right to the use of such peculiarly advantageous localities without paying for it than have thousands of others. And so, not thinking or not caring for the interests of the community, they make no objection to the system.

It recently came to light in New York that a man having no title whatever had been for years collecting rents on a piece of land that the growth of the city had made very valuable. Those who paid these rents had never stopped to ask whether he had any right to them. They felt that they had no right to land that so many others would like to have, without paying for it, and did not think of, or did not care for, the rights of all.

5. *That private property in land has the support of the common opinion of mankind, and has conduced to peace and tran-*

quillity, and that it is sanctioned by Divine Law. (11.)

Even were it true that the common opinion of mankind has sanctioned private property in land, this would no more prove its justice than the once universal practice of the known world would have proved the justice of slavery.

But it is not true. Examination will show that wherever we can trace them the first perceptions of mankind have always recognized the equality of right to land, and that when individual possession became necessary to secure the right of ownership in things produced by labor some method of securing equality, sufficient in the existing state of social development, was adopted. Thus, among some peoples, land used for cultivation was periodically divided, land used for pasturage and wood being held in common. Among others, every family was permitted to hold what land it needed for a dwelling and for cultivation, but the moment that such use and cultivation stopped any one else could step in and take it on like tenure. Of the same nature were the land laws of the Mosaic code. The land, first fairly divided among the people, was made inalienable by the provision of the jubilee, under which, if sold, it reverted every fiftieth year to the children of its original possessors.

Private property in land as we know it, the attaching to land of the same right of ownership that justly attaches to the products of labor, has never grown up anywhere save by usurpation or force. Like slavery, it is the result of war. It comes to us of the modern world from your ancestors, the Romans, whose civilization it corrupted and whose empire it destroyed.

It made with the freer spirit of the northern peoples the combination of the feudal system, in which, though subordination was substituted for equality, there was still a rough recognition of the principle of common rights in land. A fief was a trust, and to enjoyment was annexed some obligation. The sovereign, the representative of the whole people, was the only owner of land. Of him, immediately or mediately, held tenants, whose possession involved duties or payments, which, though rudely and imperfectly, embodied the idea that we would carry out in the single tax, of taking land values for public uses. The crown lands maintained the sovereign and the civil list; the church lands defrayed the cost of public worship and instruction, of the relief of the sick, the destitute and the wayworn; while the military tenures provided for public defense and bore the costs of war. A fourth and very large portion of the land remained in common, the people of the neighborhood being free to pasture it, cut wood on it, or put it to other common uses.

In this partial yet substantial recognition of common rights to land is to be found the reason why, in a time when the industrial arts were rude, wars frequent, and the great discoveries and inventions of our time unthought of, the condition of the laborer was devoid of that grinding poverty which despite our marvelous advances now exists. Speaking of England, the highest authority on such subjects, the late Professor Thorold Rogers, declares that in the thirteenth century there was no class so poor, so helpless, so pressed and degraded as are millions of Englishmen in our boasted nineteenth century; and that, save in times of actual famine, there was no laborer so poor as to fear that his wife and children might come to want even were he taken from them. Dark and rude in many respects as they were, these were the times when the cathedrals and churches and religious houses whose ruins yet excite our admiration were built; the times when England had no national debt, no poor law, no standing army, no hereditary paupers, no thousands and thousands of human beings rising in the morning without knowing where they might lay their heads at night.

With the decay of the feudal system, the system of private property in land that had destroyed Rome was extended.

As to England, it may briefly be said that the crown lands were for the most part given away to favorites; that the church lands were parceled among his courtiers by Henry VIII, and in Scotland grasped by the nobles; that the military dues were finally remitted in the seventeenth century, and taxation on consumption substituted; and that by a process beginning with the Tudors and extending to our own time all but a mere fraction of the commons were enclosed by the greater landowners; while the same private ownership of land was extended over Ireland and the Scottish Highlands, partly by the sword and partly by bribery of the chiefs. Even the military dues, had they been commuted, not remitted, would today have more than sufficed to pay all public expenses without one penny of other taxation.

Of the New World, whose institutions but continue those of Europe, it is only necessary to say that to the parceling out of land in great tracts is due the backwardness and turbulence of Spanish America; that to the large plantations of the Southern States of the Union was due the persistence of slavery there, and that the more northern settlements showed the earlier English feeling, land being fairly well divided and the attempts to establish manorial estates coming to little or nothing. In this lies the secret of the more vigorous growth of the Northern States. But the idea that land was to be treated as private property had been thoroughly established in English thought before the colonial period ended, and it has been so treated by the United States and by the several States. And though land was at first sold cheaply, and then given to actual settlers, it was also sold in large quantities to speculators, given away in great tracts for railroads and other purposes, until now the public domain of the United States, which a generation ago seemed illimitable, has practically gone. And this, as the experience of other countries shows, is the natural result in a growing community of making land private property. When the possession of land means the gain of unearned wealth, the strong and unscrupulous will secure it. But when, as we propose, economic rent, the "unearned increment of wealth," is taken by the state for the use of the community, then land will pass into the hands of users and remain there, since no matter how great its value, its possession will be profitable only to users.

As to private property in land having conduced to the peace and tranquillity of human life, it is not necessary more than to allude to the notorious fact that the struggle for land has been the prolific source of wars and of lawsuits, while it is the poverty engendered by private property in land that makes the prison and the workhouse the unfailing attributes of what we call Christian civilization.

Your Holiness intimates that the Divine Law gives its sanction to the private ownership of land, quoting from Deuteronomy, "Thou shalt not covet thy neighbor's wife, nor his house, nor his field, nor his man-servant, nor his maid-servant, nor his ox, nor his ass, nor anything which is his"

If, as your Holiness conveys, this inclusion of the words, "nor his field," is to be taken as sanctioning private property in land as it exists today, then, but with far greater force, must the words, "his man-servant, nor his maid-servant," be taken to sanction chattel slavery; for it is evident from other provisions of the same code that these terms referred both to bondsmen for a term of years and to perpetual slaves. But the word "field" involves the idea of use and improvement, to which the right of possession and ownership does attach without recognition of property in the land itself. And that this reference to the "field" is not a sanction of private property in land as it exists today is proved by the fact that the Mosaic code expressly denied such unqualified ownership in land, and with the declaration, "the land also shall not be sold forever, because it is mine, and you are strangers and sojourners with me," provided for its reversion every fiftieth year; thus, in a way adapted to the primitive industrial conditions of the time, securing to all of the chosen people a foothold in the soil.

Nowhere in fact throughout the Scriptures can the slightest justification be found for the attaching to land of the same right of property that justly attaches to the things produced by labor. Everywhere is it treated as the free bounty of God, "the land which the Lord thy God giveth thee."

6. *That fathers should provide for their children and that private property in land is necessary to enable them to do so.* (14-17.)

With all that your Holiness has to say of the sacredness of the family relation we are in full accord. But how the obligation of the father to the child can justify private property in land we cannot see. You reason that private property in land is necessary to the discharge of the duty of the father, and is therefore requisite and just, because —

> It is a most sacred law of nature that a father must provide food and all necessaries for those whom he has begotten; and, similarly, nature dictates that a man's children, who carry on, as it were, and continue his own personality, should be provided by him with all that is needful to enable them honorably to keep themselves from want and misery in the uncertainties of this mortal life. Now, in no other way can a father effect this except by the ownership of profitable property, which he can transmit to his children by inheritance. (14.)

Thanks to Him who has bound the generations of men together by a provision that brings the tenderest love to greet our entrance into the world and soothes our exit with filial piety, it is both the duty and the joy of the father to care for the child till its powers mature, and afterwards in the natural order it becomes the duty and privilege of the child to be the stay of the parent. This is the natural reason for that relation of marriage, the groundwork of the sweetest, tenderest and purest of human joys, which the Catholic Church has guarded with such unremitting vigilance.

We do, for a few years, need the providence of our fathers after the flesh. But how small, how transient, how narrow is this need, as compared with our constant need for the providence of Him in whom we live, move and have our being — Our Father who art in Heaven! It is to Him, "the giver of every good and perfect gift," and not to our fathers after the flesh, that Christ taught us to pray, "Give us this day our daily bread." And how true it is that it is through Him that the generations of men exist! Let the mean temperature of the earth rise or fall a few degrees, an amount as nothing compared with differences produced in our laboratories, and mankind would disappear as ice disappears under a tropical sun, would fall as the leaves fall at the touch of frost. Or, let for two or three seasons the earth refuse her increase, and how many of our millions would remain alive?

The duty of fathers to transmit to their children profitable property that will enable them to keep themselves from want and misery in the uncertainties of this mortal life! What is not possible cannot be a duty. And how is it possible for fathers to do that? Your Holiness has not considered how mankind really lives from hand to mouth, getting each day its daily bread; how little one generation does or can leave another. It is doubtful if the wealth of the civilized world all told amounts to anything like as much as one year's labor, while it is certain that if labor were to stop and men had to rely on existing accumulation, it would be only a few days ere in the richest countries pestilence and famine would stalk.

The profitable property your Holiness refers to is private property in land. Now profitable land, as all economists will agree, is land superior to the land that the ordinary man can get. It is land that will yield an income to the owner, as owner, and therefore that will permit the owner to appropriate the products of labor without doing labor, its profitableness to the individual involving the robbery of other individuals. It is therefore possible only for some fathers to leave their children profitable land. What therefore your Holiness practically declares is, that it is the duty of all fathers to struggle to leave their children what only the few peculiarly strong, lucky or unscrupulous can leave; and that, a something that involves the robbery of others — their deprivation of the material gifts of God.

This anti-Christian doctrine has been long in practice throughout the Christian world. What are its results?

Are they not the very evils set forth in your Encyclical? Are they not, so far from enabling men to keep themselves from want and misery in the uncertainties of this mortal life, to condemn the great masses of men to want and misery that the natural conditions of our mortal life do not entail; to want and misery deeper and more widespread than exist among heathen savages? Under the régime of private property in land and in the richest countries not five per cent of fathers are able at their death to leave anything substantial to their children, and probably a large majority do not leave enough to bury them! Some few children are left by their fathers richer than it is good for them to be, but the vast majority not only are left nothing by their fathers, but by the system that makes land private property are deprived of the bounty of their Heavenly Father; are compelled to sue others for permission to live and to work, and to toil all their lives for a pittance that often does not enable them to escape starvation and pauperism.

What your Holiness is actually, though of course inadvertently, urging, is that earthly fathers should assume the functions of the Heavenly Father. It is not the business of one generation to provide the succeeding generation "with all that is needful to enable them honorably to keep themselves from want and misery." That is God's business. We no more create our children than we create our fathers. It is God who is the Creator of each succeeding generation as fully as of the one that preceded it. And, to recall your own words (7), "Nature [God], therefore, owes to man a storehouse that shall never fail, the daily supply of his daily wants. And this he finds only in the inexhaustible fertility of the earth." What you are now assuming is, that it is the duty of men to provide for the wants of their children by appropriating this storehouse and depriving other men's children of the unfailing supply that God has provided for all.

The duty of the father to the child — the duty possible to all fathers! Is it not so to conduct himself, so to nurture and teach it, that it shall come to manhood with a sound body, well-developed mind, habits of virtue, piety and industry, and in a state of society that shall give it and all others free access to the bounty of God, the providence of the All-Father?

In doing this the father would be doing more to secure his children from want and misery than is possible now to the richest of fathers — as much more as the providence of God surpasses that of man. For the justice of God laughs at the efforts of men to circumvent it, and the subtle law that binds humanity together poisons the rich in the sufferings of the poor. Even the few who are able in the general struggle to leave their children wealth that they fondly think will keep them from want and misery in the uncertainties of this mortal life — do they succeed? Does experience show that it is a benefit to a child to place him above his fellows and enable him to think God's law of labor is not for him? Is not such wealth oftener a curse than a blessing, and does not its expectation often destroy filial love and bring dissensions and heartburnings into families? And how far and how long are even the richest and strongest able to exempt their children from the common lot? Nothing is more certain than that the blood of the masters of the world flows today in *lazzaroni* and that the descendants of kings and princes tenant slums and workhouses.

But in the state of society we strive for, where the monopoly and waste of God's bounty would be done away with and the fruits of labor would go to the laborer, it would be within the ability of all to make more than a comfortable living with reasonable labor. And for those who might be crippled or incapacitated, or deprived of their natural protectors and breadwinners, the most ample provision could be made out of that great and increasing fund with which God in his law of rent has provided society — not as a matter of niggardly and degrading alms, but as a matter of right, as the assurance which in a Christian state society owes to all its members.

Thus it is that the duty of the father, the obligation to the child, instead of giving any support to private property in land, utterly condemns it, urging us by the most powerful considerations to abolish it in the simple and efficacious way of the single tax.

This duty of the father, this obligation to children, is not confined to those who have actually children of their own, but rests on all of us who have come to the powers and responsibilities of manhood.

For did not Christ set a little child in the midst of the disciples, saying to them that the angels of such little ones always behold the face of his Father; saying to them that it were better for a man to hang a millstone about his neck and plunge into the uttermost depths of the sea than to injure such a little one?

And what today is the result of private property in land in the richest of so-called Christian countries? Is it not that young people fear to marry; that married people fear to have children; that children are driven out of life from sheer want of proper nourishment and care, or compelled to toil when they ought to be at school or at play; that great numbers of those who attain maturity enter it with undernourished bodies, overstrained nerves, undeveloped minds — under conditions that foredoom them, not merely to suffering, but to crime; that fit them in advance for the prison and the brothel?

If your Holiness will consider these things we are confident that instead of defending private property in land you will condemn it with anathema!

7. *That the private ownership of land stimulates industry, increases wealth, and attaches men to the soil and to their country.* (51)

The idea, as expressed by Arthur Young, that "the magic of property turns barren sands to gold" springs from the confusion of ownership with possession, of which I have before spoken, that attributes to private property in land what is due to security of the products of labor. It is needless for me again to point out that the change we propose, the taxation for public uses of land values, or economic rent, and the abolition of other taxes, would give to the user of land far greater security for the fruits of his labor than the present system and far greater permanence of possession. Nor is it necessary further to show how it would give homes to those who are now homeless and bind men to their country. For under it every one who wanted a piece of land for a home or for productive use could get it without purchase price and hold it even without tax, since the tax we propose would not fall on all land, nor even on all land in use, but only on land better than the poorest land in use, and is in reality not a tax at all, but merely a return to the state for the use of a valuable privilege. And even those who from circumstances or occupation did not wish to make permanent use of land would still have an equal interest with all others in the land of their country and in the general prosperity.

But I should like your Holiness to consider how utterly unnatural is the condition of the masses in the richest and most progressive of Christian countries; how large bodies of them live in habitations in which a rich man would not ask his dog to dwell; how the great majority have no homes from which they are not liable on the slightest misfortune to be evicted; how numbers have no homes at all, but must seek what shelter chance or charity offers. I should like to ask your Holiness to consider how the great majority of men in such countries have no interest whatever in what they are taught to call their native land, for which they are told that on occasions it is their duty to fight or to die. What right, for instance, have the majority of your country-men in the land of their birth? Can they live in Italy out-side of a prison or a poorhouse except as they buy the privilege from some of the exclusive owners of Italy? Can-not an Englishman, an American, an Arab or a Japanese do as much? May not what was said centuries ago by Tiberius Gracchus be said today: "Men of Rome! you are called the lords of the world, yet have no right to a square foot of its soil! The wild beasts have their dens, but the soldiers of Italy have only water and air!"

What is true of Italy is true of the civilized world — is becoming increasingly true. It is the inevitable effect as civi-lization progresses of private property in land.

8. *That the right to possess private property in land is from nature, not from man; that the state has no right to abolish it, and that to take the value of landownership in taxation would be un-just and cruel to the private owner.* (51)

This, like much else that your Holiness says, is masked in the use of the indefinite terms "private property" and "private owner" — a want of precision in the use of words that has doubtless aided in the confusion of your own thought. But the context leaves no doubt that by private property you mean private property in land, and by private owner, the private owner of land.

The contention, thus made, that private property in land is from nature, not from man, has no other basis than the confounding of ownership with possession and the ascription to property in land of what belongs to its contradictory, property in the proceeds of labor. You do not attempt to show for it any other basis, nor has any one else ever attempted to do so. That private property in the products of labor is from nature is clear, for nature gives such things to labor and to labor alone. Of every article of this kind, we know that it came into being as nature's response to the exertion of an individual man or of individual men – given by nature directly and exclusively to him or to them. Thus there inheres in such things a right of private property, which originates from and goes back to the source of ownership, the maker of the thing. This right is anterior to the state and superior to its enactments, so that, as we hold, it is a violation of natural right and an injustice to the private owner for the state to tax the processes and products of labor. They do not belong to Cæsar. They are things that God, of whom nature is but an expression, gives to those who apply for them in the way he has appointed by labor.

But who will dare trace the individual ownership of land to any grant from the Maker of land? What does nature give to such ownership? How does she in any way recognize it? Will any one show from difference of form or feature, of stature or complexion, from dissection of their bodies or analysis of their powers and needs, that one man was intended by nature to own land and another to live on it as his tenant? That which derives its existence from man and passes away like him, which is indeed but the evanescent expression of his labor, man may hold and transfer as the exclusive property of the individual; but how can such individual ownership attach to land, which existed before man was, and which continues to exist while the generations of men come and go — the unfailing storehouse that the Creator gives to man for "the daily supply of his daily wants"?

Clearly, the private ownership of land is from the state, not from nature. Thus, not merely can no objection be made on the score of morals when it is proposed that the state shall abolish it altogether, but insomuch as it is a violation of natural right, its existence involving a gross injustice on the part of the state, an "impious violation of the benevolent intention of the Creator," it is a moral duty that the state so abolish it.

So far from there being anything unjust in taking the full value of landownership for the use of the community, the real injustice is in leaving it in private hands — an injustice that amounts to robbery and murder.

And when your Holiness shall see this I have no fear that you will listen for one moment to the impudent plea that before the community can take what God intended it to take — before men who have been disinherited of their natural rights can be restored to them, the present owners of land shall first be compensated.

For not only will you see that the single tax will directly and largely benefit small landowners, whose interests as laborers and capitalists are much greater than their interests as landowners, and that though the great landowners — or rather the propertied class in general among whom the profits of landownership are really divided through mortgages, rent-charges, etc. — would relatively lose, they too would be absolute gainers in the increased prosperity and improved morals; but more quickly, more strongly, more peremptorily than from any calculation of gains or losses would your duty as a man, your faith as a Christian, forbid you to listen for one moment to any such paltering with right and wrong.

Where the state takes some land for public uses it is

only just that those whose land is taken should be compensated, otherwise some landowners would be treated more harshly than others. But where, by a measure affecting all alike, rent is appropriated for the benefit of all, there can be no claim to compensation. Compensation in such case would be a continuance of the same injustice in another form — the giving to landowners in the shape of interest of what they before got as rent. Your Holiness knows that justice and injustice are not thus to be juggled with, and when you fully realize that land is really the storehouse that God owes to all his children, you will no more listen to any demand for compensation for restoring it to them than Moses would have listened to a demand that Pharaoh should be compensated before letting the children of Israel go.

Compensated for what? For giving up what has been unjustly taken? The demand of landowners for compensation is not that. We do not seek to spoil the Egyptians. We do not ask that what has been unjustly taken from laborers shall be restored. We are willing that bygones should be bygones and to leave dead wrongs to bury their dead. We propose to let those who by the past appropriation of land values have taken the fruits of labor to retain what they have thus got. We merely propose that for the future such robbery of labor shall cease — that for the future, not for the past, landholders shall pay to the community the rent that to the community is justly due.

III.

I HAVE SAID ENOUGH TO SHOW YOUR HOLINESS the injustice into which you fall in classing us, who in seeking virtually to abolish private property in land seek more fully to secure the true rights of property, with those whom you speak of as socialists, who wish to make all property common. But you also do injustice to the socialists.

There are many, it is true, who feeling bitterly the monstrous wrongs of the present distribution of wealth are animated only by a blind hatred of the rich and a fierce desire to destroy existing social adjustments. This class is indeed only less dangerous than those who proclaim that no social improvement is needed or is possible. But it is not fair to confound with them those who, however mistakenly, propose definite schemes of remedy.

The socialists, as I understand them, and as the term has come to apply to anything like a definite theory and not to be vaguely and improperly used to include all who desire social improvement, do not, as you imply, seek the abolition of all private property. Those who do this are properly called communists. What the socialists seek is the state assumption of capital (in which they vaguely and erroneously include land), or more properly speaking, of large capitals, and state management and direction of at least the larger operations of industry. In this way they hope to abolish interest, which they regard as a wrong and an evil; to do away with the gains of exchangers, speculators, contractors and middlemen, which they regard as waste; to do away with the wage system and secure general cooperation; and to prevent competition, which they deem the fundamental cause of the impoverishment of labor. The more moderate of them, without going so far, go in the same direction, and seek some remedy or palliation of the worst forms of poverty by government regulation. The essential character of socialism is that it looks to the extension of the functions of the state for the remedy of social evils; that it would substitute regulation and direction for competition; and intelligent control by organized society for the free play of individual desire and effort.

Though not usually classed as socialists, both the trades-unionists and the protectionists have the same essential character. The trades-unionists seek the increase of wages, the reduction of working-hours and the general improvement in the condition of wage-workers, by organizing them into guilds or associations which shall fix the rates at which they will sell their labor; shall deal as one body with employers in case of dispute; shall use on occasion their necessary weapon, the strike; and shall accumulate funds for such purposes and for the purpose of assisting members when on a strike, or (sometimes) when out of employment. The protectionists seek by governmental prohibitions or taxes on imports to regulate the industry and control the exchanges of each country, so as, they imagine, to diversify home industries and prevent the competition of people of other countries.

At the opposite extreme are the anarchists, a term which, though frequently applied to mere violent destructionists, refers also to those who, seeing the many evils of too much government, regard government in itself as evil, and believe that in the absence of coercive power the mutual interests of men would secure voluntarily what cooperation is needed.

Differing from all these are those for whom I would speak. Believing that the rights of true property are sacred, we would regard forcible communism as robbery that would bring destruction. But we would not be disposed to deny that voluntary communism might be the highest possible state of which men can conceive. Nor do we say that it cannot be possible for mankind to attain it, since among the early Christians and among the religious orders of the Catholic Church we have examples of communistic societies on a small scale. St. Peter and St. Paul, St. Thomas of Aquin and Fra Angelico, the illustrious orders of the Carmelites and Franciscans, the Jesuits, whose heroism carried the cross among the most savage tribes of American forests, the societies that wherever your communion is known have deemed no work of mercy too dangerous or too repellent — were or are communists. Knowing these things we cannot take it on ourselves to say that a social condition may not be possible in which an all-embracing love shall have taken the place of all other motives. But we see that communism is only possible where there exists a general and intense religious faith, and we see that such a state can be reached only through a state of justice. For before a man can be a saint he must first be an honest man.

With both anarchists and socialists, we, who for want of a better term have come to call ourselves single-tax men, fundamentally differ. We regard them as erring in opposite directions — the one in ignoring the social nature of man, the other in ignoring his individual nature. While we see that man is primarily an individual, and that nothing but evil has come or can come from the interference by the state with things that belong to individual action, we also see that he is a social being, or, as Aristotle called him, a political animal, and that the state is requisite to social advance, having an indispensable place in the natural order. Looking on the bodily organism as the analogue of the social organism, and on the proper functions of the state as akin to those that in the human organism are discharged by the conscious intelligence, while the play of individual impulse and interest performs functions akin to those discharged in the bodily organism by the unconscious instincts and involuntary motions, the anarchists seem to us like men who would try to get along without heads and the socialists like men who would try to rule the wonderfully complex and delicate internal relations of their frames by conscious will.

The philosophical anarchists of whom I speak are few in number, and of little practical importance. It is with socialism in its various phases that we have to do battle.

With the socialists we have some points of agreement, for we recognize fully the social nature of man and believe that all monopolies should be held and governed by the state. In these, and in directions where the general health, knowledge, comfort and convenience might be improved, we, too, would extend the functions of the state.

But it seems to us the vice of socialism in all its degrees is its want of radicalism, of going to the root. It takes its theories from those who have sought to justify the impoverishment of the masses, and its advocates generally teach the preposterous and degrading doctrine that slavery was the first condition of labor. It assumes that the tendency of wages to a minimum is the natural law, and seeks to abolish wages; it assumes that the natural result of competition is to grind down workers, and seeks to abolish competition by restrictions, prohibitions and extensions of governing power. Thus mistaking effects for causes, and childishly blaming the stone for hitting it, it wastes strength in striving for remedies that when not worse are futile. Associated though it is in many places with democratic aspiration, yet its essence is the same delusion to which the children of Israel yielded when against the protest of their prophet they insisted on a king; the delusion that has everywhere corrupted democracies and enthroned tyrants — that power over the people can be used for the benefit of the people; that there may be devised machinery that through human agencies will secure for the management of individual affairs more wisdom and more virtue than the people themselves possess.

This superficiality and this tendency may be seen in all

the phases of socialism.

Take, for instance, protectionism. What support it has, beyond the mere selfish desire of sellers to compel buyers to pay them more than their goods are worth, springs from such superficial ideas as that production, not consumption, is the end of effort; that money is more valuable than money's worth, and to sell more profitable than to buy; and above all from a desire to limit competition, springing from an unanalyzing recognition of the phenomena that necessarily follow when men who have the need to labor are deprived by monopoly of access to the natural and indispensable element of all labor. Its methods involve the idea that governments can more wisely direct the expenditure of labor and the investment of capital than can laborers and capitalists, and that the men who control governments will use this power for the general good and not in their own interests. They tend to multiply officials, restrict liberty, invent crimes. They promote perjury, fraud and corruption. And they would, were the theory carried to its logical conclusion, destroy civilization and reduce mankind to savagery.

Take trades-unionism. While within narrow lines trades-unionism promotes the idea of the mutuality of interests, and often helps to raise courage and further political education, and while it has enabled limited bodies of working men to improve somewhat their condition, and gain, as it were, breathing-space, yet it takes no note of the general causes that determine the conditions of labor, and strives for the elevation of only a small part of the great body by means that cannot help the rest. Aiming at the restriction of competition — the limitation of the right to labor, its methods are like those of an army, which even in a righteous cause are subversive of liberty and liable to abuse, while its weapon, the strike, is destructive in its nature, both to combatants and noncombatants, being a form of passive war. To apply the principle of trades-unions to all industry, as some dream of doing, would be to enthrall men in a caste system.

Or take even such moderate measures as the limitation of working-hours and of the labor of women and children. They are superficial in looking no further than to the eagerness of men and women and little children to work unduly, and in proposing forcibly to restrain overwork while utterly ignoring its cause — the sting of poverty that forces human beings to it. And the methods by which these restraints must be enforced, multiply officials, interfere with personal liberty, tend to corruption, and are liable to abuse.

As for thoroughgoing socialism, which is the more to be honored as having the courage of its convictions, it would carry these vices to full expression. Jumping to conclusions without effort to discover causes, it fails to see that oppression does not come from the nature of capital, but from the wrong that robs labor of capital by divorcing it from land, and that creates a fictitious capital that is really capitalized monopoly. It fails to see that it would be impossible for capital to oppress labor were labor free to the natural material of production; that the wage system in itself springs from mutual convenience, being a form of cooperation in which one of the parties prefers a certain to a contingent result; and that what it calls the "iron law of wages" is not the natural law of wages, but only the law of wages in that unnatural condition in which men are made helpless by being deprived of the materials for life and work. It fails to see that what it mistakes for the evils of competition are really the evils of restricted competition — are due to a one-sided competition to which men are forced when deprived of land. While its methods, the organization of men into industrial armies, the direction and control of all production and exchange by governmental or semi-governmental bureaus, would, if carried to full expression, mean Egyptian despotism.

We differ from the socialists in our diagnosis of the evil and we differ from them as to remedies. We have no fear of capital, regarding it as the natural handmaiden of labor; we look on interest in itself as natural and just; we would set no limit to accumulation, nor impose on the rich any burden that is not equally placed on the poor; we see no evil in competition, but deem unrestricted competition to be as necessary to the health of the industrial and social organism as the free circulation of the blood is to the health of the bodily organism — to be the agency whereby the fullest cooperation is to be secured. We would simply take for the community what belongs to the community, the value that attaches to land by the growth of the community; leave sacredly to the individual all that belongs to the individual; and, treating necessary monopolies as functions of the state, abolish all restrictions and prohibitions save those required for public health, safety, morals and convenience.

But the fundamental difference — the difference I ask your Holiness specially to note, is in this: socialism in all its phases looks on the evils of our civilization as springing from the inadequacy or inharmony of natural relations, which must be artificially organized or improved. In its idea there devolves on the state the necessity of intelligently organizing the industrial relations of men; the construction, as it were, of a great machine whose complicated parts shall properly work together under the direction of human intelligence. This is the reason why socialism tends toward atheism. Failing to see the order and symmetry of natural law, it fails to recognize God.

On the other hand, we who call ourselves single-tax men (a name which expresses merely our practical propositions) see in the social and industrial relations of men not a machine which requires construction, but an organism which needs only to be suffered to grow. We see in the natural social and industrial laws such harmony as we see in the adjustments of the human body, and that as far transcends the power of man's intelligence to order and direct as it is beyond man's intelligence to order and direct the vital movements of his frame. We see in these social and industrial laws so close a relation to the moral law as must spring from the same Authorship, and that proves the moral law to be the sure guide of man where his intelligence would wander and go astray. Thus, to us, all that is needed to remedy the evils of our time is to do justice and give freedom. This is the reason why our beliefs tend toward, nay are indeed the only beliefs consistent with a firm and reverent faith in God, and with the recognition of His law as the supreme law which men must follow if they would secure prosperity and avoid destruction. This is the reason why to us political economy only serves to show the depth of wisdom in the simple truths which common people heard gladly from the lips of Him of whom it was said with wonder, "Is not this the Carpenter of Nazareth?"

And it is because that in what we propose — the securing to all men of equal natural opportunities for the exercise of their powers and the removal of all legal restriction on the legitimate exercise of those powers — we see the conformation of human law to the moral law, that we hold with confidence that this is not merely the sufficient remedy for all the evils you so strikingly portray, but that it is the only possible remedy.

Nor is there any other. The organization of man is such, his relations to the world in which he is placed are such — that is to say, the immutable laws of God are such, that it is beyond the power of human ingenuity to devise any way by which the evils born of the injustice that robs men of their birthright can be removed otherwise than by doing justice, by opening to all the bounty that God has provided for all.

Since man can live only on land and from land, since land is the reservoir of matter and force from which man's body itself is taken, and on which he must draw for all that he can produce, does it not irresistibly follow that to give the land in ownership to some men and to deny to others all right to it is to divide mankind into the rich and the poor, the privileged and the helpless? Does it not follow that those who have no rights to the use of land can live only by selling their power to labor to those who own the land? Does it not follow that what the socialists call "the iron law of wages," what the political economists term "the tendency of wages to a minimum," must take from the landless masses — the mere laborers, who of themselves have no power to use their labor — all the benefits of any possible advance or improvement that does not alter this unjust division of land? For having no power to employ themselves, they must, either as labor-sellers or as land-renters, compete with one another for permission to labor. This competition with one another of men shut out from God's inexhaustible storehouse has no limit but starvation, and must ultimately force wages to their lowest point, the point at which life can just be maintained and reproduction carried on.

This is not to say that all wages must fall to this point, but that the wages of that necessarily largest stratum of laborers who have only ordinary knowledge, skill and aptitude must so fall. The wages of special classes, who are fenced off from the pressure of competition by peculiar knowledge, skill or other causes, may remain above that ordinary level. Thus, where the ability to read and write is rare its possession enables a man to obtain higher wages than the ordinary laborer. But as the diffusion of education makes the ability to read and write general this advantage is lost. So when a vocation requires special training or skill, or is made difficult of access by artificial restrictions, the checking of competition tends to keep wages in it at a higher level. But as the progress of invention dispenses with peculiar skill, or artificial restrictions are broken down, these higher wages sink to the ordinary level. And so, it is only so long as they are special that such qualities as industry, prudence and thrift can enable the ordinary laborer to maintain a condition above that which gives a mere living. Where they become general, the law of competition must reduce the earnings or savings of such qualities to the general level — which, land being monopolized and labor helpless, can be only that at which the next lowest point is the cessation of life.

Or, to state the same thing in another way: Land being necessary to life and labor, its owners will be able, in return for permission to use it, to obtain from mere laborers all that labor can produce, save enough to enable such of them to maintain life as are wanted by the landowners and their dependents.

Thus, where private property in land has divided society into a landowning class and a landless class, there is no possible invention or improvement, whether it be industrial, social or moral, which, so long as it does not affect the ownership of land, can prevent poverty or relieve the general conditions of mere laborers. For whether the effect of any invention or improvement be to increase what labor can produce or to decrease what is required to support the laborer, it can, so soon as it becomes general, result only in increasing the income of the owners of land, without at all benefiting the mere laborers. In no event can those possessed of the mere ordinary power to labor, a power utterly useless without the means necessary to labor, keep more of their earnings than enough to enable them to live.

How true this is we may see in the facts of today. In our own time invention and discovery have enormously increased the productive power of labor, and at the same time greatly reduced the cost of many things necessary to the support of the laborer. Have these improvements anywhere raised the earnings of the mere laborer? Have not their benefits mainly gone to the owners of land — enormously increased land values?

I say mainly, for some part of the benefit has gone to the cost of monstrous standing armies and warlike preparations; to the payment of interest on great public debts; and, largely disguised as interest on fictitious capital, to the owners of monopolies other than that of land. But improvements that would do away with these wastes would not benefit labor; they would simply increase the profits of landowners. Were standing armies and all their incidents abolished, were all monopolies other than that of land done away with, were governments to become models of economy, were the profits of speculators, of middlemen, of all sorts of exchangers saved, were every one to become so strictly honest that no policemen, no courts, no prisons, no precautions against dishonesty would be needed — the result would not differ from that which has followed the increase of productive power.

Nay, would not these very blessings bring starvation to many of those who now manage to live? Is it not true that if there were proposed today, what all Christian men ought to pray for, the complete disbandment of all the armies of Europe, the greatest fears would be aroused for the consequences of throwing on the labor market so many unemployed laborers?

The explanation of this and of similar paradoxes that in our time perplex on every side may be easily seen. The effect of all inventions and improvements that increase productive power, that save waste and economize effort, is to lessen the labor required for a given result, and thus to save labor, so that we speak of them as labor-saving inventions or improvements. Now, in a natural state of society where the rights of all to the use of the earth are acknowledged, labor-saving improvements might go to the very utmost that can be imagined without lessening the demand for men, since in such natural conditions the demand for men lies in their own enjoyment of life and the strong instincts that the Creator has implanted in the human breast. But in that unnatural state of society where the masses of men are disinherited of all but the power to labor when opportunity to labor is given them by others, there the demand for them becomes simply the demand for their services by those who hold this opportunity, and man himself becomes a commodity. Hence, although the natural effect of labor-saving improvement is to increase wages, yet in the unnatural condition which private ownership of the land begets, the effect, even of such moral improvements as the disbandment of armies and the saving of the labor that vice entails, is, by lessening the commercial demand, to lower wages and reduce mere laborers to starvation or pauperism. If labor-saving inventions and improvements could be carried to the very abolition of the necessity for labor, what would be the result? Would it not be that landowners could then get all the wealth that the land was capable of producing, and would have no need at all for laborers, who must then either starve or live as pensioners on the bounty of the landowners?

Thus, so long as private property in land continues — so long as some men are treated as owners of the earth and other men can live on it only by their sufferance — human wisdom can devise no means by which the evils of our present condition may be avoided. Nor yet could the wisdom of God.

By the light of that right reason of which St. Thomas speaks we may see that even he, the Almighty, so long as his laws remain what they are, could do nothing to prevent poverty and starvation while property in land continues.

How could he? Should he infuse new vigor into the sunlight, new virtue into the air, new fertility into the soil, would not all this new bounty go to the owners of the land, and work not benefit, but rather injury, to mere laborers? Should he open the minds of men to the possibilities of new substances, new adjustments, new powers, could this do any more to relieve poverty than steam, electricity and all the numberless discoveries and inventions of our time have done? Or, if he were to send down from the heavens above or cause to gush up from the subterranean depths, food, clothing, all the things that satisfy man's material desires, to whom under our laws would all these belong? So far from benefiting man, would not this increase and extension of his bounty prove but a curse, enabling the privileged class more riotously to roll in wealth, and bringing the disinherited class to more widespread starvation or pauperism?

IV.

Believing that the social question is at bottom a religious question, we deem it of happy augury to the world that in your Encyclical the most influential of all religious teachers has directed attention to the condition of labor.

But while we appreciate the many wholesome truths you utter, while we feel, as all must feel, that you are animated by a desire to help the suffering and oppressed, and to put an end to any idea that the church is divorced from the aspiration for liberty and progress, yet it is painfully obvious to us that one fatal assumption hides from you the cause of the evils you see, and makes it impossible for you to propose any adequate remedy. This assumption is, that private property in land is of the same nature and has the same sanctions as private property in things produced by labor. In spite of its undeniable truths and its benevolent spirit, your Encyclical shows you to be involved in such difficulties as a physician called to examine one suffering from disease of the stomach would meet should he begin with a refusal to consider the stomach.

Prevented by this assumption from seeing the true cause, the only causes you find it possible to assign for the growth of misery and wretchedness are the destruction of working men's guilds in the last century, the repudiation in public institutions and laws of the ancient religion, rapacious usury, the custom of working by contract, and the concentration of trade.

Such diagnosis is manifestly inadequate to account for evils that are alike felt in Catholic countries, in Protestant countries, in countries that adhere to the Greek communion and in countries where no religion is professed by the state; that are alike felt in old countries and in new countries; where industry is simple and where it is most elaborate; and amid all varieties of industrial customs and relations.

But the real cause will be clear if you will consider that since labor must find its workshop and reservoir in land, the labor question is but another name for the land question, and will reexamine your assumption that private property in land is necessary and right.

See how fully adequate is the cause I have pointed out. The most important of all the material relations of man is his relation to the planet he inhabits, and hence, the "impious resistance to the benevolent intentions of his Creator," which, as Bishop Nulty says, is involved in private property in land, must produce evils wherever it exists. But by virtue of the law, "unto whom much is given, from him much is required," the very progress of civilization makes the evils produced by private property in land more widespread and intense.

What is producing throughout the civilized world that condition of things you rightly describe as intolerable is not this and that local error or minor mistake. It is nothing less than the progress of civilization itself; nothing less than the intellectual advance and the material growth in which our century has been so preëminent, acting in a state of society based on private property in land; nothing less than the new gifts that in our time God has been showering on man, but which are being turned into scourges by man's "impious resistance to the benevolent intentions of his Creator."

The discoveries of science, the gains of invention, have given to us in this wonderful century more than has been given to men in any time before; and, in a degree so rapidly accelerating as to suggest geometrical progression, are placing in our hands new material powers. But with the benefit comes the obligation. In a civilization beginning to pulse with steam and electricity, where the sun paints pictures and the phonograph stores speech, it will not do to be merely as just as were our fathers. Intellectual advance and material advance require corresponding moral advance. Knowledge and power are neither good nor evil. They are not ends but means — evolving forces that if not controlled in orderly relations must take disorderly and destructive forms. The deepening pain, the increasing perplexity, the growing discontent for which, as you truly say, some remedy must be found and quickly found, mean nothing less than that forces of destruction swifter and more terrible than those that have shattered every preceding civilization are already menacing ours — that if it does not quickly rise to a higher moral level; if it does not become in deed as in word a Christian civilization, on the wall of its splendor must flame the doom of Babylon: "Thou art weighed in the balance and found wanting! One false assumption prevents you from seeing the real cause and true significance of the facts that have prompted your Encyclical. And it fatally fetters you when you seek a remedy. You state that you approach the subject with confidence, yet in all that greater part of the Encyclical (39-67) devoted to the remedy, while there is an abundance of moral reflections and injunctions, excellent in themselves but dead and meaningless as you apply them, the only definite practical proposals for the improvement of the condition of labor are:

1. That the state should step in to prevent overwork, to restrict the employment of women and children, to secure in workshops conditions not unfavorable to health and morals, and, at least where there is danger of insufficient wages provoking strikes, to regulate wages (39-40).

2. That it should encourage the acquisition of property (in land) by working men (50-51).

3. That working men's associations should be formed (52-67).

These remedies so far as they go are socialistic, and though the Encyclical is not without recognition of the individual character of man and of the priority of the individual and the family to the state, yet the whole tendency and spirit of its remedial suggestions lean unmistakably to socialism — extremely moderate socialism it is true; socialism hampered and emasculated by a supreme respect for private possessions; yet socialism still. But, although you frequently use the ambiguous term "private property" when the context shows that you have in mind private property in land, the one thing clear on the surface and becoming clearer still with examination is that you insist that whatever else may be done, the private ownership of land shall be left untouched.

I have already referred generally to the defects that attach to all socialistic remedies for the evil condition of labor, but respect for your Holiness dictates that I should speak specifically, even though briefly, of the remedies proposed or suggested by you.

Of these, the widest and strongest are that the state should restrict the hours of labor, the employment of women and children, the unsanitary conditions of workshops, etc. Yet how little may in this way be accomplished.

A strong, absolute ruler might hope by such regulations

to alleviate the conditions of chattel slaves. But the tendency of our times is toward democracy, and democratic states are necessarily weaker in fraternalism, while in the industrial slavery, growing out of private ownership of land, that prevails in Christendom today, it is not the master who forces the slave to labor, but the slave who urges the master to let him labor. Thus the greatest difficulty in enforcing such regulations comes from those whom they are intended to benefit. It is not, for instance, the masters who make it difficult to enforce restrictions on child labor in factories, but the mothers, who, prompted by poverty, misrepresent the ages of their children even to the masters, and teach the children to misrepresent.

But while in large factories and mines regulations as to hours, ages, etc., though subject to evasion and offering opportunities for extortion and corruption, may be to some extent enforced, how can they have any effect in those far wider branches of industry where the laborer works for himself or for small employers?

All such remedies are of the nature of the remedy for overcrowding that is generally prescribed with them — the restriction under penalty of the number who may occupy a room and the demolition of unsanitary buildings. Since these measures have no tendency to increase house accommodation or to augment ability to pay for it, the overcrowding that is forced back in some places goes on in other places and to a worse degree. All such remedies begin at the wrong end. They are like putting on brake and bit to hold in quietness horses that are being lashed into frenzy; they are like trying to stop a locomotive by holding its wheels instead of shutting off steam; like attempting to cure smallpox by driving back its pustules. Men do not overwork themselves because they like it; it is not in the nature of the mother's heart to send children to work when they ought to be at play; it is not of choice that laborers will work under dangerous and unsanitary conditions. These things, like overcrowding, come from the sting of poverty. And so long as the poverty of which they are the expression is left untouched, restrictions such as you indorse can have only partial and evanescent results. The cause remaining, repression in one place can only bring out its effects in other places, and the task you assign to the state is as hopeless as to ask it to lower the level of the ocean by bailing out the sea.

Nor can the state cure poverty by regulating wages. It is as much beyond the power of the state to regulate wages as it is to regulate the rates of interest. Usury laws have been tried again and again, but the only effect they have ever had has been to increase what the poorer borrowers must pay, and for the same reasons that all attempts to lower by regulation the price of goods have always resulted merely in increasing them. The general rate of wages is fixed by the ease or difficulty with which labor can obtain access to land, ranging from the full earnings of labor, where land is free, to the least on which laborers can live and reproduce, where land is fully monopolized. Thus, where it has been comparatively easy for laborers to get land, as in the United States and in Australasia, wages have been higher than in Europe and it has been impossible to get European laborers to work there for wages that they would gladly accept at home; while as monopolization goes on under the influence of private property in land, wages tend to fall, and the social conditions of Europe to appear. Thus, under the partial yet substantial recognition of common rights to land, of which I have spoken, the many attempts of the British Parliament to reduce wages by regulation failed utterly. And so, when the institution of private property in land had done its work in England, all attempts of Parliament to raise wages proved unavailing. In the beginning of this century it was even attempted to increase the earnings of laborers by grants in aid of wages. But the only result was to lower commensurately what wages employers paid.

The state could maintain wages above the tendency of the market (for as I have shown labor deprived of land becomes a commodity), only by offering employment to all who wish it; or by lending its sanction to strikes and supporting them with its funds. Thus it is, that the thorough-going socialists who want the state to take all industry into its hands are much more logical than those timid socialists who propose that the state should regulate private industry — but only a little.

The same hopelessness attends your suggestion that working-people should be encouraged by the state in obtaining a share of the land. It is evident that by this you mean that, as is now being attempted in Ireland, the state shall buy out large landowners in favor of small ones, establishing what are known as peasant proprietors. Supposing that this can be done even to a considerable extent, what will be accomplished save to substitute a larger privileged class for a smaller privileged class? What will be done for the still larger class that must remain, the laborers of the agricultural districts, the workmen of the towns, the proletarians of the cities? Is it not true, as Professor De Laveleye says, that in such countries as Belgium, where peasant proprietary exists, the tenants, for there still exist tenants, are rack-rented with a mercilessness unknown in Ireland? Is it not true that in such countries as Belgium the condition of the mere laborer is even worse than it is in Great Britain, where large ownerships obtain? And if the state attempts to buy up land for peasant proprietors will not the effect be, what is seen today in Ireland, to increase the market value of land and thus make it more difficult for those not so favored, and for those who will come after, to get land? How, moreover, on the principle which you declare (36), that "to the state the interests of all are equal, whether high or low," will you justify state aid to one man to buy a bit of land without also insisting on state aid to another man to buy a donkey, to another to buy a shop, to another to buy the tools and materials of a trade — state aid in short to everybody who may be able to make good use of it or thinks that he could? And are you not thus landed in communism — not the communism of the early Christians and of the religious orders, but communism that uses the coercive power of the state to take rightful property by force from those who have, to give to those who have not? For the state has no purse of Fortunatus; the state cannot repeat the miracle of the loaves and fishes; all that the state can give, it must get by some form or other of the taxing power. And whether it gives or lends money, or gives or lends credit, it cannot give to those who have not, without taking from those who have.

But aside from all this, any scheme of dividing up land while maintaining private property in land is futile. Small holdings cannot coexist with the treatment of land as private property where civilization is materially advancing and wealth augments. We may see this in the economic tendencies that in ancient times were the main cause that transformed world-conquering Italy from a land of small farms to a land of great estates. We may see it in the fact that while two centuries ago the majority of English farmers were owners of the land they tilled, tenancy has been for a long time the all but universal condition of the English farmer. And now the mighty forces of steam and electricity have come to urge concentration. It is in the United States that we may see on the largest scale how their power is operating to turn a nation of landowners into a nation of tenants. The principle is clear and irresistible. Material progress makes land more valuable, and when this increasing value is left to private owners land must pass from the ownership of the poor into the ownership of the rich, just as diamonds so pass when poor men find them. What the British government is attempting in Ireland is to build snow-houses in the Arabian desert! To plant bananas in Labrador!

There is one way, and only one way, in which working people in our civilization may be secured a share in the land of their country, and that is the way that we propose — the taking of the profits of landownership for the community.

As to workingmen's associations, what your Holiness seems to contemplate is the formation and encouragement of societies akin to the Catholic sodalities, and to the friendly and beneficial societies, like the Odd Fellows, which have had a large extension in English-speaking countries. Such associations may promote fraternity, extend social intercourse and provide assurance in case of sickness or death, but if they go no further they are powerless to affect wages even among their members. As to trades-unions proper, it is hard to define your position, which is, perhaps, best stated as one of warm approbation provided that they do not go too far. For while you object to strikes; while you reprehend societies that "do their best to get into their hands the whole field of labor and to force working men either to join them or to starve;" while you discountenance the coercing of employers and seem to think that arbitration might take the place of strikes; yet you use expressions and assert principles that are all that the trades-unionist would ask, not merely to justify the strike and the boycott, but even the use of violence where only violence would suffice. For you speak of the insufficient wages of workmen as due to the greed of rich employers; you assume the moral right of the workman to obtain employment from others at wages greater than those others are willing freely to give; and you deny the right of anyone to work for such wages as he pleases, in such a way as to lead Mr. Stead, in so widely read a journal as the *Review of Reviews*, approvingly to declare that you regard "blacklegging," i.e., the working for less than union wages, as a crime.

To men conscious of bitter injustice, to men steeped in poverty yet mocked by flaunting wealth, such words mean more than I can think you realize.

When fire shall be cool and ice be warm, when armies shall throw away lead and iron, to try conclusions by the pelting of rose-leaves, such labor associations as you are thinking of may be possible. But not till then. For labor associations can do nothing to raise wages but by force. It may be force applied passively, or force applied actively, or force held in reserve, but it must be force. They must coerce or hold the power to coerce employers; they must coerce those among their own members disposed to straggle; they must do their best to get into their hands the whole field of labor they seek to occupy and to force other working men either to join them or to starve. Those who tell you of trades-unions bent on raising wages by moral suasion alone are like those who would tell you of tigers that live on oranges.

The condition of the masses today is that of men pressed together in a hall where ingress is open and more are constantly coming, but where the doors for egress are closed. If forbidden to relieve the general pressure by throwing open those doors, whose bars and bolts are private property in land, they can only mitigate the pressure on themselves by forcing back others, and the weakest must be driven to the wall. This is the way of labor-unions and trade-guilds. Even those amiable societies that you recommend would in their efforts to find employment for their own members necessarily displace others.

For even the philanthropy which, recognizing the evil of trying to help labor by alms, seeks to help men to help themselves by finding them work, becomes aggressive in the blind and bitter struggle that private property in land entails, and in helping one set of men injures others. Thus, to minimize the bitter complaints of taking work from others and lessening the wages of others in providing their own beneficiaries with work and wages, benevolent societies are forced to devices akin to the digging of holes and filling them up again. Our American societies feel this difficulty, General Booth encounters it in England, and the Catholic societies which your Holiness recommends must find it, when they are formed.

Your Holiness knows of, and I am sure honors, the princely generosity of Baron Hirsch toward his suffering coreligionists. But, as I write, the New York newspapers contain accounts of an immense meeting held in Cooper Union, in this city, on the evening of Friday, September 4, in which a number of Hebrew trades-unions protested in the strongest manner against the loss of work and reduction of wages that are being effected by Baron Hirsch's generosity in bringing their own countrymen here and teaching them to work. The resolution unanimously adopted at this great meeting thus concludes:

> We now demand of Baron Hirsch himself that he release us from his "charity" and take back the millions, which, instead of a blessing, have proved a curse and a source of misery.

Nor does this show that the members of these Hebrew labor-unions — who are themselves immigrants of the same class as those Baron Hirsch is striving to help, for in the next generation they lose with us their distinctiveness — are a whit less generous than other men.

Labor associations of the nature of trade-guilds or unions are necessarily selfish; by the law of their being they must fight for their own hand, regardless of who is hurt; they ignore and must ignore the teaching of Christ that we should do to others as we would have them do to us, which a true political economy shows is the only way to the full emancipation of the masses. They must do their best to starve workmen who do not join them, they must by all means in their power force back the "blackleg" — as the soldier in battle must shoot down his mother's son if in the opposing ranks. And who is the blackleg? A fellow-creature seeking work — a fellow creature in all probability more pressed and starved than those who so bitterly denounce him, and often with the hungry pleading faces of wife and child behind him.

And, in so far as they succeed, what is it that trade guilds and unions do but to impose more restrictions on natural rights; to create "trusts" in labor; to add to privileged classes other somewhat privileged classes; and to press the weaker closer to the wall?

I speak without prejudice against trades-unions, of which for years I was an active member. And in pointing out to your Holiness that their principle is selfish and incapable of large and permanent benefits, and that their methods violate natural rights and work hardship and injustice, I am only saying to you what, both in my books and by word of mouth, I have said over and over again to them. Nor is what I say capable of dispute. Intelligent trades-unionists know it, and the less intelligent vaguely feel it. And even those of the classes of wealth and leisure who, as if to head off the demand for natural rights, are preaching trades-unionism to workingmen, must needs admit it.

Your Holiness will remember the great London dock strike of two years ago, which, with that of other influential men, received the moral support of that Prince of the Church whom we of the English speech hold higher and dearer than any prelate has been held by us since the blood of Thomas ä Becket stained the Canterbury altar.

In a volume called "The Story of the Dockers' Strike," written by Messrs. H. Llewellyn Smith and Vaughan Nash, with an introduction by Sydney Buxton, M.P., which advocates trades-unionism as the solution of the labor question, and of which a large number were sent to Australia as a sort of official recognition of the generous aid received from there by the strikers, I find in the summing up, on pages 164-165, the following:

> *If the settlement lasts, work at the docks will be more regular, better paid, and carried on under better conditions than ever before. All this will be an unqualified gain to those who get the benefit from it. But another result will undoubtedly be to con-tract the field of employment and lessen the number of those for whom work can be found. The lower-class casual will, in the end, find his position more precarious than ever before, in proportion to the increased regularity of work which the "fit-ter" of the laborers will secure. The effect of the organization of dock labor, as of all classes of labor, will be to squeeze out the residuum. The loafer, the cadger, the failure in the indus-trial race – the members of "Class B" of Mr. Charles Booth's hierarchy of social classes – will be no gainers by the change, but will rather find another door closed against them, and this in many cases the last door to employment.*

I am far from wishing that your Holiness should join in that pharisaical denunciation of trades-unions common among those who, while quick to point out the injustice of trades-unions in denying to others the equal right to work, are themselves supporters of that more primary injustice that denies the equal right to the standing-place and natu-ral material necessary to work. What I wish to point out is that trades-unionism, while it may be a partial palliative, is not a remedy; that it has not that moral character which could alone justify one in the position of your Holiness in urging it as good in itself. Yet, so long as you insist on pri-vate property in land what better can you do?

V.

In the beginning of the Encyclical you declare that the responsibility of the apostolical office urges your Holiness to treat the question of the condition of labor "expressly and at length in order that there may be no mistake as to the principles which truth and justice dictate for its settlement." But, blinded by one false assumption, you do not see even fundamentals.

You assume that the labor question is a question between wage-workers and their employers. But working for wages is not the primary or exclusive occupation of labor. Primarily men work for themselves without the intervention of an employer. And the primary source of wages is in the earnings of labor, the man who works for himself and consumes his own products receiving his wages in the fruits of his labor. Are not fishermen, boatmen, cab drivers, peddlers, working farmers all, in short, of the many workers who get their wages directly by the sale of their services or products without the medium of an employer, as much laborers as those who work for the specific wages of an employer? In your consideration of remedies you do not seem even to have thought of them. Yet in reality the laborers who work for themselves are the first to be considered, since what men will be willing to accept from employers depends manifestly on what they can get by working for themselves.

You assume that all employers are rich men, who might raise wages much higher were they not so grasping. But is it not the fact that the great majority of employers are in reality as much pressed by competition as their workmen, many of them constantly on the verge of failure? Such employers could not possibly raise the wages they pay, however they might wish to, unless all others were compelled to do so.

You assume that there are in the natural order two classes, the rich and the poor, and that laborers naturally belong to the poor.

It is true as you say that there are differences in capacity, in diligence, in health and in strength, that may produce differences in fortune. These, however, are not the differences that divide men into rich and poor. The natural differences in powers and aptitudes are certainly not greater than are natural differences in stature. But while it is only by selecting giants and dwarfs that we can find men twice as tall as others, yet in the difference between rich and poor that exists today we find some men richer than other men by the thousandfold and the millionfold.

Nowhere do these differences between wealth and poverty coincide with differences in individual powers and aptitudes. The real difference between rich and poor is the difference between those who hold the tollgates and those who pay toll; between tribute-receivers and tribute-yielders.

In what way does nature justify such a difference? In the numberless varieties of animated nature we find some species that are evidently intended to live on other species. But their relations are always marked by unmistakable differences in size, shape or organs. To man has been given dominion over all the other living things that tenant the earth. But is not this mastery indicated even in externals, so that no one can fail on sight to distinguish between a man and one of the inferior animals? Our American apologists for slavery used to contend that the black skin and woolly hair of the negro indicated the intent of nature that the black should serve the white; but the difference that you assume to be natural is between men of the same race. What difference does nature show between such men as would indicate her intent that one should live idly yet be rich, and the other should work hard yet be poor? If I could bring you from the United States a man who has $200,000,000, and one who is glad to work for a few dollars a week, and place them side by side in your antechamber, would you be able to tell which was which, even were you to call in the most skilled anatomist? Is it not clear that God in no way countenances or condones the division of rich and poor that exists today, or in any way permits it, except as having given them free will he permits men to choose either good or evil, and to avoid heaven if they prefer hell. For is it not clear that the division of men into the classes rich and poor has invariably its origin in force and fraud; invariably involves violation of the moral law; and is really a division into those who get the profits of robbery and those who are robbed; those who hold in exclusive possession what God made for all, and those who are deprived of his bounty? Did not Christ in all his utterances and parables show that the gross difference between rich and poor is opposed to God's law? Would he have condemned the rich so strongly as he did, if the class distinction between rich and poor did not involve injustice — was not opposed to God's intent?

It seems to us that your Holiness misses its real significance in intimating that Christ, in becoming the son of a carpenter and himself working as a carpenter, showed merely that "there is nothing to be ashamed of in seeking one's bread by labor." To say that is almost like saying that by not robbing people he showed that there is nothing to be ashamed of in honesty. If you will consider how true in any large view is the classification of all men into working men, beggar-men and thieves, you will see that it was morally impossible that Christ during his stay on earth should have been anything else than a working man, since he who came to fulfill the law must by deed as well as word obey God's law of labor.

See how fully and how beautifully Christ's life on earth illustrated this law. Entering our earthly life in the weakness of infancy, as it is appointed that all should enter it, he lovingly took what in the natural order is lovingly rendered, the sustenance, secured by labor, that one generation owes to its immediate successors. Arrived at maturity, he earned his own subsistence by that common labor in which the majority of men must and do earn it. Then passing to a higher — to the very highest — sphere of labor, he earned his subsistence by the teaching of moral and spiritual truths, receiving its material wages in the love-offerings of grateful hearers, and not refusing the costly spikenard with which Mary anointed his feet. So, when he chose his disciples, he did not go to landowners or other monopolists who live on the labor of others, but to common laboring men. And when he called them to a higher sphere of labor and sent them out to teach moral and spiritual truths, he told them to take, without condescension on the one hand or sense of degradation on the other, the loving return for such labor, saying to them that "the laborer is worthy of his hire," thus showing, what we hold, that all labor does not consist in what is called manual labor, but that whoever helps to add to the material, intellectual, moral or spiritual fullness of life is also a laborer.*

In assuming that laborers, even ordinary manual laborers, are naturally poor, you ignore the fact that labor is the

------

* "Nor should it be forgotten that the investigator, the philosopher, the teacher, the artist, the poet, the priest, though not engaged in the production of wealth, are not only engaged in the production of utilities and satisfactions to which the production of wealth is only a means, but by acquiring and diffusing knowledge, stimulating mental powers and elevating the moral sense, may greatly increase the ability to produce wealth. For man does not live by bread alone.... He who by any exertion of mind or body adds to the aggregate of enjoyable wealth, increases the sum of human knowledge, or gives to human life higher elevation or greater fullness — he is, in the large meaning of the words, a "producer," a "workingman," a "laborer," and is honestly earning honest wages. But he who without doing aught to make mankind richer, wiser, better, happier, lives on the toil of others — he, no matter by what name of honor he may be called, or how lustily the priests of Mammon may swing their censers before him, is in the last analysis but a beggar man or a thief." — *Protection or Free Trade*, Chapter 7.

producer of wealth, and attribute to the natural law of the
Creator an injustice that comes from man's impious violation of his benevolent intention. In the rudest stage of the
arts it is possible, where justice prevails, for all well men to
earn a living. With the labor-saving appliances of our time,
it should be possible for all to earn much more. And so, in
saying that poverty is no disgrace, you convey an unreasonable implication. For poverty ought to be a disgrace, since
in a condition of social justice, it would, where unsought
from religious motives or unimposed by unavoidable misfortune, imply recklessness or laziness.

The sympathy of your Holiness seems exclusively directed to the poor, the workers. Ought this to be so? Are
not the rich, the idlers, to be pitied also? By the word of the
gospel it is the rich rather than the poor who call for pity,
for the presumption is that they will share the fate of Dives.
And to anyone who believes in a future life, the condition
of him who wakes to find his cherished millions left behind must seem pitiful. But even in this life, how really
pitiable are the rich. The evil is not in wealth in itself — in
its command over material things; it is in the possession of
wealth while others are steeped in poverty; in being raised
above touch with the life of humanity, from its work and its
struggles, its hopes and its fears, and above all, from the
love that sweetens life, and the kindly sympathies and generous acts that strengthen faith in man and trust in God.
Consider how the rich see the meaner side of human nature; how they are surrounded by flatterers and sycophants;
how they find ready instruments not only to gratify vicious
impulses, but to prompt and stimulate them; how they must
constantly be on guard lest they be swindled; how often
they must suspect an ulterior motive behind kindly deed or
friendly word; how if they try to be generous they are beset
by shameless beggars and scheming impostors; how often

the family affections are chilled for them, and their deaths anticipated with the ill-concealed joy of expectant possession. The worst evil of poverty is not in the want of material things, but in the stunting and distortion of the higher qualities. So, though in another way, the possession of unearned wealth likewise stunts and distorts what is noblest in man.

God's commands cannot be evaded with impunity. If it be God's command that men shall earn their bread by labor, the idle rich must suffer. And they do. See the utter vacancy of the lives of those who live for pleasure; see the loathsome vices bred in a class who surrounded by poverty are sated with wealth. See that terrible punishment of ennui, of which the poor know so little that they cannot understand it; see the pessimism that grows among the wealthy classes — that shuts out God, that despises men, that deems existence in itself an evil, and fearing death yet longs for annihilation.

When Christ told the rich young man who sought him to sell all he had and to give it to the poor, he was not thinking of the poor, but of the young man. And I doubt not that among the rich, and especially among the self-made rich, there are many who at times at least feel keenly the folly of their riches and fear for the dangers and temptations to which these expose their children. But the strength of long habit, the prompting of pride, the excitement of making and holding what have become for them the counters in a game of cards, the family expectations that have assumed the character of rights, and the real difficulty they find in making any good use of their wealth, bind them to their burden, like a weary donkey to his pack, till they stumble on the precipice that bounds this life.

Men who are sure of getting food when they shall need it eat only what appetite dictates. But with the sparse tribes who exist on the verge of the habitable globe life is either a famine or a feast. Enduring hunger for days, the fear of it prompts them to gorge like anacondas when successful in their quest of game. And so, what gives wealth its curse is what drives men to seek it, what makes it so envied and admired — the fear of want. As the unduly rich are the corollary of the unduly poor, so is the soul-destroying quality of riches but the reflex of the want that embrutes and degrades. The real evil lies in the injustice from which unnatural possession and unnatural deprivation both spring.

But this injustice can hardly be charged on individuals or classes. The existence of private property in land is a great social wrong from which society at large suffers, and of which the very rich and the very poor are alike victims, though at the opposite extremes. Seeing this, it seems to us like a violation of Christian charity to speak of the rich as though they individually were responsible for the sufferings of the poor. Yet, while you do this, you insist that the cause of monstrous wealth and degrading poverty shall not be touched. Here is a man with a disfiguring and dangerous excrescence. One physician would kindly, gently, but firmly remove it. Another insists that it shall not be removed, but at the same time holds up the poor victim to hatred and ridicule. Which is right?

In seeking to restore all men to their equal and natural rights we do not seek the benefit of any class, but of all. For we both know by faith and see by fact that injustice can profit no one and that justice must benefit all.

Nor do we seek any "futile and ridiculous equality." We recognize, with you, that there must always be differences and inequalities. In so far as these are in conformity with the moral law, in so far as they do not violate the command, "Thou shalt not steal," we are content. We do not seek to better God's work; we seek only to do his will. The equality we would bring about is not the equality of fortune, but the equality of natural opportunity; the equality that reason and religion alike proclaim — the equality in usufruct of all his children to the bounty of Our Father who art in Heaven.

And in taking for the uses of society what we clearly see is the great fund intended for society in the divine order, we would not levy the slightest tax on the possessors of wealth, no matter how rich they might be. Not only do we deem such taxes a violation of the right of property, but we see that by virtue of beautiful adaptations in the economic laws of the Creator, it is impossible for any one honestly to acquire wealth, without at the same time adding to the wealth of the world.

To persist in a wrong, to refuse to undo it, is always to become involved in other wrongs. Those who defend private property in land, and thereby deny the first and most important of all human rights, the equal right to the material substratum of life, are compelled to one of two courses. Either they must, as do those whose gospel is "Devil take the hindermost," deny the equal right to life, and by some theory like that to which the English clergyman Malthus has given his name, assert that nature (they do not venture to say God) brings into the world more men than there is provision for; or, they must, as do the socialists, assert as rights what in themselves are wrongs.

Your Holiness in the Encyclical gives an example of this. Denying the equality of right to the material basis of life, and yet conscious that there is a right to live, you assert the right of laborers to employment and their right to receive from their employers a certain indefinite wage. No such rights exist. No one has a right to demand employment of another, or to demand higher wages than the other is willing to give, or in any way to put pressure on another to make him raise such wages against his will. There can be no better moral justification for such demands on employers

by working men than there would be for employers demanding that working men shall be compelled to work for them
when they do not want to and to accept wages lower than
they are willing to take. Any seeming justification springs
from a prior wrong, the denial to working men of their
natural rights, and can in the last analysis rest only on that
supreme dictate of self-preservation that under extraordinary circumstances makes pardonable what in itself is theft,
or sacrilege or even murder.

A fugitive slave with the bloodhounds of his pursuers
baying at his heels would in true Christian morals be held
blameless if he seized the first horse he came across, even
though to take it he had to knock down the rider. But this
is not to justify horse-stealing as an ordinary means of traveling.

When his disciples were hungry Christ permitted them
to pluck corn on the Sabbath day. But he never denied the
sanctity of the Sabbath by asserting that it was under ordinary circumstances a proper time to gather corn.

He justified David, who when pressed by hunger committed what ordinarily would be sacrilege, by taking from
the temple the loaves of proposition. But in this he was far
from saying that the robbing of temples was a proper way of
getting a living.

In the Encyclical however you commend the application to the ordinary relations of life, under normal conditions, of principles that in ethics are only to be tolerated
under extraordinary conditions. You are driven to this assertion of false rights by your denial of true rights. The natural right which each man has is not that of demanding
employment or wages from another man; but that of employing himself — that of applying by his own labor to the
inexhaustible storehouse which the Creator has in the land
provided for all men. Were that storehouse open, as by the
single tax we would open it, the natural demand for labor

would keep pace with the supply, the man who sold labor and the man who bought it would become free exchangers for mutual advantage, and all cause for dispute between workman and employer would be gone. For then, all being free to employ themselves, the mere opportunity to labor would cease to seem a boon; and since no one would work for another for less, all things considered, than he could earn by working for himself, wages would necessarily rise to their full value, and the relations of workman and employer be regulated by mutual interest and convenience.

This is the only way in which they can be satisfactorily regulated.

Your Holiness seems to assume that there is some just rate of wages that employers ought to be willing to pay and that laborers should be content to receive, and to imagine that if this were secured there would be an end of strife. This rate you evidently think of as that which will give working men a frugal living, and perhaps enable them by hard work and strict economy to lay by a little something.

But how can a just rate of wages be fixed without the "higgling of the market" any more than the just price of corn or pigs or ships or paintings can be so fixed? And would not arbitrary regulation in the one case as in the other check that interplay that most effectively promotes the economical adjustment of productive forces? Why should buyers of labor, any more than buyers of commodities, be called on to pay higher prices than in a free market they are compelled to pay? Why should the sellers of labor be content with anything less than in a free market they can obtain? Why should working-men be content with frugal fare when the world is so rich? Why should they be satisfied with a lifetime of toil and stinting, when the world is so beautiful? Why should not they also desire to gratify the higher instincts, the finer tastes? Why should they be forever content to travel in the steerage when others find the cabin more enjoyable?

Nor will they. The ferment of our time does not arise merely from the fact that working men find it harder to live on the same scale of comfort. It is also and perhaps still more largely due to the increase of their desires with an improved scale of comfort. This increase of desire must continue. For working men are men. And man is the unsatisfied animal.

He is not an ox, of whom it may be said, so much grass, so much grain, so much water, and a little salt, and he will be content. On the contrary, the more he gets the more he craves. When he has enough food then he wants better food. When he gets a shelter then he wants a more commodious and tasty one. When his animal needs are satisfied then mental and spiritual desires arise.

This restless discontent is of the nature of man — of that nobler nature that raises him above the animals by so immeasurable a gulf, and shows him to be indeed created in the likeness of God. It is not to be quarreled with, for it is the motor of all progress. It is this that has raised St. Peter's dome and on dull, dead canvas made the angelic face of the Madonna to glow; it is this that has weighed suns and analyzed stars, and opened page after page of the wonderful works of creative intelligence; it is this that has narrowed the Atlantic to an ocean ferry and trained the lightning to carry our messages to the remotest lands; it is this that is opening to us possibilities beside which all that our modern civilization has as yet accomplished seem small. Nor can it be repressed save by degrading and embruting men; by reducing Europe to Asia.

Hence, short of what wages may be earned when all restrictions on labor are removed and access to natural opportunities on equal terms secured to all, it is impossible to fix any rate of wages that will be deemed just, or any rate of wages that can prevent working men striving to get more.

So far from it making working men more contented to improve their condition a little, it is certain to make them more discontented.

Nor are you asking justice when you ask employers to pay their working men more than they are compelled to pay — more than they could get others to do the work for. You are asking charity. For the surplus that the rich employer thus gives is not in reality wages, it is essentially alms.

In speaking of the practical measures for the improvement of the condition of labor which your Holiness suggests, I have not mentioned what you place much stress upon — charity. But there is nothing practical in such recommendations as a cure for poverty, nor will any one so consider them. If it were possible for the giving of alms to abolish poverty there would be no poverty in Christendom.

Charity is indeed a noble and beautiful virtue, grateful to man and approved by God. But charity must be built on justice. It cannot supersede justice.

What is wrong with the condition of labor through the Christian world is that labor is robbed. And while you justify the continuance of that robbery it is idle to urge charity. To do so — to commend charity as a substitute for justice, is indeed something akin in essence to those heresies, condemned by your predecessors, that taught that the gospel had superseded the law, and that the love of God exempted men from moral obligations.

All that charity can do where injustice exists is here and there to mollify somewhat the effects of injustice. It cannot cure them. Nor is even what little it can do to mollify the effects of injustice without evil. For what may be called the superimposed, and in this sense, secondary virtues, work evil where the fundamental or primary virtues are absent. Thus sobriety is a virtue and diligence is a virtue. But a sober and diligent thief is all the more dangerous. Thus patience is a virtue. But patience under wrong is the condoning of wrong. Thus it is a virtue to seek knowledge and to endeavor to cultivate the mental powers. But the wicked man becomes more capable of evil by reason of his intelligence. Devils we always think of as intelligent.

And thus that pseudo-charity that discards and denies justice works evil. On the one side, it demoralizes its recipients, outraging that human dignity which as you say "God himself treats with reverence," and turning into beggars and paupers men who to become self-supporting, self-respecting citizens need only the restitution of what God has given them. On the other side, it acts as an anodyne to the consciences of those who are living on the robbery of their fellows, and fosters that moral delusion and spiritual pride that Christ doubtless had in mind when he said it was easier for a camel to pass through the eye of a needle than for a rich man to enter the Kingdom of Heaven. For it leads men steeped in injustice, and using their money and their influence to bolster up injustice, to think that in giving alms they are doing something more than their duty toward man and deserve to be very well thought of by God, and in a vague way to attribute to their own goodness what really belongs to God's goodness. For consider: Who is the All-Provider? Who is it that as you say, "owes to man a storehouse that shall never fail," and which "he finds only in the inexhaustible fertility of the earth." Is it not God? And when, therefore, men, deprived of the bounty of their God, are made dependent on the bounty of their fellow-creatures, are not these creatures, as it were, put in the place of God, to take credit to themselves for paying obligations that you yourself say God owes?

But worse perhaps than all else is the way in which this substituting of vague injunctions to charity for the clear-cut demands of justice opens an easy means for the professed teachers of the Christian religion of all branches and communions to placate Mammon while persuading themselves that they are serving God. Had the English clergy not subordinated the teaching of justice to the teaching of charity — to go no further in illustrating a principle of which the whole history of Christendom from Constantine's time to our own is witness — the Tudor tyranny would never have arisen, and the separation of the church been averted; had the clergy of France never substituted charity for justice, the monstrous iniquities of the ancient régime would never have brought the horrors of the Great Revolution; and in my own country had those who should have preached justice not satisfied themselves with preaching kindness, chattel slavery could never have demanded the holocaust of our civil war.

No, your Holiness; as faith without works is dead, as men cannot give to God his due while denying to their fellows the rights he gave them, so charity unsupported by justice can do nothing to solve the problem of the existing condition of labor. Though the rich were to "bestow all their goods to feed the poor and give their bodies to be burned," poverty would continue while property in land continues.

Take the case of the rich man today who is honestly desirous of devoting his wealth to the improvement of the condition of labor. What can he do?

Bestow his wealth on those who need it? He may help some who deserve it, but will not improve general conditions. And against the good he may do will be the danger of doing harm.

Build churches? Under the shadow of churches poverty festers and the vice that is born of it breeds.

Build schools and colleges? Save as it may lead men to see the iniquity of private property in land, increased education can effect nothing for mere laborers, for as education is diffused the wages of education sink.

Establish hospitals? Why, already it seems to laborers

that there are too many seeking work, and to save and prolong life is to add to the pressure.

Build model tenements? Unless he cheapens house accommodations he but drives further the class he would benefit, and as he cheapens house accommodations he brings more to seek employment and cheapens wages.

Institute laboratories, scientific schools, workshops for physical experiments? He but stimulates invention and discovery, the very forces that, acting on a society based on private property in land, are crushing labor as between the upper and the nether millstone.

Promote emigration from places where wages are low to places where they are somewhat higher? If he does, even those whom he at first helps to emigrate will soon turn on him to demand that such emigration shall be stopped as reducing their wages.

Give away what land he may have, or refuse to take rent for it, or let it at lower rents than the market price? He will simply make new landowners or partial landowners; he may make some individuals the richer, but he will do nothing to improve the general condition of labor.

Or, bethinking himself of those public-spirited citizens of classic times who spent great sums in improving their native cities, shall he try to beautify the city of his birth or adoption? Let him widen and straighten narrow and crooked streets, let him build parks and erect fountains, let him open tramways and bring in railroads, or in any way make beautiful and attractive his chosen city, and what will be the result? Must it not be that those who appropriate God's bounty will take his also? Will it not be that the value of land will go up, and that the net result of his benefactions will be an increase of rents and a bounty to landowners? Why, even the mere announcement that he is going to do such things will start speculation and send up the value of land by leaps and bounds.

What, then, can the rich man do to improve the condition of labor?

He can do nothing at all except to use his strength for the abolition of the great primary wrong that robs men of their birthright. The justice of God laughs at the attempts of men to substitute anything else for it.

If when in speaking of the practical measures your Holiness proposes, I did not note the moral injunctions that the Encyclical contains, it is not because we do not think morality practical. On the contrary it seems to us that in the teachings of morality is to be found the highest practicality, and that the question, What is wise? may always safely be subordinated to the question, What is right? But your Holiness in the Encyclical expressly deprives the moral truths you state of all real bearing on the condition of labor, just as the American people, by their legalization of chattel slavery, used to deprive of all practical meaning the declaration they deem their fundamental charter, and were accustomed to read solemnly on every national anniversary. That declaration asserts that

> We hold these truths to be self-evident – that all men are created equal; that they are endowed by their Creator with certain unalienable rights; that among these are life, liberty, and the pursuit of happiness.

But what did this truth mean on the lips of men who asserted that one man was the rightful property of another man who had bought him; who asserted that the slave was robbing the master in running away, and that the man or the woman who helped the fugitive to escape, or even gave him a cup of cold water in Christ's name, was an accessory to theft, on whose head the penalties of the state should be visited?

Consider the moral teachings of the Encyclical:

You tell us that God owes to man an inexhaustible storehouse which he finds only in the land. Yet you support a system that denies to the great majority of men all right of recourse to this storehouse.

You tell us that the necessity of labor is a consequence of original sin. Yet you support a system that exempts a privileged class from the necessity for labor and enables them to shift their share and much more than their share of labor on others.

You tell us that God has not created us for the perishable and transitory things of earth, but has given us this world as a place of exile and not as our true country. Yet you tell us that some of the exiles have the exclusive right of ownership in this place of common exile, so that they may compel their fellow-exiles to pay them for sojourning here, and that this exclusive ownership they may transfer to other exiles yet to come, with the same right of excluding their fellows.

You tell us that virtue is the common inheritance of all; that all men are children of God the common Father; that all have the same last end; that all are redeemed by Jesus Christ; that the blessings of nature and the gifts of grace belong in common to all, and that to all except the unworthy is promised the inheritance of the Kingdom of Heaven! Yet in all this and through all this you insist as a moral duty on the maintenance of a system that makes the reservoir of all God's material bounties and blessings to man the exclusive property of a few of their number — you give us equal rights in heaven, but deny us equal rights on earth!

It was said of a famous decision of the Supreme Court of the United States made just before the civil war, in a fugitive-slave case, that "it gave the law to the North and the nigger to the South." It is thus that your Encyclical gives the gospel to laborers and the earth to the landlords. Is it really to be wondered at that there are those who sneeringly

say, "The priests are ready enough to give the poor an equal
share in all that is out of sight, but they take precious good
care that the rich shall keep a tight grip on all that is within
sight"?

Herein is the reason why the working masses all over
the world are turning away from organized religion.

And why should they not? What is the office of religion
if not to point out the principles that ought to govern the
conduct of men toward each other; to furnish a clear, deci-
sive rule of right which shall guide men in all the relations
of life — in the workshop, in the mart, in the forum and in
the senate, as well as in the church; to supply, as it were, a
compass by which amid the blasts of passion, the aberra-
tions of greed and the delusions of a short-sighted expediency men may safely steer? What is the use of a religion that
stands palsied and paltering in the face of the most momentous problems? What is the use of a religion that whatever it may promise for the next world can do nothing to
prevent injustice in this? Early Christianity was not such a
religion, else it would never have encountered the Roman
persecutions; else it would never have swept the Roman
world. The skeptical masters of Rome, tolerant of all gods,
careless of what they deemed vulgar superstitions, were
keenly sensitive to a doctrine based on equal rights; they
feared instinctively a religion that inspired slave and prole-
tarian with a new hope; that took for its central figure a
crucified carpenter; that taught the equal Fatherhood of
God and the equal brotherhood of men; that looked for
the speedy reign of justice, and that prayed, "Thy Kingdom
come on Earth!"

Today, the same perceptions, the same aspirations, exist among the masses. Man is, as he has been called, a religious animal, and can never quite rid himself of the feeling
that there is some moral government of the world, some

eternal distinction between wrong and right; can never quite abandon the yearning for a reign of righteousness. And to-day, men who, as they think, have cast off all belief in religion, will tell you, even though they know not what it is, that with regard to the condition of labor something is wrong! If theology be, as St. Thomas of Aquin held it, the sum and focus of the sciences, is it not the business of religion to say clearly and fearlessly what that wrong is? It was by a deep impulse that of old when threatened and perplexed by general disaster men came to the oracles to ask, In what have we offended the gods? Today, menaced by growing evils that threaten the very existence of society, men, conscious that something is wrong, are putting the same question to the ministers of religion. What is the answer they get? Alas, with few exceptions, it is as vague, as inadequate, as the answers that used to come from heathen oracles.

Is it any wonder that the masses of men are losing faith?

Let me again state the case that your Encyclical presents:

What is that condition of labor which as you truly say is "the question of the hour," and "fills every mind with painful apprehension"? Reduced to its lowest expression it is the poverty of men willing to work. And what is the lowest expression of this phrase? It is that they lack bread — for in that one word we most concisely and strongly express all the manifold material satisfactions needed by humanity, the absence of which constitutes poverty.

Now what is the prayer of Christendom — the universal prayer; the prayer that goes up daily and hourly wherever the name of Christ is honored; that ascends from your Holiness at the high altar of St. Peter's, and that is repeated by the youngest child that the poorest Christian mother has taught to lisp a request to her Father in Heaven? It is, "Give us this day our daily bread!"

Yet where this prayer goes up, daily and hourly, men lack bread. Is it not the business of religion to say why? If it cannot do so, shall not scoffers mock its ministers as Elias mocked the prophets of Baal, saying, "Cry with a louder voice, for he is a god; and perhaps he is talking, or is in an inn, or on a journey, or perhaps he is asleep, and must be awaked!" What answer can those ministers give? Either there is no God, or he is asleep, or else he does give men their daily bread, and it is in some way intercepted.

Here is the answer, the only true answer: If men lack bread it is not that God has not done his part in providing it. If men willing to labor are cursed with poverty, it is not that the storehouse that God owes men has failed; that the daily supply he has promised for the daily wants of his children is not here in abundance. It is, that impiously violating the benevolent intentions of their Creator, men have made land private property, and thus given into the exclusive ownership of the few the provision that a bountiful Father has made for all.

Any other answer than that, no matter how it may be shrouded in the mere forms of religion, is practically an atheistical answer.

I have written this letter not alone for your Holiness, but for all whom I may hope it to reach. But in sending it to you personally, and in advance of publication, I trust that it may be by you personally read and weighed. In setting forth the grounds of our belief and in pointing out considerations which it seems to us you have unfortunately overlooked, I have written frankly, as was my duty on a matter of such momentous importance, and as I am sure you would have me write. But I trust I have done so without offense. For your office I have profound respect, for yourself personally the highest esteem. And while the views I have opposed seem to us erroneous and dangerous, we do not wish to be understood as in the slightest degree questioning either your sincerity or intelligence in adopting them. For they are views all but universally held by the professed religious teachers of Christendom, in all communions and creeds, and that have received the sanction of those looked to as the wise and learned. Under the conditions that have surrounded you, and under the pressure of so many high duties and responsibilities, culminating in those of your present exalted position, it is not to be expected that you should have hitherto thought to question them. But I trust that the considerations herein set forth may induce you to do so, and even if the burdens and cares that beset you shall now make impossible the careful consideration that should precede expression by one in your responsible position, I trust that what I have written may not be without use to others.

And, as I have said, we are deeply grateful for your Encyclical. It is much that by so conspicuously calling attention to the condition of labor, you have recalled the fact forgotten by so many that the social evils and problems of our time directly and pressingly concern the church. It is much that you should thus have placed the stamp of your disapproval on that impious doctrine which directly and by implication has been so long and so widely preached in the name of Christianity, that the sufferings of the poor are due to mysterious decrees of Providence which men may lament but cannot alter. Your Encyclical will be seen by those who carefully analyze it to be directed not against socialism, which in moderate form you favor, but against what we in the United States call the single tax. Yet we have no solicitude for the truth save that it shall be brought into discussion, and we recognize in your Holiness's Encyclical a most efficient means of promoting discussion, and of promoting discussion along the lines that we deem of the greatest importance — the lines of morality and religion. In this you deserve the gratitude of all who would follow truth, for it is of the nature of truth always to prevail over error where discussion goes on.

And the truth for which we stand has now made such progress in the minds of men that it must be heard; that it can never be stifled; that it must go on conquering and to conquer. Far-off Australia leads the van, and has already taken the first steps toward the single tax. In Great Britain, in the United States, and in Canada, the question is on the verge of practical politics and soon will be the burning issue of the time. Continental Europe cannot long linger behind. Faster than ever the world is moving.

Forty years ago slavery seemed stronger in the United States than ever before, and the market price of slaves — both working slaves and breeding slaves — was higher than it had ever been before, for the title of the owner seemed growing more secure. In the shadow of the Hall where the equal rights of man had been solemnly proclaimed, the manacled fugitive was dragged back to bondage, and on what to American tradition was our Marathon of freedom, the slave-master boasted that he would yet call the roll of his chattels.

Yet forty years ago, though the party that was to place Abraham Lincoln in the Presidential chair had not been formed, and nearly a decade was yet to pass ere the signal-gun was to ring out, slavery, as we may now see, was doomed.

Today a wider, deeper, more beneficent revolution is brooding, not over one country, but over the world. God's truth impels it, and forces mightier than he has ever before given to man urge it on. It is no more in the power of vested wrongs to stay it than it is in man's power to stay the sun. The stars in their courses fight against Sisera, and in the ferment of today, to him who hath ears to hear, the doom of industrial slavery is sealed.

Where shall the dignitaries of the church be in the struggle that is coming, nay that is already here? On the side of justice and liberty, or on the side of wrong and slavery? With the delivered when the timbrels shall sound again, or with the chariots and the horsemen that again shall be engulfed in the sea?

As to the masses, there is little fear where they will be. Already, among those who hold it with religious fervor, the single tax counts great numbers of Catholics, many priests, secular and regular, and at least some bishops, while there is no communion or denomination of the many into which English-speaking Christians are divided where its advocates are not to be found.

Last Sunday evening in the New York church that of all churches in the world is most richly endowed, I saw the cross carried through its aisles by a hundred choristers, and heard a priest of that English branch of the church that three hundred years since was separated from your obedience, declare to a great congregation that the labor question was at bottom a religious question; that it could only be settled on the basis of moral right; that the first and clearest of rights is the equal right to the use of the physical basis of all life; and that no human titles could set aside God's gift of the land to all men.

And as the cross moved by, and the choristers sang,

> *Raise ye the Christian's war-cry –*
> *The Cross of Christ the Lord!*

men to whom it was a new thing bowed their heads, and in hearts long steeled against the church, as the willing handmaid of oppression, rose the "God wills it!" of the grandest and mightiest of crusades.

Servant of the Servants of God! I call you by the strongest and sweetest of your titles. In your hands more than in those of any living man lies the power to say the word and make the sign that shall end an unnatural divorce, and marry again to religion all that is pure and high in social aspiration.

Wishing for your Holiness the chiefest of all blessings, that you may know the truth and be freed by the truth; wishing for you the days and the strength that may enable you by the great service you may render to humanity to make your pontificate through all coming time most glorious; and with the profound respect due to your personal character and to your exalted office, I am,

Yours sincerely,

Henry George
New York, September 11, 1891.

Index

Books by Henry George

Published by the Robert Schalkenbach Foundation

Progress and Poverty: An Inquiry into the Cause of Industrial
    Depressions and the Increase of Want with Increase of
    Wealth... The Remedy (orig. 1879)
    Unabridged Hardcover, ISBN 978-0-911312-79-9
    Unabridged Paperback, ISBN 978-0-911312-58-4
    Abridged by Arthur Madsen, Paperback, ISBN 978-0-911312-10-2
    Modernized & Abridged by Bob Drake, Pb., ISBN 978-0-911312-98-0

Social Problems (orig. 1883)
    Unabridged Hardcover, ISBN 978-0-911312-10-2

The Land Question: Viewpoint and Counterviewpoint on the
Need for Land Reform (orig. 1884)
    Unabridged Paperback, ISBN 978-0-911312-40-9

Protection or Free Trade: An Examination of the Tariff
Question, with Special Regard to the Interests of Labor (orig. 1886)
    Unabridged Hardcover, ISBN 978-0-911312-83-6
    Unabridged Paperback, ISBN 978-0-911312-84-3
    Abridged by F. C. R. Douglas, Pb., ISBN 978-0-911312-49-2

A Perplexed Philosopher: An Examination of Herbert Spencer's
    Utterances on the Land Question (orig. 1892)
    Unabridged Hardcover, ISBN 978-0-911312-80-5

The Science of Political Economy: A Reconstruction of its
Principles in Clear and Systematic Form (orig. 1898)
    Unabridged Hardcover, ISBN 978-0-911312-51-5
    Abridged by Lindy Davies, Paperback, ISBN 978-0-911312-48-5

Other works by Henry George and related authors are also
available in print, on disc, and online. Latest catalogue available
free upon request and online: **www.schalkenbach.org**

Robert Schalkenbach Foundation
90 John Street, Suite 501, New York, NY 10038-3202
Tel: 212-683-6424   Toll-free: 800-269-9555   Fax: 212-683-6454

For Further Exploration

Tuition-free courses on the economics and social philosophy of Henry George are offered by:

Henry George School of Social Science
    121 East 30th Street, New York NY 10016
    212-889-8020   www.henrygeorgeschool.org

Henry George School of Philadelphia
    413 South 10th Street; Philadelphia PA 19147
    215-922-4278   www.henrygeorgeschoolphila.org

Henry George School of Chicago
    28 East Jackson #1004, Chicago IL 60604
    312-362-9302   www.hgchicago.org

Henry George School of Los Angeles
    P.O.Box 55, Tujunga CA 94105
    818-352-4141   henrygeorgeschool@comcast.net

Henry George School of Northern California
    55 New Montgomery Street, San Francisco CA 94105
    415-543-4294   www.henrygeorgesf.org

Correspondence courses (Internet or regular mail) based on the works of Henry George are offered by the Henry George Institute, 121 East 30th Street, New York NY 10016   www.henrygeorge.org

A world-wide list of all Georgist organizations, with contact information, is available from the Council of Georgist Organizations, P.O. Box 57, Evanston IL 60204   www.cgocouncil.org

Robert Schalkenbach Foundation (RSF) was founded in 1925 to promote and develop the ideas of Henry George and keep them in the public dialogue. The foundation carries out its mission in several ways: (1) by publishing the works of Henry George and distributing the works of related authors; (2) by engaging in scholarly research projects that assess George's world-wide legacy, extend his analysis, and apply it to new circumstances; and (3) by using modern media, including film, to engage a wider public audience.

The End of Poverty? is a film produced by RSF and Cinema Libre Studio, and well received at its debut at the 2008 Cannes Film Festival. Its theatrical release in 2009 will be followed by a DVD release. For this invitation to "Think Again" about causes of poverty and how to end it, award-winning director Philippe Diaz brings together narration by celebrated actor Martin Sheen and commentary by Nobel laureate economists Amartya Sen and Joseph Stiglitz, along with experts Susan George, John Perkins, Eric Toussaint, Chalmers Johnson, and RSF's Clifford Cobb. The camera crew takes the audience to Africa and South America to visit and talk with working people struggling for their lives within a global system of economic monopolization and ecological degradation. The film is designed to move the viewer to look deeply into the question: *Why in the midst of so much wealth is there so much poverty?*

> "The principles expounded by Henry George in his immortal book entitled *Progress and Poverty* will, if enacted into law, give equal opportunity to all and tend to the betterment of the individual and of society by the abolition of involuntary poverty and its attendant evils." — *From the Will of Robert Schalkenbach*

Please visit www.schalkenbach.org to purchase published materials on paper, CD and DVD; to read and download new research and writing online, news about *The End of Poverty?* and links to Georgist websites, projects, and organizations.

Robert Schalkenbach Foundation
90 John Street, Suite 501, New York, NY 10038-3202
Tel: 212-683-6424 Toll-free 800-269-9555 Fax: 212-683-6454